VIRTUAL PLAY AND THE VICTORIAN NOVEL

Pondering the town he had invented in his novels, Anthony Trollope had 'so realised the place, and the people, and the facts' of Barset that 'the pavement of the city ways are familiar to my footsteps'. After his novels end, William Thackeray wonders where his characters now live and misses their conversation. How can we understand the novel as a form of artificial reality? Timothy Gao proposes a history of virtual realities, stemming from the imaginary worlds created by novelists such as Trollope, Thackeray, Charlotte Brontë, and Charles Dickens. Departing from established historical or didactic understandings of Victorian fiction, *Virtual Play and the Victorian Novel* recovers the period's fascination with imagined places, people, and facts. This text provides a short history of virtual experiences in literature, four studies of major novelists, and an innovative approach for scholars and students to interpret realist fictions and fictional realities from before the digital age.

TIMOTHY GAO is a Presidential Postdoctoral Fellow at Nanyang Technological University, Singapore. He previously lectured at the University of Oxford, and his work has been published in *Victorian Network* and *Victorian Literature and Culture*. This title is also available as Open Access on Cambridge Core.

CAMBRIDGE STUDIES IN NINETEENTH-CENTURY
LITERATURE AND CULTURE

Founding Editors
Gillian Beer, *University of Cambridge*
Catherine Gallagher, *University of California, Berkeley*

General Editors
Kate Flint, *University of Southern California*
Clare Pettitt, *King's College London*

Editorial Board
Isobel Armstrong, *Birkbeck, University of London*
Ali Behdad *University of California, Los Angeles*
Alison Chapman, *University of Victoria*
Hilary Fraser, *Birkbeck, University of London*
Josephine McDonagh, *University of Chicago*
Elizabeth Miller, *University of California, Davis*
Hillis Miller, *University of California, Irvine*
Cannon Schmitt, *University of Toronto*
Sujit Sivasundaram *University of Cambridge*
Herbert Tucker, *University of Virginia*
Mark Turner, *King's College London*

Nineteenth-century literature and culture have proved a rich field for interdisciplinary studies. Since 1994, books in this series have tracked the intersections and tensions between Victorian literature and the visual arts, politics, gender and sexuality, race, social organisation, economic life, technical innovations, scientific thought – in short, culture in its broadest sense. Many of our books are now classics in a field which since the series' inception has seen powerful engagements with Marxism, feminism, visual studies, post-colonialism, critical race studies, new historicism, new formalism, transnationalism, queer studies, human rights and liberalism, disability studies and global studies. Theoretical challenges and historiographical shifts continue to unsettle scholarship on the nineteenth century in productive ways. New work on the body and the senses, the environment and climate, race and the decolonisation of literary studies, biopolitics and materiality, the animal and the human, the local and the global, politics and form, queerness and gender identities, and intersectional theory is re-animating the field. This series aims to accommodate and promote the most interesting work being undertaken on the frontiers of nineteenth-century literary studies, connecting the field with the urgent critical questions that are being asked today. We seek to publish work from a diverse range of authors, and stand for anti-racism and anti-colonialism, and against discrimination in all forms.

A complete list of titles published will be found at the end of the book.

VIRTUAL PLAY AND THE VICTORIAN NOVEL

The Ethics and Aesthetics of Fictional Experience

TIMOTHY GAO

Nanyang Technological University

CAMBRIDGE
UNIVERSITY PRESS

University Printing House, Cambridge CB2 8BS, United Kingdom

One Liberty Plaza, 20th Floor, New York, NY 10006, USA

477 Williamstown Road, Port Melbourne, VIC 3207, Australia

314–321, 3rd Floor, Plot 3, Splendor Forum, Jasola District Centre, New Delhi – 110025, India

79 Anson Road, #06-04/06, Singapore 079906

Cambridge University Press is part of the University of Cambridge.

It furthers the University's mission by disseminating knowledge in the pursuit of education, learning, and research at the highest international levels of excellence.

www.cambridge.org
Information on this title: www.cambridge.org/9781108837163
DOI: 10.1017/9781108938518

© Cambridge University Press 2021

This publication is in copyright. Subject to statutory exception and to the provisions of relevant collective licensing agreements; with the exception of the Creative Commons version, the link for which is provided below, no reproduction of any part of this work may take place without the written permission of Cambridge University Press.

An online version of this work is published at doi.org/10.1017/9781108938518 under a Creative Commons Open Access licence CC-BY-NC-ND.

All versions of this work may contain content reproduced under licence from third parties. Permission to reproduce this third-party content must be obtained from these third parties directly.

When citing this work, please include a reference to the DOI 10.1017/9781108938518

First published 2021

A catalogue record for this publication is available from the British Library.

ISBN 978-1-108-83716-3 Hardback

Cambridge University Press has no responsibility for the persistence or accuracy of URLs for external or third-party internet websites referred to in this publication and does not guarantee that any content on such websites is, or will remain, accurate or appropriate.

Contents

List of Abbreviations		page vi
Introduction: How to Play the Victorian Novel		1
1	Virtual, Paracosmic, Fictional	14
2	Authorship, Omnipotence, and Charlotte Brontë	35
	The Professor	54
3	Plotting, Improvisation, and Anthony Trollope	70
	The Small House at Allington	89
4	Continuation, Attachment, and William Makepeace Thackeray	104
	The Newcomes	123
5	Description, Projection, and Charles Dickens	139
	Little Dorrit	158
Conclusion: Approaching Virtuality		174
Notes		179
Bibliography		205
Index		217

Abbreviations

This book employs a system of abbreviations for citing frequently quoted primary texts. The full reference to each work and edition is provided in a footnote on their first citation, as well as in the bibliography, with further references incorporated into the body of the argument.

AA   *An Autobiography*
AS   *Autobiographical Sketches*
BC   *Barchester Towers*
EW   *Early Writings of Charlotte Brontë*
FA   'Farewell to Angria' in *Tales of Glass Town, Angria, and Gondal*
HC   'Memoir of Hartley Coleridge' in *Poems*
JE   *Jane Eyre*
LCB   *The Last Chronicle of Barset*
LD   *Little Dorrit*
Life   *The Life of Charlotte Brontë*
NC   *The Newcomes*
NE   'Novels and their Endings' in *The Works of John Ruskin*
SH   *The Small House at Allington*
TP   *The Professor*

Introduction
How to Play the Victorian Novel

How do we play the Victorian novel? Such a verb might confound our ordinary sense of what to do or can be done with an object like the novel, and accordingly, what kind of object it is. Such a question also demands both description and instruction, a sociology and a how-to guide, implying motives both to know and to participate. If the obvious answer is that novels are read (or analysed, interrogated, unpacked), not played, ongoing debates in book history and of disciplinary methodology suggest 'reading' to be not so obvious a mode of relating. How to do it: closely or distantly, skimmed or in depth, materially or digitally, with sympathy or suspicion?[1] What is or ought to be the nature of our encounter with fiction? Sharon Marcus, Stephen Best, and Rita Felski have been the latest and most prominent critics to pose such questions as indicative of a present impasse in literary studies, raised by a growing dissatisfaction with established approaches.[2]

This book proposes an alternative mode of literary engagement to these multiplying forms of reading, a different way of doing the novel, which it recovers from a nineteenth-century practice into a critical method with distinct advantages. The authors and readers examined here recognised and exploited the form and history of the novel as an exceptional medium for artificial realities. The uses (or abuses) to which they put the text as vicarious experiences of power, fantasy, and presence compose an unorthodox tradition of literary knowledge and function which cannot be fully accommodated within existing critical approaches to the novel as an aesthetic, historical, material, or ethical object – even as recent scholarship on the phenomenology of reading suggests such experiences to be ubiquitous. Felski, for instance, has called on literary studies to 'face up to the limits of demystification as a critical method and [...] begin to engage the affective and absorptive, the sensuous and somatic qualities of aesthetic experience'.[3] Elaine Auyoung has proposed 'a form of critical attention distinct from the pursuit of interpretive meaning, focusing instead on [...] the sensory and affective properties of the represented fictional world'.[4] Brigid Lowe has advocated for a style of criticism 'not of objective examination but of subjective participation' in literature.[5] More than a matter of acknowledging popular forms of reading, criticism is catching on to fictional experience as a new way to operate the literary object, eliciting other kinds of value than those of the so-called hermeneutics of suspicion.

I take up this experiential turn in criticism and call it *play* because examples and representations of how children and adults make-believe offer us (as they offered the Victorians) exemplary models for the often ineffable process of imaginative engagement with fictions. The chief advocates of this comparison are nineteenth-century novels and novelists themselves: Charles Dickens's David Copperfield envisions that the heroes of his favourite novels 'came out, a glorious host, to keep me company', and enacts their adventures by wandering his house 'armed with the centre-piece out of an old set of boot-trees [...] in danger of being beset by savages'.[6] William Makepeace Thackeray concludes *Vanity Fair* with an image of children 'shut[ting] up the box and the puppets', putting away the narrative world and its characters now that 'our play is played out'.[7] Anthony Trollope doubts whether, had it not been for his adolescence escape into imaginative play, 'I should ever have written a novel. I learned in this way [...] to live in a world altogether outside the world of my own material life'. Jane Eyre walks back and forth along the corridors of Thornfield, acting out a version of Charlotte Brontë's own childhood habits by telling herself 'a tale my imagination created [...] with all of incident, life, fire, feeling, that I desired and had not in my actual existence'.[8] Bordering daydream and fantasy, play embodies for these authors a practice of novel fiction as the experience of imagined worlds and objects, and more suggestively still, as a supplementary reality to life beyond the traditional ends (and endings) of the literary text.

Critics, philosophers, and narratologists have similarly found a useful heuristic in play for understanding how fiction affects or is experienced by readers. Critical practice may, as Eve Sedgwick put it, be constrained by 'the limitations of present theoretical vocabularies' for articulating such experiences.[9] But when George Henry Lewes seeks to explain the felt reality of Dickens's novels, the same sense of palpability which David uses for company and excitement, he is able to turn to an analogy of the child with 'a wooden horse', who imagines the spinning of its 'wheels' as an experience of galloping.[10] In 'Creative Writers and Day-Dreaming', Freud presents the usefulness of this comparison explicitly:

> If we could at least discover [...] an activity which was in some way akin to creative writing! An examination of it would then give us a hope of obtaining the beginnings of an explanation of the creative work of writers. And, indeed, there is some prospect of this being possible. [...] Might we not say that every child at play behaves like a creative writer, in that he creates a world of his own, or rather, rearranges the things of his world in a new way which pleases him?[11]

Twentieth-century critics therefore employ an intellectual tool first developed by nineteenth-century writers when they argue, as Peter Brooks argues, that realism can be seen 'as a kind of literature and art committed to a form of play that uses carefully wrought and detailed toys'.[12] Or as Kendall Walton and Thomas Pavel propose in their studies of mimesis, that 'just as children pretending to feed dolls [...] become themselves fictional moms and dads fictionally feeding their offspring, readers of *Anna Karenina* [...] participate (as spectators) in a game of make-believe'.[13] Imaginative play as an observable practice provides what is the perhaps the most visible model for examining the immersive aspect of literary fiction.

This book reconstructs a tradition of novel practice and criticism which has long been sidelined for its prioritisation of imaginative experience, and builds on this tradition in two ways. First, it endows the play-novel analogy with historical and technical specificity, by examining an actual, material play practice. At the turn between the eighteenth and nineteenth centuries, the documented childhoods of the De Quincey brothers, the Brontë siblings, Hartley Coleridge, Anna Jameson, Thomas Malkin, and Trollope produced a phenomenon in the history of child psychology: the emergence of an unprecedented and highly specified type of make-believe, involving the elaborate construction of imaginary worlds. I investigate the mechanics of this imaginative practice, and trace its entanglements with the history of the novel, in order to better understand the novel's affordances and significance as a practice of fictional realities. Second, this book proposes how this understanding resituates the novel as an object in the history and culture of the virtual.

How is the novel virtual? Such a term draws deliberate associations with video gaming and cyber realities, domains where interactions with imaginary objects currently command widespread cultural and theoretical attention; but as many art and literary historians have now argued, virtuality represents a philosophical concept that preceded and has helped to shape its modern digital connotations. Its seminal definition, adapted by Gilles Deleuze from Marcel Proust's famous description of sensuous memory, is that which is 'real but not actual, ideal but not abstract'.[14] That this philosophical definition originates from the novelistic account of a psychological event reflects the sense in which – as John Plotz has argued – the virtual constitutes a category of mediated sensory, social, or aesthetic experiences which crosses 'genre boundaries, historical periodization, and even disciplinary logic', even as its individual expressions in art and theory are generically, historically, or discipline specific.[15] On similar lines, Jean-Marie Schaeffer has argued that the three-dimensional other-world through which we imagine digital virtual realities is modelled after 'biological systems of representation' such as memory, as well as representational technologies in the visual and verbal arts.[16] Peter Otto has identified the formalisation of these examples into a concept of the virtual within Enlightenment and Romantic ideas about the second-order realities of the senses (Hume and Kant), of social fictions (Burke and Paine), and of poetic imagination (Coleridge and Wordsworth).[17]

The virtuality explored in this book shares some of these (as Plotz calls them) 'fuzzy borders', but represents a specific instantiation of the concept in the mid-Victorian novel: the virtual as *fictional experiences and actions, or fictional realities which can be experienced and acted upon.*[18] As I will argue in my chapter on Dickens, the inherent virtuality of human perception – the mediation of the world through our senses, and our susceptibility to seeing things that are not there – is central to Victorian debates about the psychology of fictional experience, a tradition which presages William Gibson's 1982 invention of the term 'cyberspace' as a 'consensual hallucination'.[19] Conversing with his characters beyond the novel and receiving letters of concern about them, Thackeray wondered whether, as 'Madmen, you know, see visions, hold conversations with, even draw the likeness of, people invisible to you and me [...] are novel-writers at all entitled to strait-waistcoats?'[20] Can a social encounter be real but not actual? The philosopher J. David Velleman identifies this capacity in the video game *Second Life*, where digital avatars perform meaningful actions on behalf of an actual player, and also in therapeutic play:

How can there be fictional actions that a real person literally performs? Here is another example. In the psychoanalytic transference, the patient may attempt to seduce the analyst, but not literally. Patient and analyst are rather embodying fictional versions of child and parent, and the attempt by the one to seduce the other is a fictional attempt at a fictional seduction. But the patient is really making that attempt, is really the agent of that unreal action. Actions carried out within the transference are not make-believe; *they are fictional actions literally performed.*[21]

To act or experience virtually in these senses is not, as in common parlance, to nearly do something ('I was virtually in tears') or to do it digitally ('I completed the forms virtually'), but to do it with vicarious or fictional reality: to taste the memory of food or seduce an imagined person. As Auyoung has argued, such effects 'are central to literary experience but remain on the periphery of literary studies [...] how the words of a novel can seem to evoke immediate sensory experiences and how fictional persons can continue to endure in a reader's mind'.[22] Understanding the novel as a historical medium for this capacity, and moreover as its exemplary literary form, reorients our sense of its literary functions while also recovering a Victorian legacy of ongoing questions about the relation between material and imagined lives.

Why the novel? Experiences of vicarious reality or immersive participation are not exclusive to the novel, nor often what novelists claim to be providing; yet it is a literary form whose inherent characteristics afford virtuality like no other. 'Affordance' is a psychological concept which has gained recent traction in literary studies, largely through the work of Terence Cave and Caroline Levine, as a way of thinking about genre: it signifies 'the potential *uses* an object or features of the environment offers to a living creature'.[23] Importantly, the qualities of an object can afford its use – lend it to being used – in ways that may be indifferent to its intended purpose. For example, a chair can (by virtue of its shape) be used as a coat rack or (by virtue of its rigidity) as a battering ram, as much as (by virtue of its design) for sitting in, and these affordances are particular in that it is better or less suited for some of these uses than other objects. If David's 'glorious host' is sustained 'out' of his reading of actual novels, in the sense of arising and then diverging from, the sense that the novel is especially effective for producing this kind of imaginative experience belies the generic particularity of novel fiction and its literary history.

One of the novel's technical innovations, as Catherine Gallagher and Lennard Davis have argued, was a new (but now almost universal) form of fictionality which combined plausibility and specificity with nonreferentiality. That is, the early novel was distinctive for appearing to reference specific persons, places, or events in the reader's contemporary world while overtly denying any direct correspondences, in contrast to other genres which lacked either its pretended reality (such as the epic or the romance) or its accepted fictitiousness (such as news or libel). For both Gallagher and Davis, this development was the unintentional yet monumental side-effect of eighteenth-century legal pressures on the depictions of contemporaries, where the disingenuous claims of satirists to be engaging in 'an innocent alternative to libellous referential stories' created a genuine genre of 'believable stories that did not solicit belief [...] which could be enjoyed for their own sake without reference to [a] person satirised'.[24] With the realist novel's further emphasis on the recognisable, Elaine Freedgood has also suggested, this 'weird – although thoroughly naturalized – combination of fictionality and factuality [...] makes the nineteenth-century novel anomalous (and this form persists [...] in any novel that continues to be realistic and thus referential')'.[25] By this account, novel fiction invented as its special characteristic imaginary objects which, having the referential style and verisimilitude of actual instances, can be treated or taken in certain ways 'as-if' for real.

This distinctive capacity of the novel for purveying explicitly artificial realities – in other words, the novel's historical affordance for the virtual – has been obscured by two prevailing attitudes to literary representation which might be called, for our purposes, *the real as actual* and *the ideal as abstract*. In the former, inherited from Platonic suspicions of the copy and registered by recurrent anxieties about cultural consumption, literature's acknowledged persuasiveness at reproducing reality is understood as falsifying the actual. The popular contention of these arguments is that representations lead individuals to mistake fiction for life. This anxiety is embodied by cultural figures from Don Quixote to Madame Bovary to the video-game shooter, who allegedly model their behaviour in the actual world after the false standards of fictive realities, even to a certain model of the reader as interpellated subject who Davis presents as 'experiencing a fantasy not their own but which, in this autistic state, they believe in some provisional way to be true'.[26] Such a view, committed to a logical binary between actuality and deception, fails to accommodate the playful doubleness of a form that renders openly non-existent things with extravagant verisimilitude. Davis's own history of the novel as an explicitly fictional form emphasises its distinction from simply persuasive deception: its capacity for 'ironic imagination' which Michael Saler has argued to be the foundation of virtual thinking, or as Lowe explains, simply its ability to not 'confound believing with imagining', to enjoy the quality of an illusion without being deceived.[27]

The second view, more influential and specific to the critical history of the novel, holds that represented realities express or typify general truths about actuality. As a defence of the novel's ethical or empirical truthfulness, versions of this argument extend back to Henry Fielding's claim to 'describe not men, but manners; not an individual, but a species', an adaptation of Aristotelian tradition that Gallagher and others enshrine as 'The founding claim of the [novel] form [...] a nonreferentiality that could be seen as a greater referentiality'.[28] A character's private life reflect the tendencies of a social class; the outcome of a tragedy embodies the conditions of living in the world; the luxuriant description of a manor house is 'no more than code for 'upper class' [...] an extremely roundabout way of making a very general and mediated statement about the way things are'; many students running these basic drills of literary training would recognise an inherent disappointment to the act of interpretation in its movement from the fictional towards the generalisable, universal, or abstract.[29] The referential specificity and immaterial details of the novel's fictional particulars appear to most readers as overdetermined (even wasteful) for making nebulous statements about 'species'.[30] The literary tourist's arrival at architectural exemplars and biographical inspirations only belies the desire, not for manor houses in general, but for Thornfield itself; it is not a class nor genus of the actual that Dickens's readers have in mind when they beseech him 'to spare the life of Nell in his story', or for Dickens himself on writing that character's death, that 'Nobody will miss her like I shall'.[31]

What are the stakes of virtual play? Distinguishing the novel's imagined objects from both the Platonic copy and the Aristotelian universal, as possessing a kind of experiential reality in their own right, enables criticism to perceive what such fictions afford by virtue of their artifice. William Macready, the Victorian actor who petitioned for Nell's life, knew her to be a non-material person whose plausibility and referential style enabled real knowledge and attachment in response to her imagined specificity, as opposed to a general groan for the condition of orphans in the world; but although he was uncommonly affected by the narrative's outcome, it was not equivalent to the death of an actual contemporary. 'I dread to read it, but I must get it over', Macready resignedly wrote in his diary, 'I never have read printed words that gave me so much pain'.[32] Another reader was reported as having exclaimed at the page, 'Dickens [...] would *commit murder*! He killed my little Nell', his niece commenting in her account that 'anyone might have supposed she was a real living child in whose sad fate he was deeply interested'; but this supposition too is limited by the presumable fact (it would be a different kind of anecdote otherwise) that he did not then contact the police.[33] As Lesley Goodman argues, such 'indignant readers' possess a specific sense of the author's culpability as not equivalent to actual action but still 'something that authors *do to* their characters' through the explicitly imaginary medium of plot.[34] Seeing as there is much else that authors and readers might *do to* a virtual person they could or would not to an actual one, this special category of experience demands its own theorisation and analysis.

The novel's potential value as a fictional reality is distinct, fulfilling other needs and requiring other practices, from our more familiar sense of its functions as a literary work. There are different social and ethical standards to an author's killing of character than to the murder of a material person, on the one hand, and to a character's killing of characters, on the other – because vicarious acts and experiences bear different kinds of significance to actual ones. 'Reading' an alleged report or reflection on actual care or violence is again different from 'playing' and enacting care or violence towards concrete imaginary objects: to interpret Trollope's representation of Mrs Proudie is to analyse the text or its claims about the world; to kill her off in narrative, miss her dearly, and then (in Trollope's words) 'live much in company with her ghost' (*AA* 173) is to do something to her specifically. Lowe's work articulates this as a difference of approach between critical methods of objectivity or detachment and of 'Sympathetic understanding' or 'subjective participation', following in the tradition of Wayne C. Booth's desire to 'work my way into a narrative [...] begin to see as [a character] sees, to feel as she feels, to love what he loves'.[35] This project differs from theirs, as play from sympathy, by expanding from a feeling understanding of perspective as only one (and perhaps least troubling) of many possible types of vicarious participation; I argue that the experience of a novel's fictional reality affords a wider range of responses and uses.

Just as Dickens's readers felt him to be 'literally perform[ing] fictional actions' (on analogously real, non-actual persons) through plot, Dickens himself recurrently imagined the vicarious satisfaction and moral difference of violence on representational objects.[36] In the second report of the 1838 *Mudfog Papers*, Dickens's fictional association proposes a system of 'harmless and wholesome relaxation for the young gentlemen of England', involving the construction of ten square miles of artificial country with replica 'highway roads, turnpikes, bridges, miniature villages'.[37] Within this space, which has the appearance of the public world but is in fact 'inclosed, and carefully screened', inebriated viscounts could dress how they please, 'walking about without any costume at all, if they liked that better', destroy any of the easily rebuildable props, and behave freely with a population of 'automaton figures [...] a policeman, cab-driver, or old woman' who could be 'set upon and beaten by six or eight noblemen [...] utter divers groans, mingled with entreaties for mercy, [and] thus rendering the illusion complete, and the enjoyment perfect'.[38] If the social critique of this sketch is the association's inverted priorities – accommodating, rather than reforming, a social class which already treats the world as their playground – its detailed fantasy also acknowledges an 'enjoyment' in the world reproduced as toy, in an expendable semblance of reality. Dickens would later reiterate this idea, without the satirical voice, in response to less realistic figures than the automaton:

> In my opinion the Street Punch is one of those extravagant reliefs from the realities of life which would lose its hold upon the people if it were made moral and instructive. I regard it as quite harmless in its influence, and as an outrageous joke which no one in existence would think of regarding as an incentive to any course of action, or a model for any kind of conduct. It is possible, I think, that one secret source of the pleasure [...] is the satisfaction the spectator feels in the circumstance that likenesses of men and women can be so knocked about, without pain or suffering.[39]

Such examples of secret pleasure may represent the antithesis of what Dickens and most Victorian novelists explicitly claimed as the novel's function – 'IT IS TRUE', Dickens fumed about the violent death of Nancy in *Oliver Twist*, which he used as an example to incentivise public philanthropy – but at the same time, they exemplify the inherent implications of the novel's design. Much like Fielding's founding claim, 'moral and instructive' defences of the form do not diminish its givenness to other uses. If the pleasure of the puppet theatre depends simultaneously on its 'extravagant reliefs' from life and its 'likenesses', just as the enjoyment of beating an automaton is its harmless resemblance of harm, the logical structure of novel fiction epitomises this combination.

By creating a screened and enclosed world which stylistically resembles the actual, and can be treated and experienced in selective, advantageous respects like actual instances, the novel by virtue of its *fiction* may perform social and ethical functions which work with or against its goals as a *depiction* of society and ethics. As I have suggested, the work of Booth, Lowe, and Rae Greiner converge on sympathy as one of these functions, 'bind[ing] the reading of fiction to the task of endowing others, and the historical past, with virtual life'.[40] Jonathan Farina proposes epistemology as another, pointing out the uses of counterfactual analogies in Victorian literature and science as a 'combination of imaginative, sympathetic speculation *and* disavowal of speculation', coming to a new hypothetical knowledge of the actual by positing explicitly fictional circumstances 'as-if' for real.[41] For Freedgood, the vicarious fantasies intrinsic to the robinsonade provide another means of imperial domination, separate to its valorised representations of empire, by imagining the fictional colony as a virtual place which can be actualised through colonisation yet also one in which the unsavoury nature of that colonisation can be dismissed as fictional.[42] These recent approaches to nineteenth-century virtuality demonstrate an interpretive method which 'reads' not for a novel's symbolic meaning or historical representations, but for the implications of its vicarious enactments and relations, the advantages and uses available only because of its distinctive fictionality; as Nicholas Dames has argued, such studies engage 'the challenge of exploring the unique specificities of fictional, or virtual, experiences'.[43] *Virtual Play* is committed to that challenge as a pertinent enquiry into our past and present lives with fiction.

Chapter Overview

The first chapter, 'Virtual, Paracosmic, Fictional', establishes virtual play as a historical practice, and draws its parallel with eighteenth- and nineteenth-century developments in novel fictionality. It introduces the concept of *paracosmic play* or *worldplay* – a form of modern make-believe documented in the juvenilia and biographical archives of Thomas De Quincey, Anna Jameson, Hartley Coleridge, Thomas Malkin, Brontë, and Trollope – as the clearest manifestation of this practice. I review the social scientific work on this phenomenon, track its origins through the history of utopian fiction, and propose its formal significance and theoretical affinities to the nineteenth-century novel. This chapter frames and contextualises the historical argument of the book: that novel fiction comes of age by distinguishing the actual from the virtual.

This unorthodox history of the form prepares the ground for the four bipartite author studies that follow. The first part of each begins with a critical encounter, between an author and an ambivalent critic, which elucidates an obscured or disparaged facet of their fiction I then explain and re-evaluate through their potential, alternative value as functions of virtual play. These sections re-examine an aspect of the novel (authorship, plot, form, and description) through comparison to a component of worldplay (omnipotence, improvisation, emotional attachment, and sensory imagination), to form the basis of a new critical perspective. The second part of each chapter puts this perspective to work on the close reading of an exemplary text, demonstrating the practical interventions and interpretive possibilities of a more vicarious novel criticism.

The second chapter examines recurring instances in the Brontë juvenilia where the siblings intervene in their narratives as omnipotent author-gods, called the 'Chief Genii', who reshape the imaginary world by writing it. I trace this narrative and play practice back to its roots in the pseudo-Oriental tales of *The Arabian Nights* and James Ridley, but also argue for its wider significance to the literary-theoretical metaphor (employed by writers from Gustave Flaubert to Roland Barthes) of the author as divine creator of the narrative reality. In counterpoint to existing scholarship which tend to emphasise generic differences between the juvenilia and Charlotte Brontë's mature work, I offer a reading of *The Professor* as a continuation of the Genii authorship within the realist novel, and thereby defend Brontë's reputation as an author of vicarious 'wish-fulfilment'. Brontë provides a starting case for this book's larger argument about the alternative uses of the novel as a fictional reality, rather than a historical representation, an aesthetic work, or an ethical parable.

The third chapter develops this argument by examining two claims of Anthony Trollope's *Autobiography*: that his novel-writing developed out of a paracosmic play practice he called 'castle-building', and that he made up his novel plots as he wrote them. Through an analysis of his and the De Quinceys' games, I point out how the improvisational nature of play – the virtual world is 'filled in' and revised over time with little premeditation – as an obvious analogue to Trollope's construction of the fictional Barsetshire, and to his plotting of individual novels. I argue that the characters of *The Small House at Allington* behave improvisationally, inventing, revising, and 'filling in' their personhoods as they go along, offering an alternative reading of the moral logic and psychology in Trollope's realism. For Trollope, the novel is distinctive for providing this experience of fictional living, not as 'mere' escapism but as it contributes concretely to the reader's experience of their own world.

The fourth chapter compares the longevity of imaginary worlds such as Brontë's Angria and De Quincey's Gombroon to Thackeray's obsessive revisiting of a single novelistic setting over multiple works. For instance, the protagonists of *Vanity Fair*, *Pendennis*, *The Newcomes*, and *Phillip* are all alumni of a fictional Grey Friars School which connects an expanding network of characters from across his oeuvre. Through his critical writing, I show how Thackeray was concerned about the affective pull of a familiar, imaginary place on the attention of his ever-baggier serial novels; a problem I argue he explores in *The Newcomes*, a novel about past relationships into which the characters of previous novels repeatedly intrude. Thackeray's story about these affective entanglements suggests not only a reassessment of his uses of form, but also the conflicting uses of the novel in general, torn between its status as a literary work and as the medium for a fictional reality.

The fifth and final chapter addresses the concreteness of fictional experiences on which Brontë's, Trollope's, and Thackeray's various uses of the novel depend. I examine nineteenth-century medical responses to Coleridge's paracosmic play, in particular their cautions against imagined environments as precursors to hallucination, and the continuity of this discourse with more general anxieties about fictional or poetic experience; for instance, George Henry Lewes singled out Dickens as an author who shared his pseudo-hallucinations through novels. This view of novel-reading as imaginative sensory participation has since been overshadowed by the cinematic and the digital, but represents an important precedent for the everyday presence of non-material things and spaces. In a reading of *Little Dorrit*, where multiple characters form their unrealised hopes and plans into fantasised environments, I argue that play, hallucination, and fiction provided nineteenth-century critics with tools to conceptualise a phenomenology of the virtual, or even its reparative value.

This book is a project to distinguish the virtuality of the Victorian novel, both in the sense of differentiating a quality from other literary values or cultural functions, and of making a case for its significance to our understanding and use of the form. The novel's development in the eighteenth century uniquely equipped it to produce detailed, plausible, and palpable accounts of explicitly non-existent events, objects, places, and people, a capacity which has too often been subordinated to aims of 'reflecting' condition or generalities. This unprecedented practice of particularising the imaginary needs reassessment, on its own grounds, as a practice of the virtual, of making its own realities that can be experienced and interacted with through the medium of the text. What do novels distinctively do by virtue of their fictional worlds? What kinds of literal action do they vicariously afford? At stake in such questions is both a descriptive and instructive knowledge of the novel; understanding what kind of object it is and how it can help us to live imaginatively.

CHAPTER 1

Virtual, Paracosmic, Fictional

On being offered employment at a certain house 'near Millcote, ——shire', Jane Eyre 'brushed up my recollections of the map of England: yes, I saw it; both the shire and the town' (*JE* 105). Yet either the map or the England she consults must be different from our own, because while readers can only seek Thornfield abstractly, through 'historical inspirations' and filming locations, Jane unerringly places Millcote 'seventy miles nearer London' than her address at Lowood, and as 'a large manufacturing town on the banks of the A——' (105). Charlotte Brontë's *Jane Eyre* is set, of course, in a fictional part of England, but it is worth pausing on the seeming obviousness of this expectation. How can a real country have a fictional part? Novel fiction engages its readers in protocols nearly invisible for the ease with which we assume them, as natural as reading, so much a matter of course that it requires a moment of obstinate naivete to register the paradoxical logic involved in 'setting' any realist novel within, but also necessarily out of, the spaces of real life. If Jane's relocation first seems less radical than the Indian mission she would later consider, her appeal to national reference abruptly defamiliarises an ostensibly familiar backdrop, revealing the apparent interstices of English geography that only inhabitants of the novel can see or enter. Much as Rochester continually teases Jane's plainness for disguising 'a fairy [...] come from Elfland' (337), the innocuousness of Millcote or Lowood as contemporary settings, measurable in miles from London and no more exotic than Leeds, belies 'the look of another world' (149).

The *otherworldliness* of novel fiction is a determining yet unacknowledged condition of the realist mode. It is in fact difficult to imagine the Victorian novel without the plausible yet invisible annexes its narratives interlock with the reference world of the reader: from the provincial neighbourhoods of Middlemarch and Barsetshire, to domestic spaces like Bleak House and Wuthering Heights, even to individual fictional rooms set into recognisable public buildings, the famously ordinary realist setting occupies a magical or quantum existence we take extraordinarily for granted. *Bleak House*'s Mr Vhole keeps his office on the ground floor of the historical Symond's Inn, making him a close neighbour to *Pendennis*'s Captain Costigan, who lives in the fictional Shepherd's Inn, nestled 'Some where behind the black gables and smutty chimney-stacks of Wych Street, Holywell Street, Chancery Lane [...] hidden from the outer world'.[1] A national map riddled with such fairy glades, big and small – 'I saw it', says Jane, but what would such a map look like? – exemplifies the unusual, hybrid discourse which distinguishes the realist novel.

This book proposes the various ways mid-nineteenth-century novelists and readers find resources for living in this hybridity between fact and fiction, in imaginative practices I call *virtual play*. The four author studies that follow demonstrate these practices in action, exploring the implications and affordances of the novel's verisimilitude, in order to propose an alternative tradition of the novel as a medium for artificial realities. This chapter, however, lays the groundwork for these explorations by lingering on the idiosyncratic premise of fictional worlds and our naturalised capacity to entertain them, both products of the so-called rise of the novel which have become fundamental to modern fiction.

The idea that fictional discourse refers to a state of affairs outside the actual world is a philosophically intuitive and widely held model of narrative semantics: that what fictional sentences are doing when they talk as if Jane Eyre or Thornfield exist is positing an alternative reality where they do.[2] Yet such narratological models, as Michael McKeon has argued, are 'largely drawn from the concrete practice of the novel genre' which has come to dominate understandings of fiction, even as its distinctive mode of extra-actual reference is, relative to the literary history of narratives in general, a recent invention of the eighteenth century.[3] As historian of reading Jonathan Rose has stressed, not everyone even in the nineteenth century was caught up on the rules of a 'fairly sophisticated literary convention that must be learned',[4] with credulous readers taking everything from the Revelations to *Robinson Crusoe* as literally and equivalently true to one unified history of actual events, an error only further complicated by the realist novel's seamless transitions between fictional and factual modes of reference (e.g., Sherlock Holmes lives on Baker Street).[5] The capacity to virtualise narrative fiction, to engage the right protocols when encountering the realistic account of a non-actual world, enjoys the current status of a universal skill but has a specific literary history in the novel, as well as a set of practical literary functions which have become obscured by this taking for granted.

Here as elsewhere in this book, I use 'play' as a heuristic to illustrate these possibilities of a virtualising capacity, and argue for their realisation in a practice of fiction intrinsic to the novel tradition. As the necessary form of response to what Gallagher calls the novel's 'language game' of reference without correspondence, play is an apt analogy for the navigation between cognitive frames required to maintain that London is connected by road to parts of the country that do not exist.[6] More than an analogy, however, accounts of actual, specific play by nineteenth-century children also provide suggestive examples of a virtual practice in history, drawing on the same protocols of fiction as the novel form. How might play be novelistic? As Matthew Kaiser and J. Jeffrey Franklin have noted, play in its most philosophical form operated 'as the mystified kernel at the center of [Victorian] culture', uniting the disparate logics of competition, chance, fantasy, and leisure; much as it also provided for Kant the cornerstone of aesthetic judgement, and for Friedrich von Schiller the basis of human freedom.[7] But the period also recognised 'play' more literally, in the sense of a specific activity with an imaginative or psychological component, which they alternatively described through the idioms of daydream, invention, make-believe, or castle-building. In the late eighteenth and early nineteenth centuries, a special kind of play in this latter sense began to be noticed among multiple groups of English children, prompting remarks from contemporary witnesses and later biographers on both its atypicality as a phenomenon and its conformity between cases. What developmental psychologists now neologise as *paracosmic play* or *worldplay*, a practice of extended make-believe premised on the creation and documentation of imaginary lands or worlds, continued throughout the twentieth century into the present day, but appear by the strength of the evidential record to have begun with a loose generation of late Romantics and early Victorians: with Hartley Coleridge, Anna Jameson, Thomas Malkin, Anthony Trollope, the De Quincey brothers, and the Brontë siblings.

The rise of novel fiction and of worldplay are concurrent historical narratives – and, as I propose, complementary ones. Both operate on a concept of fiction as an alternative plane of reference, existing non-materially yet concretely, independently yet in parallel to the actual; a set of assumptions which McKeon and Gallagher have shown to be significant and new for concepts of narrative and truthfulness in the eighteenth century. The distinctiveness and necessary sophistication of both have been eroded by familiarity, universalised by their persistence into our present ways of imagining fiction, and as such the two phenomena suggest similar questions – sharing potentially similar answers – about the development of our naturalised practices both on the historical and the biographical scale. Attempting to get at the particularities of what 'became the norm throughout Europe and America in the nineteenth century, and we still anticipate [...] when we pick up a novel today', Gallagher turns to the eighteenth century to 'hear what the novel has to say about fictionality in its infancy'.[8] Though it may be long forgotten, at some point we all 'learned' as a culture and as individuals to cry for the death of Little Nell without believing in her material life. As Rose points out, 'We are not born with this strategy of reading'.[9] In what follows, I argue that the history of worldplay is similarly revealing about the initial adoption of the fictional mode to which we now default, particularly in the cases of Trollope and Brontë, whose early play and juvenilia embody the learning of certain narrative assumptions which would underlie their later work as realist novelists. The complex protocols of fictional reality we necessarily perform, yet often elide when talking about the 'realist' settings of Barsetshire and Millcote are being visibly gestated in the imaginary worlds of paracosms, not having yet disguised their otherworldliness; fictionality captured in its infancy.

Gombroon, Ejuxria, and Allestone

> Both my brother and myself, for the sake of varying our intellectual amusements, occupied ourselves at times in governing imaginary kingdoms. I do not mention this as any thing unusual; it is a common resource of mental activity and of aspiring energies amongst boys.[10]

Thomas De Quincey, writing about a childhood in the 1790s, goes on to explain that 'My own kingdom was an island called Gombroon', which existed in 'one eternal element of feud' (*AS* 45) with Tigrosylvania, the kingdom of his older brother. The siblings took turns to determine the geographical position of their nations, a decision De Quincey deferred in the hopes of leaving 'a monstrous world of waters between us' (45) as a buffer against his brother's expansionism: on William's declaration that his capital lay on a latitude of sixty-five degrees north (just above the Bering Strait), 'That fact being once published and settled, instantly I smacked my little kingdom of Gombroon down into the tropics, 10 deg., I think, south of the line [...] my brother never would degrade himself by fitting out a costly nautical expedition against poor little Gombroon; and how else could he get at me?' (45–46)[11] He had not counted, however, on William's riposte that Tigrosylanivan borders extended from its Arctic capital 'southwards through a matter of 80 or 90 deg. [...] vast horns and promontories ran down from all parts of his dominions towards any country whatsoever, in either hemisphere', (46) and moreover, that Gombroon's tropical forests concealed diamond mines its imperial neighbour intended to seize.

The De Quinceys' game is remarkable both for its precocity and its earnestness. For one, Gombroon and Tigrosylvania are governed by rules which support their capacity for *true facts*, information about the fictional world kept strictly consistent, specific, and accurate even while continually accumulated through play. Neither brother, in spite of their rivalry, ever attempt to reject each other's narrative claims or even to retract their own; once a fact is 'published and settled' (*AS* 45), it can be extravagantly elaborated upon but never contradicted, 'like a move at chess or draughts, which it was childish to dispute' (46). As Sally Shuttleworth has also noted, 'there is curious interplay between the concepts of the real and imaginary: although this world is one of imagination, it obeys rigid rules of physicality and social intercourse'.[12] A precise difference of seventy-five degrees in latitude is a distance which requires either 'a costly nautical expedition' (46) or an already sprawling empire to surmount; nations invade each other for concrete motives of resource-gathering, requiring a diegetic logic of the game in addition to a player's belligerence. Such details demand not only exactness but also an extensive coherence.

For another, although the siblings are clearly aware of a potential arbitrariness to facts they themselves invent (choosing, for instance, where to place landmasses), the imaginariness of objects and experiences do not diminish their value or seriousness. 'O reader, do not laugh!' De Quincey pleads in acknowledgement that, compared to his physical fights with local boys, Gombroon is 'a world purely aerial, where all the combats and the sufferings were absolute moonshine' (*AS* 47). Yet, reversing the expected hierarchy, real life 'was as nothing in comparison of that dream kingdom which rose like a vapor from my own brain', because the 'Long contemplation of a shadow, earnest study for the welfare of that shadow [...] had gradually frozen that shadow into a rigor of reality far denser than the material realities of brass or granite' (47–48). The more that the fictional world makes sense, the more it matters, and vice versa; the effort to maintain the specificity and self-consistency of the pretence renders it capable of real affective responses, just as emotional and imaginative participation in that pretence contributes to its feeling of inviolable reality.

Playing with imaginary worlds is an exemplarily and distinctively *virtual* practice, not only because it fore-'shadows' the language of digital virtual realities, but because the very concept of an imaginary world reflects the development of substantive new attitudes to literary fiction and truth in the eighteenth century. If the brothers' system of true invented facts appears as precocious but unexceptional to a modern culture where multiple print dictionaries document the Klingon language in English, Portuguese, German, Italian, and Czech, authors and readers of the early novel had arrived fitfully to the idea that a plausible report about concrete objects could be neither telling the truth nor lying about the actual, but instead relaying fictional information. Although the dishonesty of poetry has been consistently debated since Plato, the incipient genre of the novel was the first to formally frame fictional narratives as reports of real life, necessitating circumlocuitous defences like Daniel Defoe's 1719 preface to *Robinson Crusoe*, which (spuriously) claimed the tale to be 'a just History of Fact; neither is there any appearance of Fiction in it' yet also hedged his bets, 'because all such things are [disputed], that the Improvement of it, as well as the Diversion [...] will be the same'.[13] Others, like Fielding, mounted Aristotelean arguments of the novel's general or abstract truthfulness – reporting the type of thing that can happen – even as the narrative seemed to describe specific instances in what Ian Watt seminally termed as 'formal realism'.[14]

Between *Robinson Crusoe* and, exactly a century later, *The Bride of Lammermoor* lies the naturalisation of an assumption which would render Defoe and Fielding's excuses unnecessary: the novel describes its own reality, overlapping with ours but maintaining its own rigorous system of reference and fact. Walter Scott's preface in 1819 identifies the 'real source' for *Lammermoor*'s narrative but also the explicit imaginariness of his version of events. For instance, 'the death of the unfortunate bridegroom by a fall from horseback has been in the novel transferred' to a different character, and that although 'The imaginary castle of Wolf's Crag has been identified by some lover of locality with that of Fast Castle [...] The Author is not competent to judge of the resemblance betwixt the real and imaginary scenes, having never seen Fast Castle except from the sea'.[15] In the new protocols of fictionality between Scott and his readers, to attack his narrative as implausible by pointing out internal contradictions – for example, if two separate descriptions placed Wolf's Crag on opposite ends of Scotland – would be fair game, but to do so by disputing the historicity of its particulars (as Defoe once expected to be 'disputed') would not. The idea of a fictional world, to which play or narrative can refer instead of the actual world, is significant not just for its imagined space and objects but as a fundamental conceit for understanding how to read a novel in the nineteenth century.

De Quincey's account registers the acquisition of a novel literacy or cognitive skill by two particular children at the turn of the century, but larger implications about the cultural spread of these skills lie in his suggestion that such games represent a 'common resource of mental activity' (*AS* 45) in this period. He specifically cites a fellow monarch in Hartley Coleridge (the son of his erstwhile idol Samuel Taylor Coleridge), who also 'had a kingdom which he governed for many years' (45). Derwent Coleridge's posthumous memoir of his younger brother recalls the imaginary land of Ejuxria, which Hartley invented as 'a region – a realm [...] an island-continent, with its own attendant isles,– a new Australia, or newest Sea-land'.[16] Unlike William De Quincey, Derwent played confidant to his brother's fictions but did not participate, giving Hartley sole authorship over a less embattled realm than Gombroon:

> [F]urnishing a theatre and scene of action, with *dramatis personae* [...] day after day, for the space of long years, he went on evolving the complicated drama of existence. There were many nations, continental and insular, each with its separate history, civil, ecclesiastical, and literary, its forms of religion and government, and specific national character. (*HC* xliii)

Contemporaneously yet independently, De Quincey and Coleridge converged on similar yet highly specific patterns of play. Common to both cases is a focus on consistency and detail, faithfully imagining a single world and its inhabitants over years and to great specificity. Both are drawn to the setting of the island, isolated by an indeterminate ocean but still nebulously located on the globe. More fundamentally, the two games also share a fictional mode. As an ambivalent yet enraptured spectator, Derwent made an incisive theoretical distinction that, although 'the Ejuxrian world presented a complete analogon to the world of fact [...] the correspondence was free and poetical, not in the nature of a fac-simile, nor, as in *Gulliver's Travels*, of an intentional disguise' (xliii–xliv). Like the imaginary Wolf's Crag, the 'analogon' of Ejuxria may resemble certain actualities, but it constitutes a reality which is specific and complete in itself. 'I believe it to have been a work of the imagination', Derwent concludes, 'woven with wonderful minuteness, and, as I believe, with uniform consistency' (xliv).

Both pairs of brothers were in turn unaware of another contemporary in Thomas Malkin (b. 1795), the son of writer Benjamin Heath Malkin and an apparent child prodigy. After Thomas's tragic death from illness at the age of nine, the elder Malkin published in 1803 *A Father's Memoirs of His Child* to record the lost promise of his son's genius; in particular, the biography is dominated by narratives and sketches of Thomas's imagined world. This archive, which includes a fold-out facsimile of Thomas's map and an appendix of his writings (in addition to significant excerpts within the biographical text), presents a compelling model for the no longer extant 'publications' of Hartley and the De Quinceys:

> This was the idea of a visionary country, called Allestone, which was so strongly impressed on his own mind, as to enable him to convey an intelligible and lively transcript of it in description. Of this delightful territory he considered himself as king. He had formed the project of writing its history, and had executed the plan in detached parts. Neither did his ingenuity stop here; for he drew a map of the country, giving names of his own invention to the principal mountains, rivers, cities, seaports, villages, and trading towns.[17]

Besides striking congruences in the practice of 'governing imaginary kingdoms' (*AS* 45), the senior Malkin's account is also telling in its oscillation between Thomas's play as 'description' and as 'ingenuity', with the formal appearance of a referential or documentary activity (conveying a transcript, writing a history, drawing a map) belying the explicit ontology of fiction-making (assuming kingship, inventing names). All three games operate on this elaborate double structure of fictional reference. Although 'no written record remains' of Hartley's Ejuxrian writings except 'the fragment of a story' (*HC* xlii), Derwent remembers that 'an elaborate map of the country was once in existence' (xlii–xliii). De Quincey recalls another instance of brotherly cruelty in how, on encountering Lord Monboddo's pre-Darwinian theories on human ancestry, William 'published an extract from some scoundrel's travels in Gombroon, according to which the Gombroonians had not yet emerged from this early condition of apedom. They, it seems, were still *homines caudati* [humans with tails]' (*AS* 52). Such maps, histories, and travel writings, borrowed forms which encourage their reception as true or false records of the actual, depend on the context of the game to be understood as fictional works referring to a fictional world; a strategy, as I have argued, that embodies a distinctively novelistic logic.

It of course bears noting that not all play of this kind and in this period conform so exactly in their features, but that the conceit of the fictional world is nonetheless a conspicuous marker for the availability of 'a common resource' (*AS* 45). Anna Jameson (b. 1796), in her popular 1854 essay

'A Revelation of Childhood', disproves De Quincey's assumption that imaginary kingdoms are the exclusive province of boys:

> I can truly say that, from ten years old to fourteen or fifteen, I lived a double existence; one outward, linking me with the external sensible world, and other inward, creating a world to and for itself, conscious to itself only. I carried on whole years a series of action, scenes, and adventures; one springing out of another, and coloured and modified by increasing knowledge.[18]

Jameson's imagined 'world' (not named in the essay) bears generic differences from Gombroon, Ejuxria, and Allestone, designed to accommodate romances of her own adventures as 'a princess-heroine in the disguise of a knight [...] going about to redress the wrongs of the poor, fight giants, and kill dragons'.[19] Moreover, for Jameson the 'double existence' of 'inward' narration emphasises privacy over publication, noting that despite her 'very strict and very accomplished governess [...] nothing of this was known or even suspected by her, and I exulted in possessing something which her power could not reach'.[20] Her language echoes the solipsistic practices of characters such as Lucy Snowe of *Villette*, published the year before, who similarly balances 'two lives – the life of thought, and that of reality',[21] and of Jane Eyre tuning her 'inward ear to a tale that was never ended – a tale my imagination created, and narrated continuously' (*JE* 132). As we will see, such parallels to Brontë's protagonists ultimately trace back to another game of imagined worlds, but much else about Jameson's play also shares fundamental features with De Quincey, Coleridge, and Malkin: the 'founding [of] a society in some far-off solitude or desolate island', the assumption of an authority to mandate 'no tears, no tasks, and no laws, – except those which I made myself', and the continuation of the same or connected set of fictions over years.[22]

'It is an interesting question why', Shuttleworth suggests, 'at this period, children in such different households should have invested such energy in creating alternate lands [...] there are not, as far as I am aware, any earlier records of them attempting to create entire imaginary lands, complete with political, economic, and cultural systems'.[23] I have argued so far that the spread of this practice parallels the popularisation of a literary form (the novel) and its narrative conventions (applicable beyond the novel), or understood together, represents the naturalisation of a type of virtual thinking about fiction. But as her question implies, Shuttleworth herself is less persuaded on the emergence of a child psychological phenomenon 'at this period', given only a correlation without causation between 'such different households'. She proposes instead to explain an emergence of 'records', the dissemination of a mode of autobiography rather than of fictionality, wherein 'the publication of so many reflections on early childhood at the mid-[nineteenth] century [...] had a contagious effect, stimulating further revelations from writers turning to their own childhoods as a source of self-understanding'.[24] If the birthdates of these children appear to cluster in the 1780s and 90s, the publications of their 'reflections' also closely follow each other: Derwent's memoir in 1851, De Quincey's *Autobiographical Sketches* in 1853, and Jameson's essay in 1855.[25] By this account, play with imaginary worlds may have existed long before the novel, but not considered worthy of comment until a new interest in representing childhood after Wordsworth and the *bildungsroman*.

The modern inheritors of this nineteenth-century interest – developmental psychology and the social sciences – have similarly understood this form of play to be a universal cognitive schema, a hypothesis strengthened by the continued manifestation of cases into the present day. Such studies, however, are less interested in nineteenth-century records for their historiographical problems than for providing cultural ballast to a theory of complex play as signalling or encouraging creative potential. Lewis Terman's eugenic studies on intellectual giftedness, conducted longitudinally from 1921 until 1986, noted that 48 of his 643 subjects (7 percent) had 'imaginary countries', although he did not record them in any detail.[26] In 1942, Leta Hollingworth's *Children Above 180 IQ* similarly reported that three of her six prepubescent subjects played games of imaginary worlds (Center Land, Bornington, and an unnamed colony on Venus), which she interpreted as a general desire to '*organize the play* into a complicated pattern [...] in long-sustained, complicated games' that indicated their developmental acceleration.[27] David Cohen and Stephen A. MacKeith's 1991 study *The Development of the Imagination* collected case studies through a public survey, interviewing fifty-seven respondents whom they felt conformed to the characteristics of what they termed *paracosmic play* (derived from *paracosm*, a neologism for the invented world itself).[28] Noting the statistical significance of their results, Cohen and MacKeith suggested 'that if we are ever to understand how the imagination develops, we shall have to be able to understand how young children find the skill and motivation to conjure up such remarkable places'.[29] Most recently, Michele Root-Bernstein's 2014 study hypothesised that the highly creative population (represented by a survey of MacArthur Fellows) are more likely to develop what she calls *worldplay* than the average population – furthermore, that worldplay might be used as a pedagogical tool to cultivate creativity as part of a national curriculum.[30] For Root-Bernstein, examples of literary writers like De Quincey, Coleridge, and Jameson exemplify the potential of an exceptional developmental process that transcends cultural context.[31]

Yet there are good reasons to insist on the historical specificity of a genuinely emergent phenomenon taking place among children at the end of the eighteenth century. For one, although Malkin's unusual memoir of his son registers a new scientific interest in accounts of childhood, Thomas's own writings about Allestone also represent a unprecedented type of record produced by children in the course of play itself, 'live' evidence of a new imaginative practice rather than a new trend in representation after the fact. For another, both play's setting and objects, as well as the genres and ideologies which frame it, visibly draw on the available resources of its cultural environs; as Christine Alexander has argued, 'children learn largely by imitation, their early writings [...] mock, cavil, exaggerate, and explore the adult attitudes that surround them and that they encounter in their reading'.[32] William De Quincey, for example, pastiches the travel and scientific literature of his reading into an ignominious attack on Gombroon. Derwent Coleridge likewise recalls Hartley's 'wont to transfer whatever struck his fancy or stimulated his intellect in actual life' (*HC* xl) into the Ejuxrian world:

> Whatever he had seen in London – theatres, tower, laboratory, or chemistry-house, as he called it; whatever struck his fancy in reading, – armies, ships, battles by sea and land, news, negociations, alliances, diplomacy – he thought to reproduce in little in his own playground[.] (xlv)

Joetta Harty notes in particular Hartley's reproduction of 'a new Australia', contextualising these children's interests in latitudes and cartography within 'the various shapes and forms of a geography-centred, colonialist, culturally imperialist discourse': James Cook had charted and claimed the coast of New South Wales in 1770, concluding the age of aggressive colonial expansion and imagination Joseph Conrad would call 'Geography Militant'.[33] Such materials provided fresh impetus to childish fascinations with the 'desolate island' and with fantasies of sovereignty, which clearly rehearse older, yet still popular narratives such as *Robinson Crusoe*.[34]

As I propose, this learning by imitation included a mode of reading and writing *Robinson Crusoe* which no longer seriously entertained (nor required) Defoe's claim to 'a just History of Fact'.[35] The acquisition and naturalisation of a fictional mode represents a less abstract form of development than of 'giftedness' or creative capacity, and a less visible example of cultural practice in play than the tropes of political news or colonial adventure. The ability to conceptualise fictional worlds lies at the intersection between a kind of inventive cognition and a literary conceit of undiscovered lands. For two of the novelists examined in this book, from a succeeding generation of children born in the early nineteenth century, little of the contents of their imaginary countries survive into their later works – one reason the significance of their play has been underacknowledged or misunderstood in discussions of their literary practices – but a way of doing fiction does. Charlotte Brontë's (b. 1816) and Anthony Trollope's (b. 1815) realist novels do not resemble travel narratives, nor feature the 'armies, ships, battles by sea or land' (*HC* xlv) to which this generation of children are drawn. What they learn from and demonstrate in play, however, is a conceptualisation of where novel fictions take place: in imaginary worlds adjoined to ours.

Glass Town, Angria, Gondal, and Gaaldine

The archive known as the Brontë juvenilia is undoubtedly the best preserved and most well-known example of imaginary worlds in this period. Composed roughly between 1829 and 1839, an extant collection of poems, narratives, histories, catalogues, maps, and drawings detail the four Brontë siblings' collaborative creation of the nations of Glass Town, Angria, Gondal, and Gaaldine, both resembling and dwarfing the archive of mixed media assembled by Thomas Malkin's father. As the critic Kate Brown points out, Charlotte Brontë's prose contributions to this game 'exceed in length [...] all of Brontë's novels put together', and as Elizabeth Gaskell estimated when she uncovered them in 1856, 'would make more than 50 vols of print'.[36] Yet since the publication of these voluminous early writings – first in excerpt by Gaskell's *Life of Charlotte Brontë* in 1857, then more completely by Fannie Ratchford's scholarly edition in 1941 – critics have been largely ambivalent about their literary function or significance. In a letter to George Smith, Gaskell raised concerns about the manuscripts she had discovered and deemed 'the wildest & most incoherent things [...] creative power carried to the verge of insanity'.[37] Ratchford's work, which exhaustively traces prototypes for the Brontës' canonical plots and characters back to this early writing, locates their value in being 'the laboratory in which developed all the elements that in their several combinations make up *The Professor, Jane Eyre, Shirley*, and *Villette*'.[38]

Alexander, the most recent editor of this material for the 1987 edition, similarly suggests their function as 'both workshop and playground' for novelists-in-development.[39] Such approaches, tending to debate the juvenilia's significance in the biographical context of the Brontës as a distinct group of novelists, leave open the possibility for a wider interpretation of this material in the context of the paracosmic phenomenon, of fictional or imaginative practices in general, and of the novel as a form.

As I have argued, games of imaginary worlds embody a novelistic logic and history of fiction; in their juvenilia, the Brontës not only work up the materials of their later novels, but they learn the basic protocols of novel discourse. Their procedures of play, which are also procedures of narrative, reflect fundamental assumptions about the relation between fact and fiction. Like the De Quinceys with their latitudes and Coleridge with his new Australia, the Brontës created their new lands in between the literal lines of geographical reference. In the Brontë Parsonage's copy of Rev. J. Goldsmith's *A Grammar of General Geography*, in the gazetteer of place names at the back of the volume, after the printed entry for 'Eurestenburg; a principality of the Grand Duchy of Baden' and before that of 'Gareta; a celebrated town of Naples', a childish script inserts 'Gaaldine a large island newly discovered in the south pacific'; and again, between Gomera (one of the Canary Islands) and Gondar (a city in modern Ethiopia), 'Gondal a large island in the north pacific'.[40] Again deceptively easy to dismiss as imaginative precocity, such annotations in fact make substantive ontological claims for the narrative, visually insisting that Gondal and Gaaldine are places formally equivalent to actual places, with an equivalent capacity to be specified, documented, and indexed. Moreover, they are explicitly not disguises for an actual place (in which case they would replace or modify an existing entry), nor an elaborate hoax to deceive future users of the gazette, nor the symptoms of a delusional belief. Rather, the Brontës are playing at verisimilitude, supplementing a work of reference *as if* Gaaldine has been 'newly discovered' in the material world represented by Goldsmith.[41]

The Brontës' additions to the *Grammar* are strange but true examples of the 'discoveries' intrinsic to the discursive game of the novel, where we pretend to accrue knowledge about unheard-of people and places *as if* the text is documenting rather than inventing this information. To open Dickens's eighth novel, *The Personal History, Adventures, Experience and Observation of David Copperfield the Younger of Blunderstone Rookery (Which He Never Meant to Publish on Any Account)*, is to pretend in this way that we have 'newly discovered' the life story of an individual encounterable in the world. Nicholas D. Paige has argued that the formal boundary between the early novel and its generic predecessors is marked by this 'pseudofactual posture [...]' of memoirs, letters, or occasionally eyewitness histories by or about contemporaries of whom no one had heard'.[42] Readers had to develop a new sophistication about fictions which became increasing indistinguishable from fact on the textual level – as Rose has shown, different populations of readers 'caught on' at uneven historical speeds – learning to perform the cognitive trick that when 'we meet a merely fictional character in a novel [...] we fold them into the world we inhabit without inconsistency'.[43] This trick is not so much an operation of counterfactual thinking – as some narratologists posit – as of extrafactuality, imagining more than is strictly true about the world.[44]

Due to the social and legal stakes of reputation in the period, literary historians have tended to emphasise the imagined contemporary as an example of the novel's unique interlocking of fiction and fact. 'The key mode of nonreferentiality in the novel was, and still is, that of proper names', Gallagher argues, tracking the rise of novel fiction through its movement from 'a previous language game that assumed a correspondence between a proper name in a believable narrative and an embodied individual in the world' to the modern understanding that 'proper names do not take specific individuals as their referents, and hence none of the specific assertions made about them can be verified or falsified'.[45] The titles of David Copperfield's favourite eighteenth-century books seem accordingly to hinge their narrative claims upon the existences of 'Roderick Random, Peregrine Pickle, Humphrey Clinker, Tom Jones, the Vicar of Wakefield, Don Quixote, Gil Blas, and Robinson Crusoe'[46] – a convention which *David Copperfield* and *Jane Eyre* themselves follow, and which Watt has argued as the novel's 'significant break with tradition'.[47] The presence or absence of such persons in the world, and then a developing sense of their pretended reality despite the world, has become 'key' to the critical history of novel fiction.

The Brontë juvenilia remind us, however, that proper names can denote more than persons. What it means to give proper names to specific but non-actual *places* rather than characters, in fact an older literary practice, has its own, under-examined implications for how the novel came to conceive its particular fictionality. Geography is a different kind of index for truth, as the young Jane Eyre reflects in the process of learning to read:

> I considered [*Gulliver's Travels*] a narrative of facts, and discovered in it a vein of interest deeper than what I found in fairy tales: for as to the elves, having sought them in vain among foxglove leaves and bells [...] I had at length made up my mind to the sad truth, that they were all gone out of

England to some savage country where the woods were wilder and thicker, and the population more scant; whereas, Lilliput and Brobdignag being, in my creed, solid parts of the earth's surface, I doubted not that I might one day, by taking a long voyage, see with my own eyes the little fields, houses, and trees, the diminutive people[.] (*JE* 20)

If Jane has not yet learned the rules of fiction, still credulously believing that the realities named by literature have actual correspondences, her strategy for accommodating a growing sense of disbelief is to relocate this referentiality to 'some savage country' where they might still be true. (Brontë's sentence produces a moment where 'the sad truth' to which Jane has made up her mind threatens to be the non-existence of fairies, which is then comically defused by her continued faith in them through a leap of childish logic.) The advantage that the young Brontës – and the reader of *Jane Eyre* – have over Jane is the ability to *make-believe* what she actually believes, acting *as if* Gondal or Thornfield are 'solid parts of the earth's surface' just out of our knowledge, while also explicitly knowing otherwise. If the fictional contemporary always leaves some margin of possibility that they may have actually existed, given the impossibility of a complete knowledge of all historical individuals in early nineteenth-century England (there is no alphabetised roster into which the Brontës can insert the names of their characters), the rigorousness of geography demands a more explicit acknowledgement of novel fiction's non-correspondence to actuality. Inventing an imaginary country is a cognitive shortcut to inhabiting this logical space.

Jane's childish progress towards fictional sophistication might suggest an alternative reading of the complex narratological developments in the eighteenth century, the age of 'fictionality in its infancy'.[48] Naïve readers from the nineteenth century onwards only needed an atlas to realise that places in the novel are not all out there in the world: as a child, Jeremy Bentham too 'admired 'Gulliver's Travels;' [. . .] would have vouched them to be all true',[49] but as a philosopher, could breezily dismiss the existences of 'countries, such as El Dorado; seas, such as the Strait of Anian; fountains, such as the fountain of Jouvence'.[50] Bentham's wider philosophical project is to eradicate these kinds of speculative or imaginary existences from the systems of truth that govern society and the law, where he believes them to introduce ambiguity and irrationality into just distinctions between facts and lies. But the story of his own maturation recalls a third category of assertion – beliefs and possible truths – which characterises the longer respective histories of these places as speculative actualities. The Fountain of Youth, a trope which originated with Herodotus, was already regarded as mythical by the sixteenth century, but until it was replaced by the actual Bering Strait further north, the Strait of Anian featured in published maps as late as 1728. Similarly, expeditions to El Dorado, which famously engrossed Walter Raleigh, continued until 1804. By the time they became Bentham's examples of 'fabulous entities', two of the three had only recently fallen off the map, their possibility to be 'newly discovered' diminishing as the empirical world filled in over time. If Jane must eventually accept the imaginariness of fairies when she fails to find them anywhere (but realise also that the diversion of the tale is still the same), reports of Lilliput *graduate into impossibility* over the eighteenth and nineteenth centuries, requiring either Derwent Coleridge's interpretation of 'an intentional disguise' (*HC* xliv) or a different way of entertaining its reality.

Explicitly fictional worlds become conceptually useful only if the actual world has become (*à la* Bentham) a complete matter of fact; the creation of Gondal is a deliberately fictional act because it must intrude between the authoritative lines of Goldsmith's gazette.[51] In other words, the practice of pretence begins where the possibility for speculation ends. As Jason Pearl has argued, naval exploration in the period between 1660 and 1740 rendered 'largely obsolete [. . .] the once-crucial convention of the sea voyage through unknown waters to unmapped lands', as well as the early modern conceptualisation of 'utopia [. . .] as a concurrent reality separated from us only laterally'.[52] Although the elder Malkin recognised an eminent precedent for his son in Thomas More, describing Allestone as 'an imaginary country, somewhat similar to Utopia', Pearl's argument about the decline of utopian fictions marks the difference in historical conditions between the two.[53] While More and his circle of humanist correspondents kept up a coyness about Utopia's material reality which appears properly pseudofactual, they also had recourse to a persuasive rhetoric of speculative possibility.[54] More's contributor Peter Giles, in a letter appended to *Utopia*'s first edition, suggests an explanation for why the country 'is not to be found among the cosmographers': that perhaps 'they never discovered the island at all. Nowadays we find all sorts of lands turning up that the old geographers never mentioned'.[55] This is exactly the kind of explanation which became foreclosed by the end of the eighteenth century and represents a different kind of fictional claim (provisional possibility) to that which I argue distinguishes the novel and Allestone (explicit impossibility).

Gombroon, Ejuxria, Allestone, and Angria mark the point of transition between other worlds as a narrative subject, on the one hand, and as an imagined ontology for narrative, on the other. For Pearl, the lateral relation to alterity inherent to the utopian romance, made untenable by new geographical knowledge, diverges into two succeeding tropes: the euchronias (utopias in the future) of Edward Bellamy and William Morris, precursors to the utopias of science fiction, and an internalisation of the genre's conventions into cognition, 'reimagining utopias as a state of mind available anywhere'.[56] Drawing from Defoe's under-examined third instalment, *Serious Reflections During the Life and Surprising Adventures of Robinson Crusoe*, Pearl notes the solitude of Crusoe's later life in London and its practice of:

> [A] kind of interiority that is a remnant of geographic utopias. Imaginary lands engage the imagination and then, disproven, ironically legitimise it [...] the failure of utopian geography establishes interior space as oppositional and counterfactual, a site of recuperative possibility.[57]

The imagined worlds which manifest in play at the end of the eighteenth century, due partly to the popularity of *Crusoe*, suggest how Pearl's 'utopian remainder' is more widely introjected as a way of enacting fictionality, than of the social and political idealism originally associated with the utopia. By and large, the worlds of play lack ideality in the sense of normative perfectionism or desirability – Gombroon has more problems than most actual countries – but are instead 'ideal' in the sense of 'Existing only in idea, confined to thought or imagination; imaginary: opposed to *real* or *actual*'.[58] Rather than for its possibilities as a model for reorganising life, the imaginary land becomes appealing for its narrative conceit and make-believe logic of the 'new discovery', for an available space of invention made plausible.

If the Victorian novel may be the most unlikely place to search for these remnants of utopia, they are nonetheless powerfully present in its rules of reality and imagining – its mode of play. The historical nadir of stories about fantastical lands between the late eighteenth and late nineteenth century, when the novel became almost synonymous with the interiorities of subjectivity and domesticity, is also a period of ascendancy for realist protocols which proliferated imaginary instances and regions of contemporary life. How can a real country have a fictional part (or fictional citizens, or fictional events)? The travel fiction of *Robinson Crusoe* and *Gulliver's Travels* propagated the conceit of imagining lands 'out there' over a period when geographical elsewheres were in fact becoming increasingly knowable and disprovable. Closer to home, the imaginary worlds of early nineteenth-century childhoods distilled the logic of utopian speculation and transformed it into a more virtual relation between reference and invention – in other words, into novel fiction.

The Castle in the Air

The goal of this chapter, however, is not to chart (by however unusual a route) the novel's arrival at a familiar endpoint of modern fiction, but rather to defamiliarise our sense of its destination. Drawing connections between a history of play and the development of fiction might account for how things came to be, but it may also move the ground under our feet, revealing utopian foundations beneath the too easily accepted premises of an extra manufacturing town or country house, slipped between lines of reference. A make-believe logic of the fictional world underlies the most basic yet substantive assumptions of novel discourse, from the appropriateness of grieving for Nell to the futility of searching for Thornfield. By inhabiting this logic as a matter of course and taking such assumptions for granted, we often play the novel without knowing it, requiring accounts of its incipient development or initial acquisition to bring their specificity and effects more fully into attention.

For Anthony Trollope, acknowledging what the novel owes to play is a means of articulating a theory of the novel. Trollope has an unorthodox view of the form's function and distinction, which certain of his contemporaries exemplify more than others with novels that afford particular modes of vicarious response he calls, idiosyncratically, 'living with'. As he took measure in a chapter of his *Autobiography*, 'On English Novelists of the Present Day': Dickens, 'in his best days, always *lived with* his characters'; Brontë '*lived with* those characters' of Jane Eyre and Rochester; Thackeray '*lived with* the characters he was creating' (*AA* 152–57, emphasis added). Yet for all that he advocates an experience of imaginative reality as a critical standard for the novel, Trollope's own practice began with a more ambivalent childhood habit: 'I myself often regarded with dismay when I thought of the hours devoted to it', he confesses, 'but which, I suppose, must have tended to make me what I have been' (*AA* 33). By his own reckoning in *An Autobiography* (published posthumously in 1883), from roughly the age of twelve to twenty-eight,[59] Trollope engaged in a form of private play he describes as 'always going about with some castle in the air firmly built within my mind':

> Nor were these efforts in architecture spasmodic, or subject to constant change from day to day. For weeks, for months, if I remember rightly, from year to year, I would carry on the same tale, binding myself down to certain

laws, to certain proportions, and proprieties, and unities. Nothing impossible was ever introduced, – nor even anything which, from outward circumstances, would seem to be violently improbable. (33)

Consciously or not, Trollope's account takes on the language of play from the 1850s, echoing Derwent Coleridge's description of Hartley 'day after day, for the space of long years [...] evolving the complicated drama of existence' (*HC* xliii), Jameson's admission of having 'carried on for whole years a series of actions, scenes, and adventures',[60] and as I have suggested, Jane Eyre's internal narration of 'a tale that was never ended' (*JE* 132). Alongside such accounts, Trollope emphasises the rigorous qualities of play – detail, specificity, and self-consistency over time – which he considers particular to his practice, and which psychologists such as Cohen, MacKeith, and Root-Bernstein would later identify (almost exactly along these lines) as a criteria for the paracosm.

The 'hours invested' in this form of sustained engagement with a specific and continuous fiction, if dismaying to reflect on for the time spent, comes nonetheless to embody Trollope's demand for novelists to remain 'in perpetual intercourse' (*AA* 152) with characters. As J. Hillis Miller has also noted, 'The young Anthony Trollope's daydreams were remarkably like the grown-up Trollope's novels' in their shared projection of an ongoing and self-consistent imaginary world, presaging his Chronicles of Barsetshire and its accumulative creation of a fictional county in six novels written over thirteen years.[61] This connection between imaginative and literary practices is drawn explicitly by Trollope himself, in his contemplation of how play has made him 'what I have been' – a novelist:

I have often doubted whether, had [this play] not been my practice, I should ever have written a novel. I learned in this way to maintain an interest in a fictitious story, to dwell on a work created by my own imagination, and to live in a world altogether outside the world of my own material life. (*AA* 33)

For Trollope, the stakes of play are nothing less than the novel itself, contingent upon the cultivation of a capacity to 'dwell on' fiction. As Cohen and MacKeith suggest, in contrast to games of temporary make-believe, where 'nothing remains of [children's] efforts and imagination [...] Once the play is over', worldplay is distinctive for representing 'games that didn't disappear and weren't meant to', to which children 'kept returning' over long periods of time.[62] Root-Bernstein, too, distinguishes her cases for their 'consistent return over some period of time to a specific scenario, as evidenced by the naming of place and characters or the elaboration of a continuous narrative'.⁶³ This sense of the imaginary world as something that can be returned to, as if it were the same continuous object each time, or something independently 'out there' to be accessed, is for Trollope an indispensable quality of novel fiction; or put otherwise, the inherently virtual effect of formal realism's premise to document what it invents.

This quality therefore consists not just in the remarkable length of the single narrative, typical to records of play, but the assumption or pretence of what Eric Hayot has called the 'persistence' of a virtual world. As Hayot argues, literary works which imply the passing of time between instances of representation, such as 'between individual works set in the same world [like the Barsetshire novels], or even between individual chapters in the same work', suggest 'the 'persistence' of elements of the diegesis beyond the immediate attention of the controlling narrative',⁶⁴ an experience more commonly associated with digital virtuality:

> The continued existence of imaginary objects beyond their immediate apprehension by a living audience is known among users of contemporary online virtual worlds as 'persistence'. The term describes the fact that such worlds [...] continue to exist when the individual player stops playing [...] disconnecting narrative and descriptive viability from any single or collective act of perception. Continuity without human presence is thus part of the nature of such games, which could theoretically run on servers long after the extinction of the human race.⁶⁵

The affective experience De Quincey described as a shadow or vapour hardening 'into a rigor of reality' (*AS* 47) also constituted, along these lines, a way of considering even the worlds of other children for which he cared much less than his own. Imagining the state of things in Ejuxria after Hartley Coleridge had ceased to play it, De Quincey envisions 'sailing past' to see a realm continuing to run in his absence, where 'the public service must have languished deplorably for want of the royal signature [...] throats there are to be cut, from the product of ten jail deliveries, and nobody dares to cut them, for want of the proper warrant; archbishoprics there are to be filled; and, because they are *not* filled, the whole nation is running helter skelter into heresy' (45). In what sense does Ejuxria survive the 'extinction' of the mind that made it? Only by the terms of the game in which it was originally played, the same make-believe rules by which novel characters possess a past and future beyond the represented narrative.

Actually, *Jane Eyre* does not take place anywhere. The worlds of play and the novel do not have servers or far-off islands where they might keep ticking over by themselves without human attention (unless one thinks of the material book in this way). Yet part of their imaginative design is the pretence that they do; as if fiction is located on some utopian plane external to subjectivity, or in the language of the digital, stored on an external memory.[66] As I have shown, this is an experience of form which is also a logical-imaginative structure, without which novels make little sense, much as children playing appear equally nonsensical from outside the agreed-upon fantasy of their game. If, in Paige's objection, certain kinds of cultural theorisation about fiction have been too grandiose in connecting 'the nuts and bolts of literary form' to 'a change in worldview, a cultural mutation, a revolution in what is thinkable by humans',[67] the formal study of novels is and has been necessarily incomplete without an examination of their preconditions to participation, the fundamental as-ifs to which we must consent (often without thinking) in order even to move the gears of narrative. Moreover, because this as-if-ness is now so naturalised in modern expectations and practices of fiction, the novel's alternative functions and implications as a kind of make-believe – in addition to being a linguistic composition or cultural artefact – have also been underexamined or dismissed as mere escapism.

The accounts of historical play collected here allow us to draw speculative connections between the development of novel fiction and the emergence of a virtual play phenomenon at the turn between the eighteenth and nineteenth centuries, and show how these complementary narratives can help to defamiliarise a modern logic of fictional worlds. Tracing back to how we first learned the rules of a novelistic language game enables us to take fuller stock of their distinctiveness and complexity, their origins and usefulness. In the following author studies, I take up more specific comparisons between specific shared practices between play and the novel: between omnipotence and authorship; improvisation and plot; persistence and narrative closure; sensory imagination and description. Although all the children and novelists in the book employ these practices, each of the following chapters will isolate a single aspect, and pose exemplary cases of play, in order to analyse the greater play-novel analogy in parts – and from that analogy, to propose the critical implications in so foregrounding make-believe as a founding feature of the form.

CHAPTER 2

Authorship, Omnipotence, and Charlotte Brontë

In *The Life of Charlotte Brontë*, Elizabeth Gaskell qualified her earlier reaction to Brontë's juvenilia – 'they are the wildest & most incoherent things'[1] – into a more specific discomfort with 'the character of her purely imaginative writing'.[2] She sets out the problem in terms of a generic division: 'While her description of any real occurrence is [...] homely, graphic, and forcible, when she gives way to her powers of creation, her fancy and her language alike run riot, sometimes to the very borders of apparent delirium' (*Life* 69). Cutting a clean distinction not only between content which is 'real occurrence' and which is 'purely imaginative', but between the nature of writing as 'description' and as 'creation', what Gaskell isolates for praise is the *realistic* as both subject and mode of representation. The juvenilia, she argued, were exercises from which Brontë 'formed those habits of close observation, and patient analysis of cause and effect, which served so well in after-life as handmaids to her genius' (68), or in other words, those habits of empirical description exemplified by the *Life* itself:

> To counterbalance this tendency in Charlotte [for the imaginative], was the strong common sense natural to her, and daily called into exercise by the requirements of her practical life [...] to brush rooms, to run errands, to help in the simpler forms of cooking, to be by turns play-fellow and monitress to her younger sisters and brother, to make and to mend, and to study economy under her careful aunt. Thus we see that, while her imagination received powerful impressions, her excellent understanding had full power to rectify them before her fancies became realities. (70–71)

Just as this passage itself embodies the attention to everyday details and practicalities it seeks to establish in the young Brontë's performance of household chores, a clear parallel is drawn between Brontë's commitment to 'practical life' and to her writing of 'real occurrence' – that is, to the 'homely, graphic, and forcible' representations of life at the Parsonage which Gaskell's biography therefore comes to double. Like a hall of mirrors, the mimetic loop between Brontë's life, Brontë's writing of her life, and Gaskell's writing of the *Life* reflects and reinforces an analogy between domestic and literary work, emphatically revealing the female author as attentive rather than creative, responsible rather than frivolous, at work and not at play – whether in the home or on the page.

Gaskell's anxiousness 'to rectify' such a domestic portrait of the female novelist is representative of a cultural anxiety, particularly in fiction by women, about the novel's vicarious or virtualising functions. Her implication, that establishing Brontë's legitimacy as an artist requires emphasising 'common sense' over 'imagination', is more explicitly articulated by George Eliot's 1856 polemic against 'the most trashy and rotten kind of feminine literature', contemptible for being 'less the result of labour than of busy idleness' and for lacking 'those moral qualities that contribute to literary excellence – patient diligence, a sense of the responsibility involved in publication, and an appreciation for the sacredness of the writer's art'.[3] At stake in their common appeal to 'labour', 'responsibility', and 'patient diligence' is the professional and cultural recognition of novel-writing as *real work*, performing duties and necessitating effort, a claim which is vulnerable to dismissal not only because of the precarious place of women in the cultural marketplace, but also due to the form's paradoxical logic of fiction. If the novel aspires *as literature* to difficult standards of excellence and seriousness, closely observing human nature or social reality in the abstract, the novel also produces *as fiction* a reality of invented particulars, where the omnipotent word of a silly novelist can make any heroine 'an heiress, probably a peeress', 'perfectly well dressed and perfectly religious', with 'a superb *contralto* and a superb intellect'.[4] Gaskell and Eliot's insistence on 'practical life', not only as the proper subject of novel-writing but also its nature as an activity, legitimises an ostensibly documentary form by obscuring its obvious, concomitant function: the free creation of fictional lives.

This chapter reinstates the figure of the capricious, irresponsible, and omnipotent author – the author 'run riot' – to the foundations of Brontë's novel-writing. As Gaskell was probably aware, her suggestion of a 'counterbalance' between the real and the imaginative is misleading, belying an alternative but equally formative practice at play in Brontë's childhood: autobiographical accounts of 'real occurrence' are vastly outnumbered in the juvenilia by narratives about the imaginary worlds over which the Brontës ruled as massive, omnipotent gods called the Chief Genii, modelled after the whimsical spirits from James Ridley's popular *Arabian Nights* pastiche, *The Tales of the Genii*. Brontë's 'genius', a word Gaskell uses to mean a talent for 'close observation' and 'patient analysis', evokes in the context of these worlds the very opposite: the power of the author to create and determine fictional realities, to magically interfere with narrative 'cause and effect', and even to kill or resurrect characters with unabashed favouritism. The radical ambivalence of 'genius' undermines the careful characterisation Gaskell constructs around the origins of Brontë's writing as a domestic, laborious, and attentive activity – a realism of handmaids, service, and chores – suggesting instead the inseparability between two models of authorship: the author who treats writing as the dutiful 'description of any real occurrence', and on the flip side, the author who writes to exercise (or abuse) their 'powers of creation' (*Life* 69).

Understanding this other side of genius as an integral part of Brontë's literary training and practice, no less essential to her authorship than truthful representation or diligent empiricism, enables us to recover an underexamined (because disavowed) side to the realist tradition. The Genii mode of authorship does not disappear from Brontë's writing as an adult, but inheres in a vicarious quality to her novels which has been recognised both as a major condition of their appeal and as aesthetically embarrassing. For one thing, I think an author who writes fiction as a power fantasy or vicarious game is probably a more 'realistic' picture of a thirteen-year-old than that of a canonical artist in training. For another, defensive characterisations of the novel like Q. D. Leavis's (of *Jane Eyre*) as a 'fable of wish-fulfilment [...] a favourite form of self-indulgence' also suggest the inextricability of the child at play from the novelist at work.[5] That this kind of novel-writing can only be acknowledged as disparagement reveals Leavis's inheritance of a critical attitude towards 'Silly Novels by Lady Novelists'; but what if we approached vicariousness and self-indulgence not as charges from which Brontë requires rescuing, but as motives essential to her practice and experience of fiction? Rather than holding the novelist to their apparent responsibilities to depict and engage in 'practical life', I argue that such uses of writing as biographical escapism or 'wish-fulfilment' are intrinsic to the tradition and value of realist fiction, even while they are repudiated as immature or inartistic.

'A Divine Game'

'[W]e must always bear in mind', Vladimir Nabokov lectured in the 1950s, 'that art is a divine game. These two elements – the elements of the divine and that of the game – are equally important. It is divine because this is the element in which man comes nearest to God through becoming a true creator in his own right. And it is a game, because it remains art only as long as we are allowed to remember that, after all, it is all make-believe'.[6] For Nabokov as (more recently) for Lowe, literature's persuasiveness has been overrated as a factor of its function and power, at the cost of proper attention to literature's artificiality. As Lowe argues, the concept of *belief* is a distracting non-starter for understanding how literature makes us *imagine*, a difference which is more than 'a mistake as to the degree of conviction involved. Imagining the heat of the sun on your back is about as different an activity as can be from believing that tomorrow it will be sunny'.[7] As Nabokov suggests, to lose a distinction of fiction's imaginariness and how 'we are, as readers or as spectators, participating in an elaborate and enchanting game' is no longer to experience something as art, but as that 'which should belong in a newspaper instead'.[8] Maintaining this double consciousness of an explicitly imaginary reality is partly a matter of cognitive attitude, something to 'always bear in mind', but also partly of literary form, of being 'allowed to remember' that it has all been made up. And if, as this book argues throughout, games of make-believe are an effective analogy for framing this essential logic of fiction, Nabokov's other 'equally important' analogy draws more specific attention to authorship as a mode of fictional action.

An analogy of the author as divine creator assumes by implication the nature of authorship as a form of action upon virtual worlds – most notably, the act of genesis. In his 1939 essay 'On Fairy-Stories', J. R. R. Tolkien famously described the storyteller as a '"sub-creator" [...] mak[ing] a Secondary World which your mind can enter. Inside it, what he relates is "true": it accords with the laws of that world'.[9] This model of mythological or more generally literary production, he argues, involving 'sub-creation, rather than either representation or symbolic interpretation [...] is, I think, too little considered'.[10] Similarly, M. H. Abrams's 1953 study *The Mirror and the Lamp* proposed as its central thesis that eighteenth-century poetic theory underwent 'the replacement of the metaphor of the poem as imitation, as "mirror of nature", by that of a poem as heterocosm, a "second nature", created by the poet in an act analogous to God's creation of the World'.[11] Abrams in turn cites Elder Olsen's more radical argument in 1942 that, to the material world depicted by the narrative, the author's word constitutes miracle:

> [E]very poem is a microcosmos, a discrete and independent universe with its laws provided by the poet; his decision is absolute; he can make things good or bad, great or small, powerful or weak, just as he wills; he may make men taller than mountains or smaller than atoms [...] he may destroy

creation or re-form it; within his universe the impossible becomes the possible, the necessary the contingent – if he but says they do.[12]

In such formulations, figuring the author as god is really to make two analogies, inseparable from figuring fiction as a world upon which divinity acts, first by its creation and then – more problematically – with omnipotent control. If the rhetorical stakes of this analogy are sometimes construed as an argument for freedom of expression, particularly regarding the choice of fantastical subjects in literature, its greater implications concern this sense or pretence in which authors *do something* to fictional objects by making narrative decisions about them.

As we have seen, however, playing god can be an uncomfortable analogy for the professional activity of authorship; the divine poet has their counterpart in the silly novelist. However valorised as a metaphor of literature's power to create, the practice of fiction by say-so represents exactly the kind of irresponsible authorship Eliot saw as rendering all heroines immoderately fortunate and beautiful. In his footnote to Olsen, Abrams therefore appends a 'warning against the advisability of utter freedom, in the fashion of miracle', implying that what a poet *can* do in a fictional world may not be what they *should* do in a literary work.[13] This conflict between fiction and literature – between the omnipotent freedom of the author and their empirical, moral, or social duties – is especially intensified for the novel, committed at the same time to fiction's non-correspondence with actuality and to a referential plausibility that might well 'belong in a newspaper'.[14] More so than the poem or the fairy-tale, the novel must negotiate between these inseparable antitheses of its form; as Gallagher argues, 'If a genre can be thought of as having an attitude, the novel has seemed ambivalent towards its fictionality – at once [...] coax[ing] readers to accept the imaginative status of their characters [...] and conceal[ing] fictionality by locking it inside the confines of the credible'.[15] An omnipotence over the credible makes the novel in particular more ethically troubling than Nabokov's experience of 'art' in general, because the novelist exercises their imagined power over a world that resembles our own (rather than of unicorns or elves), over recognisable causes and effects which are not ordinarily so compliant to human will. The novel's attempt to be simultaneously reality-shaping and real-seeming is a powerful component of its appeal, but also an inherently unstable combination of values and functions.

Charlotte Brontë's career affords a uniquely literal case of this negotiation between 'a divine game' and the realist novel, embodied by her uneasy personal transition between childhood play and literary work. In correspondence with William Smith Williams, the literary adviser for Smith, Elder & Co., Brontë the professional novelist conceived 'The first duty of an Author' to be 'a faithful allegiance to Truth and Nature [...] a conscientious study of Art as shall enable him to interpret eloquently and effectively the oracles delivered by those two great deities'.[16] To these household gods, Thackeray's social satires particularly ordained him in her opinion as 'the legitimate High Priest of Truth'; the second edition of *Jane Eyre* is dedicated to the author of *Vanity Fair*. But if Brontë's views in 1848 presage her own posthumous portrayal by Gaskell and Eliot, representing authorship as an empirical duty performed with hard-honed skill, the overwrought language of their expression evokes neither naturalistic observation nor Christian revelation, but a more fantastical process of divining truth from art. Like Gaskell, too, Brontë's praise of another's realism finds an ambivalent foundation in the developing novelist, in what she further identifies as Thackeray's 'inherent *genius*: the thing that made him – I doubt not different as a child from other children [...] that now makes him a writer, unlike other writers'.[17] These two characterisations – observant oracle and creative genius – again suggest not one cohesive ideal of the novelist but a set of contradictory positions, the receiving of 'delivered' truth and its production from within, drawn together by an origin myth that clearly recalls Brontë's own unique making as a child writer.

Youthful High Spirits

The Brontë of the juvenilia is not so much interested in attendance upon other, abstract deities as in what Gaskell would call her own 'powers of creation' (*Life* 69). In the second earliest extant manuscript by any of the Brontë siblings (the earliest is a fragmentary narrative from 1826–28), a document dated March 12th, 1829 and entitled 'The History of the Year', Brontë presents another, very different oracular account of authorship. Even as a text that inaugurates a textual history of the Brontës, as its title implies, the 'History' is itself already preoccupied with examining a moment of origination. Looking back over the 'three great plays' of make-believe that Brontë and her siblings (Branwell, eleven; Emily, ten; Anne, nine) had formed since 1826, the document attempts to 'sketch out the origin of our plays more explicitly if I can':

> *Young Men*, June 1826 [...] Branwell came to our door with a box of soldiers. Emily and I jumped out of bed and I snatched one up and

exclaimed, 'This is the Duke of Wellington! It shall be mine!' When I said this, Emily likewise took one and said it should be hers [...] Emily's was a grave-looking fellow. We called him 'Gravey'. Anne's was a queer little thing, very much like herself. He was called 'Waiting Boy'. Branwell chose 'Bonaparte'.

Our Fellows [later referred to as *The O'Deans*], July 1827 [...] The origin of the O'Deans was as follows: we pretended we had each a large island inhabited by people six miles high. The people we took out of Aesop's *Fables*. Hay Man was my chief man, Boaster Branwell's, Hunter Anne's and Clown Emily's. Our chief men were ten miles high except Emily's who was only four.

Islanders, December 1827 [...] The origin of the Islanders was as follows. It was one wet night in December, we were all sitting round the fire and had been silent some time, and at last I said, 'Suppose we had each an Island of our own'. Branwell chose the Isle of Man, Emily Isle of Arran and Bute Isle, Anne, Jersey, and I chose the Isle of Wight. We then chose who should live in our Islands. The chief of Branwell's were John Bull, Astley Cooper, Leigh Hunt, etc.; Emily's Walter Scott [...] etc.; Anne's Michael Sadler [...] etc.; and I chose Duke of Wellington and son, North and Co.; 30 officers, Mr Abernethy, etc.[18]

Taken together, these accounts represent the 'History' of a developing process of worldplay; more fundamentally, they also capture the Brontës' initial assumption of a distinctive fictional mode. For one, these accounts emphasise possessiveness, reflective of children who clearly want to own things ('It shall be mine!'), but also of a developing power to handle fictional objects. The siblings graduate in the types of things they claim: bodily acts of seizure in 1826, as Brontë 'jumped out' and 'snatched [...] up' the toy she claims as the Duke of Wellington, are followed by more abstract but explicitly analogous acts of selection – 'Emily *likewise* took' and 'Branwell *chose*' their respective wooden figures – which also later describe indisputably non-material acts of how 'we *took* out of Aesop's *Fables*' and 'I *chose* the Isle of Wight'. If the siblings' games become greedier over time, growing from a single wooden soldier apiece to '30 officers' and a private island, the common pool represented by Branwell's toy box also expands to transform everything the siblings encounter in their reading – literary works, national newspapers, world history and geography – into potential resources of play, options from which to take and choose.

The Brontës move from an autobiographical world of material toys towards a fictional world of referential objects. Not only do they begin to use the names of persons and places as possessions to be shared, the siblings were also obviously aware that these references had real-world (or intertextual) referents about which or whom they were *not* writing truthfully, deceitfully, or ironically. By making fictional copies to play, they intuitively grasp the language game of reference without correspondence; if one of the most visible innovations of the early novel is the invocation of proper names that strongly appeared – but explicitly did not – refer to real individuals, the Brontë juvenilia magnify this paradox by severing any correspondence between even the proper name of an embodied individual from any referential claim about that person. Arthur Wellesley, the Duke of Wellington – who in the world of the 'plays' colonises Africa, swallows poison, fights kidnappers, and dies twenty-three years before his historical death – becomes a detachable identity applied over the anonymous body of the wooden soldier, imbued with the real duke's resemblance but not his ontological status. As Firdous Azim has also argued, while 'resemblances between the fictional world of the Brontë juvenilia and its journalistic sources are easy to draw', this process of 'wholesale incorporation into the juvenilia (albeit in a fictionalised form) [...] shows the participation of the juvenilia in the fact/fiction dichotomies of the novelistic genre'.[19] Only by these generically distinctive protocols of make-believe reference can one afford the temerity to specify 'the Isle of Wight' as a fantasised personal domain.

For another, these origins mark the beginning of an expanding set of possible fictional actions. If the Brontës learn over 1826–27 a licence to borrow the images of actual objects for fiction, the siblings also come to understand their broader power as authors over imagined states of affairs, starting with the creation of such states and then with the making of choices about them. Games of make-believe, as Pavel has noted, require an understanding of actions in two perspectives:

> Now when a group of children play with mud, they simultaneously touch globs of mud – in the really real world – *and* offer one another tasty pies in the world of make-believe [...] to account for our participation during such games, in both the really real world and the fictionally real worlds, we must distinguish between the two distinct levels on which the game takes places and show the links between them.[20]

Brontë's interest in going over old acts of play is motivated by exactly such an attempt to 'show the links' between perspectives, between acts of play in the Parsonage and their consequences in the imagined world. Inverting Gaskell's separation between 'real occurrence' and the 'purely imaginative' (*Life* 69), the 'History' repeatedly pinpoints moments where actions in 'the really real world' bring 'fictionally real worlds' into being: 'The origin of the Islanders', for example, is divided into a distinct (yet linked) *before* and *after* by a point over which autobiographical observations suddenly give way to much more unusual statements. Captured between the two radically different sentences of 'we were all sitting round the fire and had been silent some time' and of 'Branwell chose the Isle of Man' (*EW* 6) is the creation of a second perspective to whose objects the latter refers; textually caught between them is the sentence which 'at last' breaks both the silence of the room and the strict factuality of the account, 'Suppose we had each an Island of our own' (6). Brontë's imperative calls in the moment on her siblings, and afterwards on readers of the 'History', to assume the structures of pretence that allow the otherwise incoherent statements that follow – 'I chose Duke of Wellington and son' (6) – to function meaningfully and effectively as decisions (or for the 'History', as an account of decisions). 'Suppose' makes available something to be decided about in the first place, creating the world, reality, or paracosm in which fictional actions become available to be literally performed.

Authorship of the juvenilia consists both in the literary production of texts, an act to which the Brontës aspired with great seriousness by handwriting and -binding their manuscripts, and in the production of fictional consequences, the more extravagant actions of another world which uses 'writing itself as a vehicle of magical power'.[21] This double perspective persisted beyond Brontë's initial fascination with how her language had brought realities into paracosmic existence, and she continued experimentally to flex this power with another composition four months later. A letter written from the perspective of a 'Young Men' character, this is the one example of Brontë's 'wild weird writing' Gaskell chose to excerpt into the *Life*, and with which she evidently struggled, hazarding that it 'may have had some allegorical or political reference, invisible to our eyes, but very clear to the bright little minds for whom it was intended' (*Life* 70). Rather than a clever satire, however, the letter depicts 'the bright little minds' themselves in the guises of the Chief Genii – named Tallii, Brannii, Emii, and Annii – creators of the narrator's world who also periodically threaten its destruction:

> It is well known that the Genii have declared [...] that by their magic might they can reduce the world to a desert, the purest Waters to streams of livid poison, and the clearest lakes to stagnant waters, the pestilential vapours of which shall slay all living creatures except the blood-thirsty beast of the forest, and the ravenous bird of the rock. But that in the midst of this desolation the palace of the Chief Genii shall rise sparkling in the wilderness [...] they shall have their annual feast over the bones of the dead, and shall

yearly rejoice with the joy of victors. I think, sir, that the horrible wickedness of this needs no remark and therefore I haste to subscribe myself, etc. (*EW* 39)

The omnipotence of the Chief Genii strikingly anticipate what Olson would theorise as the right of the divine poet 'to make things good or bad, great or small [...] destroy creation or re-form it', expressed in similarly hyperbolic and hypothetical oppositions from 'the world to a desert', from 'purest Waters' to 'livid poison', from 'all living creatures' to only 'the ravenous bird'.[22] The letter's playful adoption of a view from the ground suggests how such a theory of artistic licence might appear to those unfortunate enough to live in the 'microcosmos' of the literary work, for whom the potential arbitrariness of authorial whims is not only (as for Eliot) aesthetically silly but actively dangerous, revealing the narrative or ontological precarity of their existence as imagined beings.[23]

The Chief Genii are metafictional self-portraits of the juvenilia's authors which reflect an exultation in the freedom of fictional possibility or action, and simultaneously, their consciousness of how such freedom might infringe upon an implicit code of behaviour. As the character in the letter protests, comically moralising their own author, 'the horrible wickedness' of writing a destructive, meaningless apocalypse 'needs no remark' (*EW* 39); a position which critics of the juvenilia have tended too readily to echo. Laura Forsberg, who likewise reads the Genii letter as exploring 'the consequences of imaginative authorship', chooses to emphasise Brontë's transition away from 'childhood fantasies of supreme power' to becoming more 'involved in imagining her characters' experience of powerlessness [...] how her arbitrary power over the world of Glass Town impacts its citizens'.[24] An implicit privileging of the latter position, of arbitrariness as a narrative problem rather than as authorial prerogative, similarly underpins Heather Glen's argument that, while the Chief Genii 'bespeak the child's heady assertion [...] of a coveted fictional power', the perspective of the juvenilia inheres 'not, most prominently, [in] identification with power, but, far more centrally and intimately, the imagining of powerlessness [...] a sense of self not as autonomous and free, but as dependent and determined, not as omnipotent, but as potentially not existing at all'.[25] This critical inclination to disidentify Brontë from the juvenilia's acknowledged fantasies of power, and conversely to reframe them as really imagining perspectives of 'powerlessness' – even though what the characters are powerless against is the figure of the author herself – is for one, not an interpretation necessarily demanded by the archive's other narratives, and for another, revealing of a discomfort with what it means for an author to act for themselves.

In the Genii letter, locating authorial sympathy and an ethical burden in the narrator's bathetic reprimands – 'horrible wickedness' – overlooks the clear relish with which the text describes the potential gratuitousness of authorial action. As Dickens writes of Punch, acting fictionally may be all the more secretly satisfying for being wicked, 'an outrageous joke' of harmless violence exempted from the need to be 'moral and instructive [. . .] or a model for any kind of conduct', allowable only in vicarious form within one's proprietary universe.[26] Even as they recognise Brontë's growing understanding of writing as a form of fictional action, Glen's and Forsberg's readings undervalue action's own satisfactions, advancing towards interpretations whereby authorship is only a means of constructing more traditional types of literary meaning. The argument that the Chief Genii only function to set up scenarios for Brontë to reflect on the experience of helplessness – as opposed to living out the indulgent experience of making her creations helpless, the exercise of authorship as an experience in itself – continues to assume a familiar model of the author which it is the juvenilia's potential to defamiliarise. We know well the literary functions and values of representing people in trouble, of reflecting on the limited agency that characterises our universal relation as historical individuals to the world. Forsberg's approach to interpretation is explicitly shaped by such an understanding of literature, connecting the juvenilia to the novel and its assumed work in expressing the urgent conditions (as Gaskell put it) of 'practical life':

> Rejecting a child's fantasy of authorship, Charlotte Brontë instead finds an opportunity, within the epic tales of empire, to explore the feelings of mental and physical constriction which would later occupy the pages of her full-length novels. Within the miniature world of Glass Town, Charlotte Brontë discovered not an escape from the realities of Haworth, but rather a reflection of her own feelings of smallness and vulnerability in the carefully constructed psychologies of her characters.[27]

But how else can we use literature than as a remodelling of the constricting relations of real experience, especially – as the Chief Genii demonstrate with their 'magic might' – when fiction affords different kinds of relation to less intransigent realities? What can one experience vicariously in a 'miniature world' they specifically cannot in 'the realities of Haworth'? Moreover, the juvenilia's place at the foundations of Brontë's writing might perform Forsberg's argument in reverse, or in backlash: might not the grown-up fictions of the novel, too, be reprimandable for irresponsible uses of power?

The Genie in the Novel

These are fundamental questions which the juvenilia not only raise as implicative examples but are themselves interested in testing. They are natural questions for an adolescent author to ask: what is fiction for, and how can it create satisfaction? Besides the joy of being able to perform it (reason enough in itself), much of the arbitrary magic in the juvenilia also serves repeatedly to bring such problems to the surface of narrative. In a tale from June 1829, set in the 'Islanders' play, the siblings again assume supernatural forms as the fairy-like 'Little King and Queens', roughly equivalent figures to their Genii identities in the 'Young Men' play. The Queens themselves narrate this story, where a character's attempt to poison the Duke of Wellington is both obstructed by the narrative and assisted by the author:

> [Ned] reached the park gate. But here, a great obstacle presented itself, for the keeper of the gate is an old veteran, who has followed the Duke through all his wars, and attended him in all his battles [...] Ned turned round and seeing us, he said, 'Little Queens, will you open that gate?'
> As we wished to see the end of this adventure, we took Raton up and threw him over the high wall, and then knocked at the gate. (*EW* 26)

By personally helping Ned (also known as Raton) overcome the 'great obstacle' which she herself wrote into the story, Brontë again alternates between two perspectives of fiction: a description of the character's helplessness to what 'presented itself' as fact, and a power to make fiction conform to what 'we wished'. This double vision also manifests in the different levels of 'seeing' at work in the passage: Ned physically 'seeing' behind him in the material reality of the story, and the Little Queens wanting to 'see the end of the adventure' (26).

To say what the author 'wants' with such tales is not to interpret a literary intention, nor even just to describe a participatory experience, but to acknowledge a will to make particular and desirable narrative outcomes occur. If the siblings are fairly impassive about Ned's aims as a character – they will help him to see what happens – they are not impartial about his success. Ultimately, Ned's poison itself proves a short-lived 'obstacle', impatiently overcome when 'His Grace's features collapsed with agony, the volume fell from his hand, and he sank into his chair. Just then, a loud yell rang in our ears, a rushing noise was heard and a Giant of Clouds [...]'

touched the Duke and new life seemed to be given him' (*EW* 28). Although the narrative builds up to Ned's assassination, it takes less than a paragraph for the Duke to fall ill and recover – the application of divine intervention 'Just' as the narrative reaches its logical conclusion is characteristic of such resurrections in the early juvenilia. In another 'Young Men' tale from August 1830, entitled 'A Day at Parry's Palace', Brontë's character Charles Wellesley writes of travelling from his native Glass Town to the territory of Emily's characters. (In a pointed comparison between Brontë's tastes and her sister's, Charles finds the town cramped and ugly, with dull and badly dressed residents.) The tale reaches its climax when one of Anne's characters, invited for dinner, almost dies unglamorously of overeating:

> All ate as if they had not seen a meal for three weeks [. . .] I expected some blow-up after the surfeit which Ross, if I might judge from his continued grunting and puffing, had evidently got, and was not disappointed. An hour subsequent to dinner, he was taken extremely sick. No doctor being at hand, death was momentarily expected and would certainly have ensued, had not the Genius Emily arrived at a most opportune period; and when the disorder reached its crisis, she cured with an incantation and vanished. (*EW* 232)

Unlike the Duke's poisoning, this example of sudden reversal clearly indicates a conflict between the sisters; but this conflict is also premised on the perceived stakes of a desired fictional outcome which is independent of, in fact contradictory to, narrative coherence. Exactly as the 'Giant of Clouds' interrupts that earlier tale 'Just' (28) as it almost resolves, the Genius's arrival 'at a most opportune period [. . .]' when the disorder reached its crisis' forestalls the twice-'expected' result of what had been developing for 'An hour' and 'would certainly have ensued', and had been carefully anticipated by descriptions of Ross 'grunting and puffing' (232). These moments of narrative short-circuiting – 'death was *momentarily* expected' – again employ and conflate two modes of authorship, the unreported 'incantation' with which Emily directly acts upon the fictional world, and the narration of objective description with which Brontë plots (both in the sense of narrative and of assassination) to kill off her sister's character. The narrative consequences for which the respective siblings 'wished' transparently motivates both modes of authorial action.

Such experiments with writing might elicit certain critical affects – embarrassment, discomfort, humour, dismissiveness – because they appear jarring, immature, or unprofessional (of course, they are); or because their yet unsettled state recalls uncertainties we tend to smooth over in the canonical realist novel. For instance, if the irresponsible omnipotence of the Chief Genii contravenes Eliot's sense of 'the sacredness of the writer's art', Eliot begins *Adam Bede* with her own distinctly non-Christian analogy: 'With a single drop of ink for a mirror, the Egyptian sorcerer undertakes to reveal to any chance comer far-reaching visions of the past [...] With this drop of ink at the end of my pen, I will show you the roomy workshop of Mr. Jonathan Burge'.[28] Frank Kermode has noted how this passage functions 'as a magical means of making present what is absent [...] a past period', but as Jane Moore has argued, the suggestion that realist representation paradoxically depends on 'magical means' constitutes a 'postmodern act of complicating and complexifying the presentation of meaning':[29]

> Ironically, an analogy comparing the magic powers of the narrator to look back into the past [...] with the conjuring tricks of an Egyptian sorcerer, that has the declared aim of testifying to the transparency of language and its corresponding realist effect, simultaneously brings realism into the foreground as a theoretical problem. It is the artificial, made-up, and in consequence un-real, nature of the story about to be told that the analogy draws to attention.[30]

As Hillis Miller also argues, 'The metaphor of the mirroring drop of ink calls attention, in the opening sentences of the novel, to puzzling aspects of mimetic theories of language [...] performative writing that creates what it seemingly only describes'.[31] Eliot's sorcerer complicates the realist project not only because magic powers are dishonest or unrealistic (they aren't if they work), but because to do things by magic is to reveal the make-believe omnipotence beneath the 'labour' or 'patient diligence' of novel-writing – the production of reality by *fiat*.

What the child knows, but the novelist will not openly admit, is that it is *no fun* to be the god of a world only to be sidelined from the action; to engage in the pleasure of pretence, only to pretend to observe the struggles of others. From their 'origin', Brontë's juvenilia continually seek ways to acknowledge the author's intrinsic power over the fictional world – because it is satisfying to do so – which is afforded only by explicitly recognising the artificiality of that world, its unique possibilities as a reality manufactured by the author. If the realist novel has traditionally been understood as disavowing such acknowledgement, these disavowals are self-conscious circumventions of the form's inherent fictional logic. Being an honest sorcerer, oracle, or genius, a novelist *could* make the narrative this or that, make it up as one pleases – but of course such powers must be used for good, and so what is being conjured is precisely what least requires conjuration, a faithful representation of life as it is. As George Levine has argued, 'the characteristic subject of realist fiction is [...] disenchantment. The single character is implicated in a world of the contingent and must make peace with society and nature or be destroyed'.[32] This is the perspective of the traditional *bildungsroman*, and of the Genii letter's narrator, confronting a world which is determined by forces beyond himself. At the same time, such narratives of contingency are 'dramatized in an entirely imagined world [...] that belies the determinist conception of the powerlessness of the imagination'.[33] The juvenilia's unembarrassed pleasure in this latter perspective, the joy of having power to make and wreck, can help to make visible the other side of the novel's ambivalent attitude: a will to exercise the rights inherent to the novelist as divine creator.

'Another Realism'

At the heart of the jarring or comical unrealism of the Brontë juvenilia is not its adoption of the 'purely imaginative' over 'real occurrence' (*Life* 69) – that is, not the violent, hyperbolic, and fantastical contents of play – but its conception of reading and writing as a form of action between two separate realities. Its most disconcerting moments share a common denominator in the physical presence of the author and her siblings in the world of the narrative. What is for children a natural inclination to participate in their own game is, for narrative theory, what Gerard Genette defines as 'metalepsis', the 'intrusion by the extradiegetic narrator or narratee into the diegetic universe'.[34] In principle, Genette notes, narration represents the only permissible type of 'transition from one narrative level to another', the world of the book speaking to the world of the reader, besides which 'Any other form of transit is, if not always impossible, at any rate always transgressive [...] [and] produces an effect of strangeness that is either comical [...] or fantastic'.[35]

Moments like Emily's intrusion into 'A Day at Parry's Palace' suggest, for one, the indifference of the juvenilia to conventional principles, and for another, a contextual account of their conventionality. Most nineteenth-century British readers had (at least notionally) a stronger philosophy than narrative theory of how authors interacted with their creations: as Gustave Flaubert advised in 1852, 'An author in his work must be like God in the universe, present everywhere and visible nowhere [...] Art being a second nature, the creator of that nature must operate with analogous procedures: let there be felt in every atom, every aspect, a hidden, infinite impassivity'.[36] As Dorothy Sayers writes in her 1941 book *The Mind of the Maker*, realism's version of the divine game is played on New Testament rules:

> Whatever we may think of the possibilities of direct divine intervention in the affairs of the universe, it is quite evident that the writer can – and often does – intervene at any moment in the development of his own story: he is absolute master, able to perform any miracle he likes [...] he can twist either character or plot from the course of its nature by an exertion of arbitrary power [...] in fact, behave exactly as, in our more egotistical and unenlightened petitions, we try to persuade God to behave.[37]

As 'egotistical and unenlightened' as they are (as even their own characters accuse them to be), the transgressions of the Chief Genii are theological as well as narratological, disconcerting the 'analogous procedures' of a godlike author modelled on the Christian God. If artistic creation is for Nabokov 'the element in which man comes nearest to God', this is a privilege which Sayers perceives as involving significant responsibilities, transforming moral questions of divine action into aesthetic ones.[38]

What writing the *real* means for realism is a fundamental assumption about how meaning, the coherence imposed by a transcendent force, is incarnated into reality; and it is this assumed relation that the Brontë juvenilia disrupts. As Jacques Rancière has argued, the philosophical backdrop to the realist novel is 'the Christian separation between individual subjectivity and an absolute that has deserted the world with the body of the resurrected Christ [...] Novelistic 'modernity' inherits as content the Christian distance between the individual and his god'.[39] His argument follows Erich Auerbach's formulation of realism as 'transcendence materialized in ordinary life':

> [T]he novel, as modern – realist – genre of literature is possible beginning at the moment when the 'totality of life' is no longer given in merely the extensive dimension of actions situated on one single level, but in which the intelligibility of gestures, words, and events recounted passes by a vertical relation to a background that arranges them in dramatic perspective and as a destination of humanity.[40]

If a 'vertical relation' between two separated but tenuously linked levels recalls Pavel's model of play, it is however one that insists on the abstraction of one level into the particularities of the other. It is this kind of authorship, dispersed into the fabric of the text, which Roland Barthes has in mind when he declares the deconstructive 'Death of the Author' as 'an activity we may call countertheological [...] for to refuse to halt meaning is finally to refuse God and his hypostases, reason, science, the law'.[41] Making little distinction between the author and 'the "message" of the Author-God', Barthes's claim to have 'buried the Author' in fact inters something oddly bodiless, a will and a presence dissolved into fiction as 'message', 'meaning', and 'hypostases'.[42]

While it is evidently possible to interpret the juvenilia's fictions along this model, as narratives in which authorial intentions express themselves through the represented circumstances of life, this is a necessarily partial tactic for locating the author in a world where the Chief Genii exist. It is likewise must more difficult for Barthes to excise from the text the authorial presences of the Little King and Queens, who are not reflecting, sympathising, or moralising invisibly over the fictional world but participating bodily in the causal events of the plot. In one of the first 'Young Men' tales from April 1829, the metaleptic rupture between ontological levels culminates in an extreme antithesis of 'the Christian distance between the individual and his god' – at least, after the death of Christ – a point of physical contact:[43]

> On the thrones sat the Princes of the Genii. In the midst of the hall hung a lamp like the sun. Around it stood genii, and fairies without, whose robes were of beaten gold sparkling with diamonds. As soon as their chiefs saw us they sprang up from their thrones, and one of them seizing A[rthur] W[ellesley] and exclaimed, 'This is the Duke of Wellington!' (*EW* 14)

This is, of course, a rewriting from a fictional perspective of the real events she had detailed in the 'History' the previous month:

> Branwell came to our door with a box of soldiers. Emily and I jumped out of bed and I snatched one up and exclaimed, 'This is the Duke of Wellington! It shall be mine!' (5)

Read together, these two accounts create a parallax of the relation between the bodies of Brontë and the Duke of Wellington – a giant Chief Genius, holding a man; a ten-year-old child, holding a wooden soldier – such that, even as the dizzyingly different senses of scale recognises the distinctness of two perspectives, their fusion through a single proportion also affirms their continuity.[44] Reading together, keeping in mind both the contingency of the character's encounter with the world and the possibilities of the author's power over fiction, is also the cognitive position upon which the juvenilia recurrently insists. Its fundamental incompatibility with orthodox approaches to the author (living or dead) suggests another way of rendering the 'intelligibility' of authorial decisions and actions, even beyond the idiosyncratic productions of children: another counter-theology, with a different mode of interpreting creation, not the death of the godlike author but their transformation into genii.

The metaleptic touch of the author is a gesture which embodies a radically alternative theory of realism and fiction to that of observation, representation, and abstraction. The uncomfortable directness, power, and potential for pleasure contained within the gesture – an author seizing their fiction by force – upends the model Levine constructs of Victorian realists who heroically 'save meaning at the sacrifice of pleasure':

> [I]n requiring a continuing alertness to the secret lust of the spirit to impose itself in the world [...] in resisting the romance forms that embody those lusts, [realism] is always on the verge of *another realism*: the recognition that the reality it most adequately represents is a subtly disguised version of its own desires.[45]

Levine's work in *The Realistic Imagination* is an attempt to rescue Victorian realism as a project 'to make contact with the world out there, and, even with their knowledge of their own subjectivity, to break from the threatening habits of solipsism, of convention, and of language'.[46] By saving pleasure (seemingly) at the sacrifice of meaning, and in making the wrong kind of 'contact' between worlds, the Brontë juvenilia passes over the 'verge' into what critics from Gaskell to Leavis, from Eliot to Levine, have represented as a surrender of the serious moral value of literature to either the solipsism of language or the selfishness of desire. Yet if 'the secret lust of the spirit' is always constitutive in the novel, part of its profound ambivalence, the case of the juvenilia offers novel criticism an opportunity to take its fulfilment seriously as a possible function of the form, rather than its collapse.[47] Play shows us that a world of desire can have its uses, especially in the formal disguise of reality; and that virtual actions can be meaningful, if we take the participatory perspective of those performing them.

The next part of this chapter applies this perspective in a reading of Brontë's first full-length novel, *The Professor*, proposing how its narrative reaches not for 'the world out there', but for the virtual world of fiction. For Brontë, critics have argued, the transition of writing into a professional practice required affecting a distance or detachment from using writing as a form of vicarious action. *The Professor* narrates the laborious career of William Crimsworth, a clerk-cum-teacher who masters social and economic obstacles through effort and discipline, and has therefore been read as a rejection of the juvenilia's excesses for a novelistic seriousness about depicting the experience of economic precarity or Victorian individualism. But as I will point out, the novel is itself excessive in its depictions of powerlessness and vindication, as the protagonist's improbable habits of self-improvement produce equally improbable results, in ways not so different from the wish-fulfilment of either the juvenilia or of Brontë's second novel, *Jane Eyre*.

This interpretation represents a significant intervention into the established picture of the generic relationship between Brontë's juvenilia and mature novels, but also more generally, demonstrates the potential interventions of a participatory criticism. Emphasising how *The Professor* fails as a historical representation, but succeeds as a historical fantasy, reveals the novel's alternative value for providing an experience of imagined power and action, instead of an accurate or inaccurate depiction of material experience. As Dames has put it:

> Contextualist work on fiction often functions as our own, lapsed form of Incarnation. The work of imaginative literature is studied for the way it betrays, reflects, expresses, or encodes [...] the History that speaks through it. At its simplest, contextualist work risks effacing the fictionality of fiction – its counterfactuality, its incomplete adherence to the historical real, its artifactuality[.][48]

Dames's reference to Hegel brings the theology of realism into contact with a question of critical methodology: if the critic can too easily reduce an imaginative experience to a historical one, realist authors may have more difficulty and less incentive in 'effacing' the unique possibilities afforded by fiction. Following Brontë from play to the novel, we will attempt to identify the submerged practice of 'another realism', interested in a different type of real.

THE PROFESSOR

I want to redeem a form of metaleptic interpretation, now thoroughly disavowed in Brontë scholarship, which reads Brontë's fiction as a combination of biographical experience and unlived fantasy. 'Charlotte Brontë *is* Jane Eyre', Mary Augusta Ward wrote in 1899, 'You cannot think of her apart from what she has written'.[49] Anne Thackeray Ritchie recalled casually in 1894 of once meeting Brontë 'when my father [William Thackeray] had invited a party to meet Jane Eyre at his house'.[50] Although part of a generally admiring mythification of the author, this critical and popular practice in the nineteenth and early twentieth century of placing Brontë into her novels had embarrassing implications from the beginning. As early as 1856, while waiting to see the unpublished manuscript of *The Professor*, Gaskell had 'dreaded lest the Prof: should involve anything with M. Heger', the Belgian schoolmaster and employer with whom Brontë had been infatuated: 'I have not seen the Professor as yet [...] but I am afraid it relates to M. Heger, even more distinctly & exclusively than Villette does'.[51] The potentially awkward comparisons between Brontë's romantic experiences, *The Professor*, and *Villette* (the novel of an English teacher's relationship with a foreign professor) were ultimately reinforced by Gaskell's own text – *The Life of Charlotte Brontë* – which despite its best intentions, informed a strongly biographical reception of *The Professor*'s posthumous publication. The reviewer for *The Examiner* surmised that 'Into the character of the Professor himself the writer has transferred much from her own nature'; the *North British Review*, that 'the Professor is a woman in disguise [...] for she is quite properly stripped of her male costume, and turned into "Lucy Snowe" in *Villette*'; and the *Critic*, that 'William Crimsworth is a Jane Eyre in petticoats'.[52] Henry Houston Bonnell's study in 1904 takes this to its logical conclusion: 'Lucy Snowe is Charlotte Brontë, as is Jane Eyre, and as is the Professor'.[53]

Critics from the 1960s onwards have rightly repudiated such equations as reductive, patronising, or disparaging of Brontë's artistry, offering instead interpretations of how her texts 'speak to' greater and more abstract realities of gender, politics, or historical conditions (or Barthes's 'hypostases': 'reason, science, the law').[54] At the same time, however, vicarious identification and pleasure remain undeniably central both to many readers' experiences of her novels and to her protagonists' own uses of narrative. The denouement of *The Professor*, for example, is fictionalised by one of its characters before it is realised by the narrative itself.

The protagonist William Crimsworth, having finally overcome his financial difficulties and able to propose marriage to his former student, enters her room to find her composing poetry. Francis Henri's poem tells an idealised narrative of their relationship, featuring a character named Jane and an unnamed schoolmaster, concluding in their separation by circumstance and with the Master's call for Jane to 'Come home to me again!'[55] For Crimsworth, what the poem makes clear is 'that "Jane" was now by my side; no child but a girl of nineteen, and she might be mine, so my heart affirmed' (*TP* 222), spurring him to propose. His interpretation simultaneously opens up and closes the gap between reality and fiction (for us, between *The Professor* and its mise en abyme): at the sentence level, Crimsworth's confident identification of Frances as Jane ('Charlotte Brontë *is* Jane Eyre') is in tension with the immediate caveat that Frances is 'no child but a girl of nineteen', and with the quotation marks that bracket out 'Jane' as only conditionally interchangeable with her author. More generally, Crimsworth's realisation that Frances is 'now by my side' and 'might be mine' is paradoxically 'affirmed' by her conflation with a fictional 'Jane' who, by the end of the poem, is in fact physically separated from her lover. Crimsworth's proposal revises in life the ending to a narrative originally based *on* his life, effecting a divergence between life and fiction by leveraging a recognition of their convergence.

This strategy of 'incomplete adherence' between fiction and reality is also employed by Frances's poem itself, which despite its recognisability as a reflection of her experiences and situation, also makes significant departures from them.[56] Although the narrative of Jane's relationship with her master and the impossibility of their union neatly summarises the events of *The Professor* so far (except that Frances is unaware of Crimsworth's good news), in a notable diversion from the real events, the poem also includes explicit declarations of love:

> They called in haste; he bade me go,
>   Then snatched me back again;
> He held me fast and murmured low
>   'Why will they part us, Jane?' (*TP* 221)

Such inclusions diverge significantly from Frances's consistently undemonstrative relationship with the taciturn Crimsworth, who even when arriving to propose, 'had shown no eagerness [. . .] we met as we had always met, as Master and pupil, nothing more' (216). The stanza's imagining of being 'snatched' and 'held [. . .] fast' in fact pre-empts and inspires an uncharacteristic outburst which elicits 'Amazement' from Frances: 'one moment

I was sitting [...] the next, I held Frances on my knees, placed there with sharpness and decision, and retained with exceeding tenacity' (222). The poem does not only encode Frances's experience of the relationship but also her wish, and in doing so, happens to become the agent of its fulfilment. Similarly, while Frances's tutelage under Crimsworth has been cut short in the novel by her dismissal from the school, the poem grants Jane her academic victory and emotional reward.

> At last our school ranks took their ground;
> The hard-fought field, I won;
> The prize, a laurel-wreath, was bound
> My throbbing forehead on. (220)

Both of these embellishments on the actual narrative events set the poem at a middle distance from Frances's life, one that even Crimsworth describes as 'not exactly the writer's own experience – but a composition by portions of that experience suggested; thus while egotism was avoided, the fancy was exercised, and the heart satisfied'. (217) The poem is located as loosely suspended on an incomplete relation between creation and description, of fiction 'suggested' by 'portions of [...] experience', and further triangulated to a space between 'egotism', 'fancy', and personal satisfaction.

It is exactly this space which criticism cannot comfortably examine or occupy. Recognitions of Brontë's own wishful or intimate involvement in her writing have historically resulted in judgements like Q. D. Leavis's disparagement of popular fiction, that 'the author is himself – more usually herself – identified with the leading character, and the reader invited to share the debauch [...] as a compensation for personal disabilities and disappointments'.[57] *Jane Eyre* in particular became a target for Leavis's powerfully embodied disgust towards self-indulgent immersion within fiction:

> *Jane Eyre* is [...] a fable of wish-fulfilment arising out of experience, in which figure such common indices as the child's burning sense of injustice, self-idealisation [...] blinding and maiming of the beloved to enhance the value of the subject's devotion, self-abasement to the verge of death followed by dramatic salvation, recognition by enviable relatives, etc [...] the appeal of the commoner day-dreams is inexhaustible – they represent both for author and reader a favourite form of self-indulgence.[58]

On the other hand, the reclamation of Brontë and her work from these charges – through emphasising her engagement with gender oppression, working-class politics, literary networks, and scientific discourse – has therefore tended to elide the features which Leavis is essentially accurate in pointing out. As Heather Glen argues in her 1989 introduction to *The Professor*, Brontë's fiction is 'more searching, more flexible, more disinterestedly intelligent' than nineteenth- and early twentieth-century accounts credit, and deserves 'a full alertness to the sophisticated literary intelligence that is manifest in its pages [...] a different Charlotte Brontë from the unreflective novelist of private love and longing that she is all too often taken to be'.[59] Yet in her 2004 study of *Jane Eyre*, Glen is also openly ambivalent about the catalogue of narrative results, an echo of Leavis's 'common indices', she compiles from the divine justice doled out to the novel's characters:

> Investigation into the affairs of Lowood produces 'a result mortifying to Mr Brocklehurst'; John Reed's is a 'shocking' death, and his mother's a desolate one. The Reed sisters are disposed of [...] Bertha Rochester dies [...] Blanche Ingram, is categorically dismissed by the man she has sought to entrap. Rochester is blinded, injured, and domesticated [...] By the end, [Jane] is paramount: those who have sought to wrong her are punished, her decisions are vindicated and her desires fulfilled.[60]

Even as modern criticism has increasingly demonstrated more context, sophistication, and criticality in *Jane Eyre* than simple vicarious 'wish-fulfilment', it seems undeniable that the novel is also one in which 'Jane's uncontested narrating voice, rewarding her friends and punishing her enemies, oddly recalls the great Genii of Glass Town' in its omnipotent removal of obstacles and realisation of desires.[61]

The following reading of *The Professor* moves backwards in critical history, stepping momentarily out of the new consensus on Brontë's disinterested reflectiveness to reappraise her use of fiction 'as a compensation for personal disabilities and disappointments'.[62] As critics have shifted focus away from the apparent biographical realities in Brontë's novels towards more abstract and structural realities, this has also been a movement towards more impassive, Flaubertian relations between reality and the novel.[63] As we have seen, however, the conceit of the Chief Genii suggests Brontë's development of 'another realism', the writing of a plausible yet explicitly conjured reality which is no less the product of a 'sophisticated literary intelligence' than more orthodox forms of realist representation.[64] Their resurfacing in *Jane Eyre*'s narration, and in the self-realising power of Frances's poem, point to something left behind by criticism: a partial yet desirable correspondence between life and fiction, '*not exactly* the writer's own experience' (*TP* 217, emphasis added), which balances the aim of vicarious satisfaction with an avoidance of direct 'egotism'. Practices of wish-fulfilment in Brontë's novels require a reassessment that does not necessarily entail a return to reductivism or disparagement. Rather, Frances and Crimsworth demonstrate the potential for producing real gratification from the very possibility of the novel's inexactness to history, and in doing so, suggest alternative means for using and valuing realism's distinctive verisimilitude.

Work Ethic and Work Aesthetic

The issue of what kind, degree, or specificity of reality enters the novel seems to have been foundational to Brontë's own attachment to her first completed, post-juvenilia work. Two months after the publication of *Jane Eyre* in 1847, the novel written after *The Professor* had been repeatedly rejected by publishers, she offered to rework her first manuscript and argued that 'the middle and latter portion of the work, all that relates to Brussels, the Belgian school etc [...] contains more pith, more substance, more reality, in my judgement, than much of "Jane Eyre"'.[65] Shortly after the publication of *Shirley* in 1849, Brontë offered it again to an unreceptive Elder and Smith, drafting a new preface which once more defended the novel on the basis of the 'real':

> I had not indeed published anything before I commenced 'The Professor' – but in many a crude effort destroyed almost as soon as composed I had got over any such taste as I might once have had for the ornamented and redundant in composition – and had come to prefer what was plain and homely [...] I said to myself that my hero should work his way through life as I had seen real living men work theirs – that he should never get a shilling he had not earned – that no sudden turns should lift him in a moment to wealth and high station – that whatever small competency he might gain should be won by the sweat of his brow – that before he could find so much as an arbour to sit down in – he should master at least half the ascent of the hill of Difficulty – that he should not even marry a beautiful nor a rich wife, nor a lady of rank. (*TP* 3–4)

Such a preface is typical of what Levine identifies as 'realism's most overt anti-literary manifestos', the pre-emptive defences which arise out of an inherent 'self-consciousness in realistic fiction [...] awareness both of other literature and of the strategies necessary to circumvent it, and – at last – its awareness of its own unreality'.[66] Here, *The Professor* takes on a 'plain and homely' opposition to both the juvenilia (misrepresented as 'destroyed') and to *Jane Eyre*.⁶⁷ As Glen points out, almost everything explicitly denied to Crimsworth – 'unearned wealth, a transformative marriage, excessive happiness' – recall those qualities which most expose *Jane Eyre* as transparently desire-driven.⁶⁸ Less explicitly, the visualisation of the plot through Bunyan's allegory – 'the hill of Difficulty' along which 'no sudden turns should lift him' (3–4) – also reads in its verticality like a harsh correction to the juvenilia's magical conception of plot: the 'great obstacle' of the park gate, over which the authors personally 'took Raton up and threw him' (*EW* 26). What 'more pith, more substance, more reality' seems to indicate in Brontë's preface is less wish-fulfilment – '*never* [. . .] a shilling he had not earned', '*no* sudden turns', '*not* even [. . .] a beautiful *nor* a rich wife' (*TP* 3–4, emphasis added) – and in its place, moderate rewards earned only through practical life.

For much of *The Professor*, this premise of a realistic narrative manifests as serial episodes of perseverance against intractable forces, or in other words, as the *bildungsroman*'s necessary confrontations with a contingent world. The introduction, which frames the first chapter as Crimsworth's letter to an old school-friend, characterises the implied reader as 'a sarcastic, observant, shrewd, cold-blooded creature' (5) whose very reading must be forced from him: as Crimsworth remembers from Eton, 'when I recurred to some sentiment of affection [. . .] your sardonic coldness did not move me – I felt myself superior to that check *then* as I do *now*' (6, original emphasis). The end of the chapter acknowledges that the letter goes unanswered, a fatal 'check' that Crimsworth overcomes by readdressing the novel to the public. The narrative's (and the novel's) own struggle to exist sets the stage for the story of Crimsworth's career, which analogously struggles to be realised within an unreceptive and hostile market. Initially employed as his brother Edward's clerk, Crimsworth is warned that 'I shall excuse you nothing on the plea of being my brother; if I find you stupid, negligent, dissipated, idle or possessed of any faults [. . .] I shall dismiss you as I would any other clerk. £90 a year are good wages and I expect to have the full value of money out of you' (19). Their mutual brotherly antipathy, which dominates this first section of the novel, is in some sense a perfectly matched relationship: Edward's intention to extract 'full value' from his brother's labour, and his aggressive abstraction of their familial relation into an economic exchange, mirrors Crimsworth's attitude on eventually receiving his wages 'possessed heart and soul with the pleasant feeling that the master, who had paid me, grudged every penny of that hard-earned pittance' (31). Both ostensibly private relationships – school-friends as cold readers who must be brought to attention; brothers as economic agents from whom profit must be maximised – are alienated into the hostilities of public readers and the market. Real life, for *The Professor*, is indeed a 'hill of Difficulty' (3–4) in which conflict is environmental and gravitational, an undifferentiated field of opposing forces resisting the individual climber.

Moreover, the reciprocity between the brothers points out that, if help is nowhere to be expected, it is also deeply not to be desired. Despite the cynicism with which he expresses it, Crimsworth is serious in his retort to Edward that 'not to expect favour from you and not to depend on you for any help but what I earn – that suits me exactly' (19). This aversion to personal favour recurs pathologically throughout the novel. In his severing of ties to his aristocratic uncles, Crimsworth describes as 'my reward' to see 'one of them [throw] down on the table before me a £5 note which I was able to leave there – saying that my travelling expenses were already provided for' (22). Later, after the plot relocates to Brussels, he thanks Victor Vandenhuten, a kind and willing patron, for writing an honest reference and for *not* offering financial assistance: 'You have made me quite happy and in a way that suits me; I do not feel an obligation irksome, conferred by your kind hand; I do not feel disposed to shun you because you have done me a favour' (212). This model of patronage is contrasted, in the same chapter, with the unexpected gift of a longed-for portrait of Crimsworth's mother, saved from auction by his rival Hunsden Yorke Hunsden, whose accompanying note teases that 'There is a sort of stupid pleasure in giving a child sweets [...] repaid by seeing the child besmear his face with sugar [...] In giving William Crimsworth his Mother's picture, I give him sweets' (209–10). Crimsworth's initially sentimental response instantly sours:

> I muffled the picture in its green baize covering, restored it to the case and having transported the whole concern to my bedroom, put it out of sight under my bed. My pleasure was now poisoned by pungent pain [...] I should have said to him 'I owe you nothing, Hunsden – not a fraction of a farthing – you have paid yourself in taunts'. (210)

As Glen puts it, 'Instead of Dickens's great metaphors of circulation and stoppage, or George Eliot's of the social web, there is a singular story of individual self-help'.[69] Given Crimsworth's rejection and disgust of outside interference in his affairs, this is indeed self-help in a literal sense, or self-help by process of elimination. The preface's implicit contribution to (and perhaps, endorsement of) this attitude is the apparent withdrawal, too, of the author's help, as if the appearance of a sudden heiress in the plot would also represent an unwanted and inappropriate gift. Realism, in the sense of the absence of supernatural and metaleptic interventions, here meets realism as characterised by a particular picture of the social – the effect of which is to leave Crimsworth solely responsible for bringing about both his career and his narrative through 'the sweat of his brow' (3).

Modern critics have read this begrudging narrative one of two ways: as either an endorsement or a critique of 'self-help' as a historical ideology, an aspect of what has long been touted as the Victorian work ethic. Although the term itself would not be popularised until Samuel Smiles's publication of *Self-Help* in 1859, Glen notes how 'the lectures that formed the basis of Smiles's best-seller [...] were first delivered to a young men's mutual improvement society in Leeds in 1845 – the year in which, very probably, only a few miles away, *The Professor* was conceived'.[70] Shuttleworth similarly argues that 'it is relatively easy to trace many tantalizing examples of [Brontë's] connections with local self-help culture'.[71] Whatever the case may be of Brontë's possible encounter with Smiles, there is clearly a shared cultural wellspring between *The Professor*'s 'hill of Difficulty' and *Self-Help*'s liberal-individualist view of life: 'The battle of life is, in most cases', Smiles writes, 'fought up-hill; and to win it without a struggle were perhaps to win it without honour. [...] The road to success may be steep to climb, and it puts to the proof the energies of him who would reach the summit'.[72] This culture of self-realisation through labour, culminating in Smiles's philosophy but circulated throughout Victorian social theory, has been widely identified by criticism as the appropriate context for understanding the premises of *The Professor*.

Yet critical interpretations have been divided on the novel's ideological stance towards this context – namely, its critique of or collusion in a self-help view of the world – which I outline here in order to offer a third solution. For Shuttleworth and Glen, on the side of critique, Brontë's representation of self-help culture exposes its inherently oppressive effects. In this interpretation, Crimsworth's commitment to a philosophy of self-improvement is a critical and ironic depiction, rather than an endorsement; as these critics point out, the efforts with which he overcomes difficulty and asserts his independence are explicitly and brutally self-directed:

> I served Edward as his second clerk faithfully, punctually, diligently. What was given me to do, I had the power and the determination to do well. [Edward] Crimsworth watched sharply for defects but found none; he set Timothy Steighton, his favourite and head-man, to watch also, Tim was baffled; I was as exact as himself, and quicker: Mr. Crimsworth

> made enquiries as to how I lived, whether I got into debt – no – my accounts were always straight [...] [from] the accumulated savings of my Eton pocket-money; for as it had ever been abhorrent to my nature to ask pecuniary assistance, I had early acquired habits of self-denying economy [.] (*TP* 22)

Such a strategy of gaining victory over surveillance (Edward's 'watch' and 'enquiries') by having nothing to hide, economising oneself into miserliness, and providing more than perfect work, stands out as an exemplary form of Foucaultian self-discipline or what Sedgwick describes as paranoid logic: '*Anything you can do (to me) I can do first* – to myself'.[73] Shuttleworth notes along these lines that 'he defeats his brother, he suggests, by his ability to police internally his own mental traits [...] Crimsworth's language underscores the interdependence of theories of interiorized selfhood and external structures of surveillance. His sense of the primacy of a pre-existent realm of selfhood is illusory'.[74] More to the point, she argues that this 'textbook account of the social and psychological value of self-control [...] functions rather to highlight the structural violence implicit in these ideological formations'.[75] Glen concurs that Crimsworth's character – explicitly like the 'dependent and determined' perspective she ascribes to the juvenilia – is 'one of abnegation and refusal [...] neither expressively self-actualizing nor freely self-determining', and therefore that 'the novel seems to be pointing to a fundamental contradiction in that self-sufficient individualism which Crimsworth seeks to affirm [...] his vaunted independent "exertion" is in fact wage slavery'.[76] For these essentially congruent readings, the novel exacerbates and makes visible the cracks in the morality it reproduces through narrative.

For other critics, taking the opposite approach, this irony is so subtle as to be absent, and the novel instead genuinely perpetuates a middle-class myth of egalitarian achievement through difficulty. Terry Eagleton's classic *Myths of Power* points out 'a dissonance between what the novel shows and what the Preface claims for it', unravelling the novel's claims to be a story of individualist effort, because Crimsworth is 'after all an aristocrat by birth, furnished with privileged accomplishments which he can put to profitable use'.[77] Catherine Malone has similarly registered the jingle of 'Eton pocket-money' (*TP* 22) jarring Crimsworth's protestations of austerity, arguing that 'Crimsworth's life is not one of true sweat or labour because throughout the novel he is able to rely on the privileges of his sex and class'.[78] This argument reaches its most explicit manifestation in

Neville Newman's (partly satirical) representation of Crimsworth as a kind of modern Oxbridge graduate:

> William Crimsworth is an Eton-educated scholar steeped in the classics who chooses to make his living by teaching in a continental private school for girls after a brief and unsuccessful attempt at commerce in the counting house at his brother's mill [...] The sweat which he is expected to expend is, in his case, metaphorical at best. Less generously, the expression illicitly seeks to equate Crimsworth with the workers (for whom the sweat of their brows can only ever be literal) while simultaneously erasing a recognition of the reality of their efforts.[79]

Here, the illusion of 'the hill of Difficulty' is not internalised but projected; what disappears from the novel under analysis is not the self but work, exemplified by the evaporation of Crimsworth's 'sweat' as being untrue or metaphorical. What reappears are the millworkers, with 'literal' sweat and a 'reality' of labour, whose indistinct presences are noted but never in focus during the protagonist's employment at the mill. Contrasted to *Shirley*, where the deprivation of millworkers' families, the violence of machine-breaking, and the financial risk of employers are all explicitly (if no less contentiously) represented, Crimsworth's miserliness and work ethic are in fact curiously disconnected from both his own material conditions and the economics of his workplace. His alleged 'wage slavery' appears purely for its own sake – or in Newman's reading, for the sake of appearance.

Both interpretive camps, wildly divergent in their conclusions, nonetheless proceed from a shared political conviction: self-help does not work. Historically and philosophically, the patient submission of individuals to exploitation does not create the self-actualisation and social security that Smiles, Crimsworth, and Carlyle claims it does. Whatever the novel's real position, its internal narrative of individualist achievement cannot realistically co-exist with its claim to represent the external reality of labour – either Crimsworth's triumphant selfhood must be revealed as 'illusory', or his labour must be exposed as 'metaphorical'. Jennifer Ruth's recent and incisive reading inverts this problem into a dilemma about the visibility of intellectual labour, noting that while Crimsworth's work is admittedly derived from an innate capital of education and skills he himself calls 'mental wealth', Brontë also 'pointedly refuses the assumption that immaterial labor does not count as real work, that metaphorical sweat cannot convey true effort'.[80]

Such contradictions in the nature of work are not easily resolvable in life, but I want to propose, as an intervention, that they *are* resolvable in fiction – if only with a form of interpretation which renders fiction unusable to this kind of political critique. *The Professor* can be read 'straight' – as the 'apparently simple story of obstacles surmounted, effort rewarded, and victory won' promised by the preface – if, instead of the self or the struggle, the disappearing trick is performed on the novel's referential relation to the actual.[81] Ruth's reading of mental work, which poses as one of its central questions how to make 'immaterial labor' and 'metaphorical sweat' gain substantiality and literality, suggestively verges onto (without addressing) another, more metafictional question: what is the literality or substantiality of representational sweat, narrative labour, and fictional work? Rather than a critique, a misrepresentation, or an exploration of 'immaterial' work in the sense of intellectual labour, what would it mean for Crimsworth's work to be immaterial in the sense of *imagined*? Another way of understanding the novel's premises, as well as its political or ethical functions relative to historical experience, lies in fiction's explicit difference from reality and its capacity for wish-fulfilment.

The Pleasure of Fictional Work

To play out the Victorian work ethic in fiction is of course much more satisfying than embodying it in real life; indeed, what Brontë and Crimsworth perhaps identify here is the proper plane on which such values are in fact operable. If Crimsworth's desire to 'have set up the image of Duty, the fetish of Perseverance in my small bed-room' as guards against 'my Cherished-in-secret, Imagination' (*TP* 30) is troubling as the representation of a historical worker, this belaboured characterisation of realistic life also belies the equivalence between its apparent opposition: as 'image' and 'fetish', the values of self-help are themselves mediated through the 'Imagination' for the reader *and* the protagonist. Moreover, Crimsworth's commitment to self-help also manifests as fetishistic in the libidinal sense; when he realises that his affections have been toyed with by Zoraide Reuter, a Belgian schoolmistress, he regains his self-esteem by choosing 'to face her with firmness' (113):

> [S]he had held her hand to me – that I did not choose to see – she had greeted me with a charming smile – it fell on my heart like light on stone [...] meeting her gaze full; arresting, fixing her glance, I shot into her eyes from my own a look where there was no respect, no love, no tenderness, no gallantry, where the strictest analysis could detect nothing but scorn, hardihood, irony; I made her bear it and feel it; her steady countenance did not change but her colour rose and she approached me as if fascinated. (113–14)

This erotic encounter is modelled on the same 'abnegation and refusal' as his economic, social, and narrative struggles, and his tactics here echo his paranoid encounters with his family's condescension and surveillance – to evade detection of injury, he renders the self barren; to reject bad offers, he learns to do without.[82] Yet this episode of sexual refusal is also remarkably similar in its method and effects to its opposite, sexual advance: 'I shot into her eyes from my own [...] I made her bear it and feel it [...] her colour rose' (113–14). Later, teaching a class of Reuter's schoolgirls who 'talked to me occasionally with their eyes, by means of which [...] [they] say very audacious and coquettish things' (118), he moralises that their immodesty meant 'I found *pleasure* in answering the glance of vanity with the gaze of stoicism' (119, emphasis added). These erotic exchanges model explicitly the way in which *all* of Crimsworth's encounters with difficulty implicitly generate what he calls 'the pleasant feeling' (31) of grudging his brother (and himself, and everyone else) – of triumphant, almost masochistic perseverance. This equivalence between erotic and professional struggle reveals their shared economy with the pleasure of fictional difficulties, overcome with imagined effort and ultimately yielding narrative pleasures.

By inverting difficulty into invigoration, self-denial into self-pleasure, the erotics of *The Professor* embody the perversities of economic individualism not to critique or to endorse, but to take vicarious part in the imaginary pay-offs the philosophy offers (but cannot really deliver). In this light, Asa Briggs's observation that sales of *Self-Help* 'far exceeded those of the great nineteenth-century novels' suggests new questions about the comparative functions of these two genres,[83] one which reverses fiction's subordination to a 'first-person version of the narrative of self-help' or a 'textbook account of [...] social and psychological value'.[84] An ideology which spells powerlessness for its historical subjects undergoes an inevitable transformation in its replication by fiction, because there it must encounter the absolute power inherent to the position of the author. To discover the preface's 'hill of Difficulty' (*TP* 3–4) echoed in the narrative itself is to recognise this metaleptic transformation: on the voyage from England to Belgium, Crimsworth echoes his creator by considering himself as 'like a morning traveller who doubts not that from the hill he is ascending he shall behold a glorious sunrise; what if the track be strait, steep and stony? he sees it not – his eyes are fixed on that summit' (56). Just as he most vividly realises the 'pleasure' of flirtation by pointedly ignoring it, his metaphor luxuriates in describing those obstacles he 'did not choose to see' (113) much more explicitly than the vanishing point to which his attention is supposedly directed:

'there were pebbles, inequalities, briars on my path, but my eyes were fixed on the crimson peak above, my imagination was with the refulgent firmament beyond, and I thought nothing of the stones turning under my feet or of the thorns scratching my face and hands' (56). Rather than ironic distance, on Brontë and Crimsworth's common 'hill of Difficulty' we might detect the shared pleasure of the author and the narrator at work (or rather, at play) in this hyperbolic combination of self-effacement and self-aggrandisement.

Rather than the oppression of real labour, *The Professor* depicts a fantastic 'image' of work and a pleasurable 'fetish' of difficulty – a game of pretend career-building. By the end of the novel, its at-first overwhelming sobriety has become a pornographic realism, in which the conventions that supposedly mark out reality – hardship, perseverance, gradualism – gratifyingly inflate and exaggerate into implausibility, just as the logic of slow ascension comes to vastly overgrow its original expectations of a 'small competency'.[85] Eventually setting up their own school, the economic discipline and diligence of Crimsworth and Frances reach superhuman levels, and produce no less amazing results:

> Ten years rush now upon me [...] years in which me and my wife, having launched ourselves in the full career of Progress [...] scarcely knew repose, were strangers to amusement, never thought of indulgence [...] harmony of thought and deed smoothed many difficulties, and finally, success bestowed every now and then encouraging reward on diligence. Our school became one of the most popular in Brussels, and as by degrees we raised our terms and elevated our system of education, our choice of pupils grew more select, and at length included the children of the best families in Belgium. (*TP* 249)

As Brown has rightly noted, if 'for Brontë, "the real" describes a vision of social (rather than divine) justice, in which labor earns its just reward [...] Such a plot can be called 'realistic' only against the marvels of Angria'.[86] Indeed, it is the tension between the instantaneous magic of writing and the protracted reality of effort, so frequently exploited and explored in the juvenilia, which such a passage recalls in its 'rush' over ten years of apparently ceaseless labour in one paragraph. Indistinct summaries like 'harmony of thought and deed smoothed many difficulties', as well as the transitional phrases 'by degrees', 'grew more', and 'at length', linguistically compact the gradualism of their labour, easily eliding the supposedly arduous effort required to make the Crimsworths' school 'one of the most popular in Belgium'. What Barthes points out in history as 'the conflict of two time spans: the time of the speech-act and the time of the material stated [...] the acceleration phenomena of history' can be felt distinctly in the ending of *The Professor* against the pace of the narration that came before it, but this relative change in speed only reveals how narrated labour has never mapped (and never could) moment-to-moment onto the experience of labour itself.[87]

By the end of the novel, Crimsworth and Francis's labour and capital have transfigured completely and self-consciously into effects of language. The way in which the narrative has noticeably grown and accelerated beyond its initial brief is acknowledged when the Crimsworths retire on the proceeds of capital investment:

> Behold us now at the close of the ten years and we have realized an independency. The rapidity with which we attained this end had its origin in three reasons. Firstly; we worked so hard for it. Secondly; we had no incumbrances to delay success. Thirdly; as soon as we had capital to invest, two well-skilled counsellors [...] gave us each a word of advice as to the sort of investment to be chosen. (*TP* 257)

There is a note of petulant defensiveness to Crimsworth's explanation about the 'rapidity' and scale of their success – '*we worked so hard for it*' – which belies the fantastical destination at which the narrative has now arrived. That this hard work is now all the more swift, noiseless, and invisible in the narrative can be attributed to the removal of the 'incumbrances to delay' that allow fictional work to be described and felt, and finally, to the disappearance of 'the sweat of his brow' (3) altogether (metaphorical or fictional) thanks to the profits of wise investment. As Ruth's analysis also notes of this passage:

> Representing investment in the market as if Crimsworth were still somehow talking about professional labor does not allow Brontë to get through the passage smoothly [...] Still she chooses this recipe for independence, as if at the last moment she *wished to write away* the dilemma that disfigures her text, as if representing labor combining with capital as unremarkable would make us less likely to remark on the uneasy combination of mental labor and mental capital that paradoxically, however necessarily, constitutes her own professional.[88]

Yet while the Crimsworths' fortunes are indeed represented as tied to the mental capital of their 'well-skilled counsellors', the exercise of these skills are also hyperbolically contracted into 'each *a word* of advice' (*TP* 257, emphasis added), the figurative singularity of which more recalls the Genii incantation, the fairy-tale benefactor, and what the author 'wished', than any application of professional expertise. Describing the novel's ending as an elision, contraction, or writing away of labour is therefore to grasp the wrong end of Brontë's wish: what is for Ruth a problem of reification, the compression of the time and effort of labour into the static and inanimate presence of objects or capital, operates in reverse for a metaleptic action, where the fictional efficiency of language can be exploited and expanded into endless amounts of fictional labour and wealth. Such a reversal epitomises the fictionalisation or play of self-help effected by *The Professor* – of difficulty made, not easy, but fun; the experience of powerlessness transformed, not into critique, but vicarious power.

The Professor is then not the novel of sober realism, the counter to *Jane Eyre*, that it claims (and is often taken) to be – but this is not an argument for its disparagement. What this reading of vicarious power-play and fictional self-aggrandisement seeks to re-evaluate is not the balance of Brontë's reputation between the 'disinterestedly intelligent' novelist and 'the unreflective novelist of private love and longing', but the validity of this critical dichotomy between which she has historically oscillated. Disinterest is not the precondition of literary intelligence, nor is private desire necessarily unreflective; rather, like Frances's redressing of 'portions of [her] experience' (*TP* 217) in poetry, *The Professor*'s transformation of the West Riding's growing self-help culture into a tool of fictional self-pleasure exemplifies the inventive, as opposed to reflective, engagements with reality that arise from personal need. In producing a fantasy of her circumstances, Frances is clearly neither misrepresenting nor unaware of her problems, but keenly conscious of (and imaginatively fulfilling) the desires which life has frustrated or made impossible. Similarly, to write an implausibly pleasurable narrative of the social rather than a 'textbook account' is not to be ignorant of reality's dissatisfactions, nor even only to be aware of them, but to actively render them satisfying, to *play* them, to create narrative gratification where no material gratification exists. 'The many ways selves and communities succeed in extracting sustenance from objects of a culture [...] whose avowed desire has often been not to sustain them', as Sedgwick has written, '[are] No less acute than a paranoid position, no less realistic, no less attached to a project of survival, and neither less nor more delusional or fantasmatic'.[89] *The Professor*'s implausible story of successful self-help is, in this sense of a strategic engagement with and within reality, a deeply realistic fiction.

This book argues for the real uses of artificial realities, functions of the novel which become operable only if we cease to evaluate its reflectiveness and begin to appreciate the distinctive advantages of fiction. As we have seen, the omnipotence of the author to dictate fictional consequences has long been dismissed or elided as an embarrassing corollary of the novel's made-up-ness, its potential exchange of moral, political, or social seriousness for indulgent or arbitrary fantasy. Yet there are ways of responding to historical or existential conditions, other than their faithful representation, which involve the imaginary as part of life and which recognise the novel as a useful object precisely for its less constrained version of the world. In the next chapter, I examine another example of fiction's utility in the novels of Anthony Trollope. For Trollope, too, it is an author's explicit prerogative to invent the narrative, an exercise which he repeatedly depicts in *An Autobiography* as improvisational – in other words, making it up as he goes along. Like the godlike author, the improviser can be arbitrary, but arbitrariness often functions as a saving grace for Trollope's characters, revealing their lives to be less rigidly determined than they realised. In their ongoing incompleteness, his narratives acknowledge and depend on the novel's concrete yet flexible reality, a perspective which they cultivate as a possible ethical attitude to life.

CHAPTER 3

Plotting, Improvisation, and Anthony Trollope

'He was the great *improvvisatore* of these latter years', Henry James declared of Anthony Trollope, in an essay written a few months after the older novelist's death.[1] This characterisation occurs midway through a notorious passage about Trollope having 'published too much [...] [and] sacrificed quality to quantity', supported by the account of a trans-Atlantic voyage he had shared with a younger James, who witnessed first-hand how 'Every day of his life he wrote a certain number of pages of his current tale [...] Trollope shut himself up in his cabin every morning [...] [and] drove his pen as steadily on the tumbling ocean as in Montague Square'.[2] Embedded within what James Kincaid has called 'James's terribly effective propaganda' or 'myth-making' of Trollope as a narrative manufacturer rather than (as James conversely implies for himself) a technical artist, the fleeting figure of the *'improvvisatore'* has often been swallowed up by the force of this broader rhetorical sweep.[3] Little to no comment has therefore been made about the oddness and specificity of an analogy that compares the English novelist, generating manuscripts of distinctly un-lyrical prose in a private cabin, with a type of Italian folk performer, traditionally known for extemporising verse in live performances on the street or stage. Within this analogy lies James's more ambivalent encounter – much like Gaskell's with the Brontë juvenilia – with a 'tumbling', playful mode of novel-writing vastly different from his own.

Like Gaskell, James is ambivalent about praising an aptitude for invention – a talent for making things up – which, if obviously necessary to novel-writing, is not so usually commended as a distinction of the novelist as, for instance, their powers of truthfulness or expression. '[W]e have no English word for a talent which in England is unknown', Anna Jameson writes in her 1826 novel *The Diary of an Ennuyée*, describing a series of seven *'improvvisazion[i]'* by the Roman performer Bartolomeo Sestini, each spontaneously composed on topics offered by the audience, with new key words and rhymes suggested moment-to-moment and incorporated in time to an accompanying musical beat.[4] *The Penny Magazine*'s 1839 article on 'The Improvvisatori' similarly extols their ability to compose within impromptu conditions:

> Mr. Rose speaks of seeing a man to whom three subjects for sonnets were proposed: one of which was Noah issuing from the Ark; another, the death of Caesar; the third, the wedding of Pantaloon. They were to be declaimed interlacedly; that is, a piece of Noah, then a piece of Caesar, then a piece of Pantaloon: returning after that for another piece of Noah, and so on. Nor were these difficulties enough; he was also to introduce a particular verse specified by one of the audiences at a particular place in each sonnet. He accomplished this task in ten minutes.[5]

If it takes remarkable skill to produce 'a certain number of pages' every day given the contingencies of circumstance and composition, especially while (as Trollope was known to do) interlacing multiple plots and novels at once, this may be a feat more striking in its performance than its results. Admirers of the *improvvisatore* commonly mount this as a defence of the improvised text: 'these extemporaneous effusions ought to be judged merely as what they are', Jameson argues, 'not as finished or correct poems, but as wonderful exercises of tenacious memory, ready wit, and quickness of imagination'.[6] Moreover, as with other improvisational arts like live jazz or freestyle rap, the work of the improviser appears arbitrary in form and subject – using whatever rhyme, metre, theme, or stipulation suggested by the audience – when reviewed apart from the artificial logic of its performance. To have witnessed Trollope's novel-writing may have been a more meaningful experience than reading his novels, recalling an essentially performative tradition at work in a genre James primarily valued for its 'finished or correct' form.

This chapter proposes improvisation as a fundamental characteristic of Trollope's fiction, an ad hoc art of the novel to which he repeatedly confessed in his autobiography: 'I never found myself thinking about the work that I had to do till I was doing it [...] trusting myself, with the narrowest thread of a plot, to work the matter out when the pen is in my hand' (*AA* 145). If we continue to lack the critical terms for a talent which has been undervalued in the novel, which might seem unsuitable for the form as we know it, paracosmic play can provide a heuristic for understanding and appreciating the uses of inventive spontaneity. Fiction, too, has an artificial logic: in his account of play, De Quincey describes the creative plotting with which he evaded or worked around the narrative traps set by his sibling, a form of authorial ad-libbing he compares to a lawyer's creative interpretation of facts. These manoeuvres obey and depend on the strict consistency yet explicit subjectivity of fictional information, a malleability which characterises the nature of facts in both imaginary worlds and novels. If an Angrian duchess's death is later shown to have been misreported, or the Gombroonians are suddenly revealed to have tails under their togas, or Mrs Proudie dies from an unsuspected heart condition, these twists might be news even to the authors themselves (who have just now thought them up), but in the absence of previous statements to the contrary, can be *newly established as having always been true*. Only an imaginary world affords this open-ended view of facts, and only an improviser's perspective can appreciate the possibilities of a fiction never finished or correct, but accumulated and adjusted.

At stake in the idea of an improvised novel is the question James poses elsewhere to the nineteenth-century novel as a whole: what do such fictions, 'with their queer elements of the accidental and the arbitrary, artistically mean?'[7] As I have argued, acknowledging the inherent arbitrariness of novel fiction can reveal new ways of performing and interpreting artistic meaning or function – in this chapter, I propose how emphasising the flexibility of fictional realities can reveal a different mechanism by which Trollope realises his reputation as an ethical novelist. If the representation of moral reasoning *through* fiction is often lauded as the sympathising, exemplary, or improving function of the realist novel, the practice of moral reasoning *as* fiction is conversely deeply suspicious. Certain types of people are particularly adept at what we sometimes call 'mental gymnastics', the too-flexible interpretations of fact or logic by which individuals arrive at specious, often self-serving conclusions – politicians, lawyers, propagandists, and so on – but also arguably improvisers, novelists, and literary critics, all of whom require a creative relation to their materials, turning unexpected results out of seemingly determined situations. If we consider ingenuity and skill to be inappropriate forms of response to ethical dilemmas, then the performance of such dilemmas in Trollope's fiction appear especially unsuitable as moral examples, because (as James suggests through the improviser) their value lies in the inventive but arbitrary working-out of made-up problems. But as the right conclusion is emphatically not the point of a gymnastics routine, is it possible to appreciate a novel's deliberately convoluted performance of ethical explanation and judgement? What does it mean for moral reasoning to be a spectator sport?

Examining cases of how characters in *The Small House* escape their moral quandaries, I argue that their diegetic decision-making is mirrored by the extradiegetic process of Trollope's writing, connected in the same endeavour 'to work the matter out' as it happens on the level of ethical choice and of narrative plot. Trollope and his characters plot solutions to moral dilemmas as if (or in the author's case, knowing) that the facts of the situation are on some level arbitrary – just a story, only pretend, explicitly artificial – and therefore open to reinterpretation. Understanding ethical deliberation as narrative invention, a specious manipulation of truths within the arbitrary world of a novel, does not diminish its responsibility but cultivates a moral perspective by other means than through exemplariness or didacticism. Improvised play, a practice of acting within the possibilities of accidental conditions, is intrinsic to the aesthetics of Trollope's novels and to their understanding of moral agency. In what follows, I propose the deliberate values of flexibility, ingenuity, and spontaneity afforded by how lightly Trollope takes the novel.

Contriving the Novel

Everything would work out, the narrator suggests midway through *Barchester Towers*, if only Eleanor Bold would cry in front of Mr Arabin: 'he would have melted at once, implored her pardon, perhaps knelt at her feet and declared his love. Everything would have been explained [...] But then where would have been my novel? She did not cry, and Mr Arabin did not melt'.[8] If some measure of contrivance is necessary to novel-writing (in the sense of being made up, all novels are contrived), the open acknowledgement of this necessity is a particular signature of Trollope's narration. In justifying the continuation of the narrative conflict, he appeals not to the psychological rationale of the characters – that this is how Eleanor would act when suffering an unjust accusation – but to the artificial logic of plot, the misunderstandings which could be spared were they not indispensable for the story to continue. As James points out, 'many more specimens' exist in Trollope's oeuvre of these 'little slaps at credulity', which he deplores as 'very discouraging [...] even more inexplicable; for they are deliberately inartistic'.[9] The second chapter of *Orley Farm* likewise reassures us that the middle-aged Lady Mason, recently introduced, is 'not intended to be the heroine. The heroine, so called, must by a certain fixed law be young and marriageable'.[10] As Kincaid rhetorically suggests, this sentence seems to exemplify an 'attachment to romantic comedy formulas, an attachment apparently so fixed that those formulas are shamelessly duplicated [...] who so set the law? And if one indeed determines to obey this law, why call our attention to it and thus increase its unnaturalness and diminish its force?'[11]

The facts and realities of Trollope's narratives often resist a naturalistic explanation (being made explicable on the level of the purely diegetic), but instead suggest metaleptic references to extradiegetic conditions (literary convention or authorial convenience) which rationalise them through an explicit logic of fiction. Even if such statements are to some extent ironic, they represent a different order of irony, for instance, to truths universally acknowledged about single men with good fortunes. When Trollope mocks the rules of his characters' world, he reveals that such a world is not only governed by social or natural laws but also subject to the practical rules of fiction-writing. The world of the novel is arbitrary, not only in the sense that social realities are arbitrary, but in the way that imaginary worlds are. For Kincaid, this anti-mimetic streak presents a problem for the seriousness of Trollope's purpose and the moral weight of his task, as calling attention to the 'unnaturalness' of narrative might diminish its relevance as an account of life. As James formulates the problem:

> [Trollope] took a suicidal satisfaction in reminding the reader that the story he was telling was only, after all, a make-believe. He habitually referred to the work in hand (in the course of that work) as a novel, and to himself, as a novelist [...] It is impossible to imagine what a novelist takes himself to be unless he regard himself as an historian and his narrative as a history [...] As a narrator of fictitious events he is nowhere; to insert into his attempt a back-bone of logic, he must relate events that are assumed to be real.[12]

Understanding this tendency in Trollope's fiction as something other than 'inartistic', 'inexplicable', or 'suicidal' requires a less pejorative attitude to the novel's artifice. Being conscious of the narrative's imaginariness, as opposed to being tricked (or tricking others) into temporary belief, is not to resign literary value or meaningfulness but to understand the distinctive uses of pretence.

Trollope has good reasons for giving up the assumption of reality in his novels, advantages gained in exchange for puncturing the suspension of disbelief, which form the foundations to his practice of fiction from their origins in childhood play. The explicit fictitiousness of narrative events, their partial freedom from the strictness of causation, allows Trollope the flexibility to plot narrative in ways that a historian could not. Habitually referring to his characters as literary constructs, formed out of conventional tropes, affords a style of psychological characterisation which renders them no less compelling as sympathetic subjects; making up the scenarios by which to practice moral judgement does not preclude their potential ethical value. Explaining Trollope's anomalies as part of a consistent history of practice, from the paracosmic to the literary, enables a sharper critical discernment about such uses of the novel distinctively and explicitly 'as a novel', or in other words, as 'make-believe'.

On the most basic level, Trollope is by nature disinclined to conceal the process of invention and compromise that lies behind literary production. As a contemporary reviewer protested in *Macmillan's Magazine*, Trollope's *An Autobiography* is uncomfortably explicit about how the sausage is made: 'When an author says that he wrote something for no other reason than to prevent a publisher from going to "another shop" for his wares, we may admit that the literary ideal is brutalized indeed'.[13] Trollope self-deprecates about his adherence to such banalities, but at the same time, suggests how such practicalities are inseparable from his narrative process. For instance, *An Autobiography* recounts the inception of *Framley Parsonage* not from an originating intention or inspiration, but from a series of problems arising out of a contract dispute. As part of Trollope's agreement with *The Cornhill Magazine* in 1859, the publishers Smith and Elder rejected the already in-progress *Castle Richmond*, as 'an Irish story would not do', and begged to stipulate 'an English tale, on English life, with a clerical flavour. On these orders I went to work [...] [on] an idea of what I meant to write – a morsel of the biography of an English clergyman' (*AA* 92). To this half-formed idea of the protagonist Mark Robarts, Trollope added further conditions:

> The love of his sister for the young lord was an adjunct necessity, because there must be love in a novel. And then by placing Framley Parsonage near Barchester, I was able to fall back upon my old friends Mrs. Proudie and the archdeacon. Out of these slight elements I fabricated a hodge-podge in which the real plot consisted at last simply of a girl refusing to marry the man she loved till the man's friends agreed to accept her lovingly. Nothing could be less efficient or artistic. (92)

What he articulates through this 'hodge-podge' of contingent needs and materials, in exactly the same voice with which his narrators insist on the necessity of certain contrivances, is an alternative (and really no less 'efficient') writing process than the premeditated composition of a naturalistic narrative. Trollope's novel is designed in response to a miscellany of external and self-imposed requirements – the publishers' 'orders', 'a clerical flavour', an emergency fall-back, 'an adjunct necessity' – which grow to constitute the plot, not as a plan with a coherent rationale, but as a set of personal, professional, and literary problems which instigates the ad hoc solution that is *Framley Parsonage*.

On another level of deliberateness, this kind of working account is also openly acknowledged within the novels themselves; in a sense, the view 'behind the scenes' provided by *An Autobiography* is a redundant one, because a transparent display of the story's mechanics is already on show in the narration. Much as Jameson's admiration for the *improvvisatore* refuses to separate the finished poem from the 'wonderful exercises' of its production, Carolyn Dever has suggested that the visible artifice of Trollope's novels is an essential component of their appeal; their reading experience does not hinge on suspending predictable outcomes but on 'a full-frontal view of the machinery of plot grinding away for hundreds of pages before this ending is realized'.[14] Critics have also registered this spectacle, the novel which shows its working, by redescribing Kincaid's 'formulas' as performances of variation: William A. Cohen argues that a tension between Trollope's progressivism and conservatism is reflected formally in 'the variations [the Palliser series] spins on a relatively narrow set of plot possibilities'; George Levine compares Trollope's works to 'an extended experiment on the human species, not complete until all the variations are played'; L. J. Swingle notes that the marriage plot 'tends to function in a Trollope novel [...] like the "theme" in a musical composition wherein the composer is intent upon developing variations on a theme'.[15] Each of these critical analogies to political, genealogical, and musical variation, albeit in service to very different arguments, reiterate James's formal observation that Trollope's plots are all 'a love-story constructed on an inveterate system'.[16] Rather than James's sense of a hidden machine producing derivative art, however, such critics suggest the working process of plot construction as an aesthetic experience in itself, producing pleasure and meaning by way (rather than in spite) of its artifice.

In other words, the bizarreries of Trollope's behaviour in and about the novel is not negligence, but an alternative practice of fiction, aiming at the different artistic methods and possibilities afforded by the novel's 'fabricated' nature. Like Brontë's experiments in Angria, Trollope's work is interested in exhibiting connections between the actual circumstances of authorship and their concrete effects in the imagined world: Framley Parsonage is located near Barchester not because this is simply the geographical fact of the matter, but because Trollope wished to reintroduce several characters from *Barchester Towers*; Lady Mason will not have a romantic affair, not because her age and station disinclines her to such adventures, but because it is not her given narrative role. Such trains of metaleptic logic are openly advertised in the novel and beyond. As Cohen, Levine, and Swingle point out, understanding the conventions, conditions, or limits within which the narrative operates is vital to a full appreciation of its inventiveness and coherence – much as the spectacle of the *improvvisatore* is incoherent to someone who has missed the challenges and prompts to which the performer is working. Why does the poem alternate between Noah, Caesar, and Pantaloon? Why obey the ridiculous law of the heroine?

To such analogies of variation and performance, the history of Trollope's play practices can offer a fuller and more biographical heuristic for his alternative art of the artificial novel. The possibilities and appeal of an explicitly fictional reality struck Trollope differently than they did Brontë: while for her such worlds afforded experiences of power and wish-fulfilment beyond ordinary limits, Trollope's accounts of his childhood conversely emphasise an interest in imaginary rules and principles, albeit not for some moral objection to imaginative excess (à la Gaskell). What Trollope discovers through play, as equally indulgent as authorial omnipotence, is the experience of flexible invention under conditions (particularly arbitrary ones), long before and anticipating the 'hodge-podge' of professional and generic obligations by which he would later formulate novels.

A literary art of (and a kind of creative addiction to) inventive problem-solving is deeply rooted in the *Autobiography*'s account on the origins of play. Like the story of inventing *Framley Parsonage*, this account also begins with a series of necessities: in place of a publisher's demand, Trollope started constructing imaginary worlds because 'other boys would not play with me. I was therefore alone, and had to form my plays within myself' (*AA* 33). If the practice is therefore a recourse, chosen because others leave him no choice, he also presents his own psychology as similarly demanding, because 'Play of some kind was necessary to me then, as it has always been. Study was not my bent, and I could not please myself by being all idle' (33). Much of this recurrent framing – he 'had' to, it was 'necessary' – mitigates responsibility for what he apologetically admits to be a 'dangerous habit' (33), but this issue of necessity also continues into his description of imaginative content and process:

> For weeks, for months, if I remember rightly, from year to year, I would carry on the same tale, binding myself down to certain laws, to certain proportions, and proprieties, and unities. Nothing impossible was ever introduced, – nor even anything which, from outwards circumstances, would seem to be violently improbable. I myself was of course my own hero. Such is a necessity of castle-building. But I never became a king, or a duke, – much less when my height and personal appearance were fixed could I be an Antinous, or six feet high. I never was a learned man, nor even a philosopher. But I was a very clever person, and beautiful young women used to be fond of me. (33)

Although Trollope too is interested in wish-fulfilment, its gratifications are remarkably constrained, taking place in-between self-imposed rubrics of 'proportions, and proprieties, and unities'. Even the acknowledgement of wanting to be 'my own hero', the ostensible purpose and pleasure of the fantasy, is expressed and externalised as 'a necessity' alongside other necessities of physical scale, realist probability, and narrative consistency; where Brontë says *I want*, Trollope says *I must want*. Just as play apparently originates from a set of needs rather than from any initiative, its contents also seem to be a series of things he cannot help more than he can. Despite the account's association between these two forms of restriction, their analogy has nothing to do with *actual* necessity – being forced to play alone has no necessary connection to choices about its imaginative scope – and more with how Trollope tends to tell stories through *apparent* necessity, including the origin story of this narrative method in play.

This history of play offers, for a start, another opportunity to reconsider what has long been taken as Trollope's self-deprecation or inartistry – that he wrote novels out of commercial need, to satisfy requirements, or following conventions – as a more consistent creative principle of 'binding myself down' to problems in order to resolve them with narrative. The language of self-restriction, whether about the discursive conditions of subject matter or the practical circumstances of literary production, recurs obsessively throughout *An Autobiography*. In addition to the fixed laws of generic conventions and plausibility with which the novelist 'binds himself by the circumstances of the world which he finds around him' (*AA* 272), as well as the psychological need or contractual obligations which motivate fiction-making, Trollope also finds it 'expedient to bind myself by certain self-imposed laws' (78) of allotted pages per day, having 'prided myself on completing my work exactly within the proposed dimensions' (79), in these ways 'acknowledging myself to be bound to the rules of labour' (199). As D. A. Miller has argued, the nineteenth-century novel reveals through its 'abundant restrictions and regulations [...] the uneasiness raised in the novel text by its *need* for controls'; but where he has in mind the discursive forces operating within the text, for Trollope, restrictions of any kind or reason suffice to produce 'the various incitements to narrative' Miller calls the 'narratable'.[17] Trollope can only seem to write if he is given (or gives himself) no choice but to do so, and moreover, a strict limit on choices about form and content, from adjunct subplots down to the wordcount. If necessities engender invention, such creative conditions can themselves be manufactured, self-binding or self-imposed, like a theme that gives rise to variation; rather than limiting his imagination, more rules can only satiate a prolific novelist's gratuitous need for controls.

Play also provides, for another, examples and models for rethinking the novel as an improvised narrative. Beyond the contentions of Trollope's individual reputation as an artist, accounting for his idiosyncratic practices helps us to reposition critical perspective: in general, acknowledging the novel's artifice over its mimetic illusions; and in particular, appreciating the open-endedness of narratives as fictions. Literally and figuratively, Trollope writes by making promises he does not yet know how to keep, whether on the length of a serial instalment, a pre-commitment to 'a clerical flavour' (*AA* 92), or some other productive stipulation of his own insistence. His determination of the narrative's requirements in advance, rather than its contents, means that 'with nothing settled in my brain as to the final development of events, with no capability of settling anything [...] I have rushed at the work as a rider rushes at a fence which he does not see' (111). Sometimes, he goes on to admit, this has led him to encounter 'what, in hunting language, we call a cropper' (111). At stake in such statements, read less as biographical slapstick and more as aesthetic intention, is a presently undervalued sense of the novel's indeterminacy or incompleteness.

In order more fully to articulate the rules of play which make such incompleteness desirable (and predetermination impossible) in its practice of fiction, I now turn briefly to the De Quincey brothers as a comparative case for Trollope. The open-endedness and arbitrariness of imaginary worlds, qualities which in novel-writing appear as signs of Trollope's unprofessionalism, did not bother these brothers so much as provided energy and opportunity for invention. By placing Trollope's art of conditions within the wider practices of paracosmic play, particularly alongside the adversarial back-and-forth through which the De Quinceys produced their paracosmic narratives, I suggest the pleasures and ethical functions such narratives most have to offer when they least know where they're going.

The Uses of Incompletion

'It is impossible to imagine what a novelist takes himself to be', James writes, 'unless he regard himself as an historian and his narrative as a history'.[18] Examining the narratives of paracosmic play makes it possible to imagine exactly this: what a novelist might do by acknowledging their narrative as a make-believe, and conversely, the creative possibilities foreclosed by refusing to do so. 'How, and to what extent', a thirteen-year-old William De Quincey demanded of his brother Thomas, 'did [you] raise taxes upon [your] subjects?' (*AS* 47). The younger brother rightly sensed a trap behind the question and restrained his 'first impulse to say, that I did not tax them at all [. . .] because it was too probable he would demand to know how, in that case, I maintained a standing army' (47). Aware of this potential follow-up, as well as of William's belligerence, De Quincey spent 'some days, therefore, to consider the point; but at last replied, that my people, being maritime, supported themselves mainly by a herring fishery, from which I deducted a part of the produce, and afterwards sold it for manure to neighboring nations' (47). This creative answer elaborates on Gombroon's already well-established island geography to deflect William's implicit and implicative threats, but in putting forward a solution that incorporates the existing facts of the game, De Quincey also exposes his people to further indignities that in turn follow or accommodate *this* new state of play. William 'inferred from this account [. . .] that the arts must be in a languishing state amongst a people that did not understand the process of salting fish', and moreover 'that a wretched ichthyophagous people must make shocking soldiers, weak as water' compared to Tigrosylvanian troops who – William now asserts – never 'condescended to any thing worse than surloins of beef' (47).

This conflict by inventive inferencing only makes sense given an ironic imagination which takes fiction seriously as a factual state of affairs, while simultaneously exploiting the constructedness of fictional facts. Like the Brontëan Genii, the authorial will of the De Quinceys have absolute effect over their sovereign territories. But in order for these children to share a singular, self-coherent, virtual object, to be talking about and acting on the same thing, all 'factual' expressions about the imaginary world must be mutually consented (or conceded) to, kept consistent between them by what De Quincey calls 'the law of the contest between us, as suggested by some instinct of propriety in my own mind':

> What [William] said was like a move at chess or draughts, which it was childish to dispute. The move being made [. . .] I proceeded as a lawyer who moves as long as he can, not by blank denial of facts, (or *coming to an issue*,) but by *demurring*, (i.e., admitting the allegations of fact, but otherwise interpreting their construction). It was the understood necessity of the case that I must passively accept my brother's statements so far as regarded their verbal expression; and, if *I* would extricate my poor islanders from their troubles, it must be by some distinction or evasion lying *within* this expression, or not blankly contradicting it. (*AS* 46–47, original emphasis)

In the *Autobiographical Sketches*, De Quincey retrospectively casts his brother as aggressively asserting, himself passively qualifying, but it is clear from this account that both players accepted each other's 'allegations' as binding conditions, or in attempting to challenge them, did so via new assertions which supplemented their information while subverting their intended purpose. If William seeks to denigrate Gombroon's military power, he must improvise within the possible implications offered by the economic system De Quincey has devised. In the process, he must acknowledge the imaginariness of the facts at hand, because information about actual objects lacks even this limited creative license for elaboration.

Unlike the material world of history, fictional worlds like Gombroon and Tigrosylvania are *radically incomplete* in their ontology, affording a correspondingly radical view of the relation between narratives and facts. A novel can choose to tell its fictional story as a history, following a naturalistic logic of causes and effects, but in doing so only ignores (rather than refutes) its inherent and partial freedom from the rules of logic as ordinarily applied. For instance, by articulating the 'law of contest' which governs the operation of facts in Gombroon, De Quincey reaffirms the axiom of Aristotelian logic known as the 'law of non-contradiction', which states that 'Nothing can both *be* and *not be*'.[19] That is, a set of contradictory statements cannot both be true. Gombroon may be large, but cannot contain multitudes; if De Quincey claims that it has a herring factory, William cannot also claim in 'blank denial of facts' (*AS* 46) that it hasn't. But if this law of consistency gives weight to fictional information, allowing subjective allegations to be objectively known, the paracosm strongly violates a complementary axiom in the 'law of the excluded middle', which states that 'Everything must either *be* or *not be*'.[20] That is, statements of fact about the material world must either be true or false. Any historical individual must ultimately be either right-handed or not right-handed, but Anna Karenina *can be neither* by virtue of her under-determination as an imagined entity. Even if Tolstoy's novel were to determine this aspect of its world, the most maximalist of narratives still cannot match the infinitely propertied nature of any material object; Karenina would still have an indeterminate shoe size, number of eyelashes, and so on, facts which are all fundamentally true or false (even when unknown) about an actual person.

Narratologists and philosophers have long debated the extent to which such gaps are filled in or left out during the reading process, especially for the novel as a genre which demands and assumes significant contextual knowledge about contemporary settings.[21] As Lewis argues in his seminal essay 'Truth in Fiction', it is safe to assume that certain facts in the fictional world created by Arthur Conan Doyle possess truth or falsity even when not directly referenced in the narrative; for instance, that the greater geography of Victorian London more-or-less exists beyond Baker Street and the settings of the adventures; or that the Second Anglo-Afghan War, where Watson is injured before the adventures, played out in a similar way to how it did historically.[22] But 'Is the world of Sherlock Holmes a world where Holmes has an even or an odd number of hairs on his head at the moment when he first meets Watson? What is Inspector Lestrade's blood type? It is absurd to suppose that these questions about the world of Sherlock Holmes have answers'.[23] For the De Quinceys, however, this ontological peculiarity matters less as a theoretical problem as for its practical implications to their fictional enterprise; already inhabiting the rules of a complex ontology by 'instinct', they are conscious of the inherent gaps in fiction as potential vulnerabilities or escape routes, where a fatal or redeeming qualifier might suddenly redefine the *status quo*.

For the De Quinceys – and for understanding the *uses* of fictionality – incompleteness is not a philosophical problem but an available space of play, the kind of productive insufficiency that provides further 'incitements to narrative'.[24] The state of Gombroon's taxation was not only *indeterminate* for the brothers but *undecided*, a still-malleable aspect of the world on which De Quincey can exercise creative invention, but which would in turn produce fresh possibilities at the new borders of 'verbal expression'. The availability of a constant indeterminacy is a feature of fictional worlds which enables paracosmic play to sustain narrative indefinitely, and represents an essential component of its wider practice: these children recurrently represent narrative progression or change as an encounter between new assertions and the facts as previously established, whether with siblings or by themselves. Jameson, for example, describes each new 'series of actions, scenes, and adventures' that arise in her private world as 'one *springing out* of another, and *coloured and modified* by increasing knowledge';[25] while Derwent Coleridge describes Hartley as '*evolving* the complicated drama of existence [...] [through] changes of government, a great progress of public opinion and a new order of things!' (*HC* xliii–xliv, emphasis added). Afforded by the nature of the paracosm as a virtual object, these accounts emphasise the act of fiction-making as outgrowing from an always mutable and never completed present, creating new excitement and stories out of accumulatively rearranging the fictional state of affairs.

Here again, the paracosm helps to upend our view of the novel by embodying, to extravagance, aspects of its fictionality more usually considered peripheral or ambivalent to the central values of the form. '[W]hat discontents the traditional novel', Miller argues, 'is its own condition of possibility. For the production of narrative [...] is possible only with a logic of insufficiency, disequilibrium, and deferral, and traditional novelists typically desire worlds of greater stability and wholeness than such a logic can intrinsically provide'.[26] But what requires recognition, too, is a tradition of fiction which enshrines the 'condition of possibility' as its primary appeal and form of sense-making, preferring worlds of inherent incompleteness over those of stability or wholeness. In the following chapter on sequels and continuations, I return to the problem of closure by examining how authors such as Thackeray were indeed seriously discontented with the need for novels to end. For the moment, however, such a problem does not come up for Jameson, Coleridge, or the De Quinceys, who have markedly different motivations for fiction-making than 'traditional novelists'. Nor for Trollope, who discovered in the imaginary world a hyperbolic source of narratability, insufficiency enough to 'carry on the same tale' for years and years, explicitly questioning 'whether, had it not been my practice, I should ever have written a novel. I learned in this way to maintain an interest in a fictitious story' (*AA* 33). Recalling the scene of Eleanor's convenient lack of tears – 'where would have been my novel?' (*BT* 241) – the indispensable condition of the novel for Trollope is its capacity to avoid a final determination of facts – 'Everything would have been explained' (241) – at least for now, if not forever.

The fun and meaningfulness of paracosmic narratives are to be found in the artificial logic of their invention, affording a continually creative relation to unexpected conditions. Such narratives are not only unplanned and unending, but inherently unplannable and open-ended, arising out of an indefinite process of elaboration whose destination can never be fully pinned down, or even more chaotically, from a back-and-forth between multiple authors who regularly contort the shared story in perverse directions. As Trollope always claimed, the Chronicles of Barsetshire was an unplanned enterprise; nonetheless, accumulating new families, townships, and narratives for his fictional county over a six-novel series, 'to go back to it and write about it again and again has been one of the delights of my life'.[27] Such revisitations not only take the narrative further along in time, but reveal Barsetshire as a world about which there is always more to say than any novel has the capacity to conclude. This is a view of the novel that, as I have argued, acknowledges its nature as a fiction; as we will see, it might also be a view of the world, a kind of moral optimism that people and situations are never beyond redemption.

'Protestations of Unpreparedness'

'[O]ur admiration of *The Last Chronicle [of Barset]* would be even greater if we were able to disregard what Trollope says', argues the critic Anthony Arthur.[28] Like James, Kincaid, and the reviewer for *Macmillan*'s, Arthur echoes a sentiment of Trollope as his own worst enemy, a committer of serial artistic suicide, which I have argued to be a misrecognition of Trollope's actual narrative values. Arthur's specific example – the life and death of Mrs Proudie – is a good final case for re-evaluating 'what Trollope says', and how we might differently admire his work. Like Lady Mason, Mrs Proudie's introduction and characterisation in *Barchester Towers* is an act of ostensible compliance with a novelistic law:

> It is ordained that all novels should have a male and a female angel and a male and a female devil. If it be considered that this rule is obeyed in these pages, the latter character must be supposed to have fallen to the lot of Mrs. Proudie. But she was not all devil. There was a heart inside that stiff-ribbed bodice, though not, perhaps, of large dimensions, and certainly not easily accessible. (*BT* 204)

If one possible implication of this passage is a realist ethical principle about the irreducibility of persons to type, what it *explicitly* argues instead is that Mrs Proudie is the way she is due to her nature as a fictional character, contingent to but incompletely defined by conventions. She is revealed as having a heart not because even devilish people have hearts, but because (radically unlike any actual person) the facts of her nature and history as a fictional character are available to be continually qualified in this way. As Sophie Ratcliffe has argued, Trollope's sense that individuals can be 'dual in character' is connected to a working process where the novelist allows himself 'to be inconsistent, to revise his opinion, and to edit [...] Trollope's writing methods enable such duality'.[29] The stark rhetorical turn of this passage, in which the passive voice of obligation ('It is ordained', 'If it is considered', '[it] must be supposed') gives way to positive declarations ('But she was', 'There was'), models this relation between the conditions of novel-writing and the qualities of a fictional personality: the narrator first establishes her necessity in the stock role of the villain, then opens a certain latitude or variability within that 'stiff-ribbed' form. Mrs Proudie owes her complex moral psychology, the narrator tells us, to the available caveats (rather than restrictive determinism) of the novel's 'romantic comedy formulas'.[30]

As narrative plot, Mrs Proudie's nature as a fiction also governs the circumstances of her demise. Although, as Arthur notes, contemporary reviewers did not seem to register Mrs Proudie's death in *The Last Chronicle* as an unusual development, *An Autobiography* later revealed its unusual causes behind the scenes of narrative. At work on *The Last Chronicle* in the Athenæum, Trollope overheard 'two clergyman [...] abuse what they were reading, and each was reading some part of some novel of mine':

> Then one of them fell foul of Mrs. Proudie. It was impossible for me not to hear their words, and almost impossible to hear them and be quiet. I got up, and standing between them, I acknowledged myself to be the culprit. 'As to Mrs. Proudie,' I said, 'I will go home and kill her before the week is over.' And so I did. The two gentlemen were utterly confounded, and one of them begged me to forget his frivolous observations. (*AA* 172)

This episode is a striking account of Trollope's working process, spinning narrative ad hoc out of unnecessary, arbitrary, and extradiegetic conditions: 'It was impossible for me not to hear [...] I could not, I think, have done it, but for a resolution taken and declared under circumstances of great momentary pressure' (172). If the decision is spontaneous and 'momentary', responding to a 'frivolous' and accidental situation, it is also a binding 'resolution' about a character who has spanned ten years and five novels of work. The account is temporally disrupted by this contrast between timescales, jumping proleptically from Trollope's conversation in the club to later in the week – 'And so I did' – and then back again to the clergyman asking, evidently in vain, to undo the damage. Within the novel itself, Mrs Proudie's body undergoes an impossibly accelerated rigor mortis that keeps it 'still resting on its legs, leaning against the end of the side of the bed, while one of the arms was close clasped round the bedpost' (*LCB* 594), as if the immediacy of authorial decision has flash-frozen her in the fictional world, and her sudden passing is attributed to that small, hidden part of her construction: 'It's her heart [...] though nobody knew it. She was very shy of talking about herself' (594).

The sudden claim that Mrs Proudie has always had a 'heart complaint' (*LCB* 594) – or rather, that she was never declared as *not* having one – exemplifies that space for 'distinction or evasion' (*AS* 47) intrinsic to all fictional information. The rumours of Mrs Proudie's heart play this function twice over the novel series, revealing within the established facts of Barsetshire the possibilities for surprising qualifications not yet determined or contradicted by narration; this is reinforced by the suggestion that her condition had been hidden because of a particular shyness, another retroactive quality to the unrepresented private life of an outspoken character. These eulogistic footnotes work against Arthur's argument that the scene represents a symbolic climax to Mrs Proudie's personal inflexibility, and a premeditated end to her character, that she 'die[d] as she had lived: rigid, unyielding, incapable even physically of registering defeat'.[31] Where this reading emphasises the inevitability of Trollope's 'calculated dispatch, not only justifiable but necessary in terms of plot and characterisation', the novel itself balances the finality of her death with the abruptness of the event, the impossible stiffness of her body with revelations of an unsuspected softness.[32] There is a certain rigidity itself to Arthur's insistence against the spontaneity of this episode, his search for justifications from the preceding narrative and novels, which overlooks the real 'appropriateness of the death in the series' as an accumulation, rather than a culmination. New surprising claims about an old familiar character exemplify how the Barsetshire novels have always followed each other: not as a systematic survey of a predetermined county, but the filling-in of gaps between known locations, and the steady addition of local families over time who have *suddenly always been* connected to characters of previous novels.[33] Even without Trollope's account in *An Autobiography*, Mrs Proudie is clearly killed in this spirit of the paracosmic ad hoc, a 'great momentary pressure' (*AA* 172) rearranging the lines of long-established fictions.

Arthur's discomfort with authorial spontaneity not only belies the wider critical ambivalence towards Trollope's accounts of himself as an artist, but a critical method at a loss for interpreting the novel as fiction – the arbitrary and incomplete, the possible rather than the inevitable, affording opportunity rather than closure. What Sedgwick has characterised as the 'anticipatory' tendency of criticism or its 'aversion to surprise' manifests here as a criteria applied to an author who systematically disclaims foreknowledge for spontaneity, and whose example suggests the forms of knowledge afforded by less knowingness.[34] In *An Autobiography*, Trollope repeatedly asserts that 'the incidents of the story [...] were created for the most part as they were described. I could never arrange a set of events before me' (*AA* 197), or with more specific reflection in his essay 'A Walk in the Wood':

> [T]o construct a plot so as to know, before the story is begun, how it is to end, has always been to me a labour of Hercules beyond my reach. I have to confess my incidents are fabricated to fit my story as it goes on [...] I wrote a novel once [*Orley Farm*] in which a lady forged a will; but I had not myself decided that she had forged it till the chapter before that it in which she confesses her guilt. In another [*The Eustace Diamonds*] a lady is made to

steal her own diamonds [...] but the brilliant idea only struck me when I was writing the page in which the theft is described. (266)

The volume and explicitness of such statements make them hard to 'disregard', even harder to separate from the narrative events they specify; defending the novelist from himself, Arthur argues that 'Trollope consistently understates throughout his *Autobiography* his commitment to a higher concept of his art than such an arbitrary action could accommodate'.[35] John Sutherland similarly argues that we 'should be sceptical of the novelist's own protestations of unpreparedness [...] Trollope's self-deprecating description of himself as charging at the plot'.[36] Such resistances, not only to the author's accounts of his work, but also to how the novels account for themselves, represent an evaluative and interpretive position from the standards of a Jamesian formalism to which Trollope is explicitly not signed up, and to which his many statements of artifice and invention necessarily register as irrational or self-critical.[37] But it is exactly in 'their queer elements of the accidental and the arbitrary' where Trollope's novels, like the narratives of play, locate the distinctive value of fictions *as* fictions – and where we must search for new critical standards.[38]

What kind of interpretive judgement do the Barsetshire novels allow of Mrs Proudie? Not one that is applicable to any historical individual, but at the same time, nor one therefore devoid of meaning. If, in the peculiar causation of novel-writing, Trollope has 'fabricated' a heart condition and justified it after the fact, it is not uncommon in actual life that the bereaved make unexpected discoveries about the deceased, aspects of their lives or personalities which have been true all along but unknown. This is not a mimetic or historical relation – what happened to Mrs Proudie could not literally happen in real life – but an analogy for our incomplete knowledge of people and the world around us. The difference, of course, is that what Trollope does not know about Barsetshire represents a creative opportunity, whereas our ignorance about the full facts of our world does not negate their objective truth and effects.

But are there advantages to thinking creatively about actual situations, especially about ethical dilemmas, in the way Trollope views narrative plot? David Russell has argued for what he calls a 'virtual sensibility' in the essays of Charles Lamb, whose anecdotal narratives recurrently depict 'an attitude of disinterest, of not wanting to know the facts, that provides the conditions for the pleasurable surprises of new experience'.[39] If this is an analogue for how Trollope generates narrative, it is also for Lamb a model of behaviour: a 'social relation of benign unknowing'.[40] Encountering a beggar in the city who is either feigning or not feigning their distress, Russell points out how 'the notion that he could know the truth of the other is quite inappropriate to the situation [. . .] Lamb refuses to decide whether the beggar really is in as much trouble as he says'.[41] Embracing an incomplete view of the world might be more ethically valuable than a deterministic view that the facts are out there (even though they are); in other words, Lamb approaches the situation as if it were fictional, imagining that the beggar is neither lying nor not lying except as you are free to entertain it.

The following reading of *The Small House at Allington* proposes the ethical value in a fictional view of the world. Trollope's characters in this novel qualify and demur; they contemplate the binding force of their principles or commitments; they believe (generally correctly) that their personal dilemmas have some hope of future exemption or change. Critics since Ruth apRoberts have characterised their mode of moral dissembling as *casuistry* or *situation ethics*, a process of considering the full specificities of the case rather than applying categorical imperatives, waiting to review more of the circumstances before giving any verdict.[42] But how does one practice 'situation ethics' on situations which are imaginary, particularly as imagined by a novelist who has not completely decided the facts of that situation when he began to write it? Acknowledging the inherently artificial logic of the novel turns the process of casuistry on its head: instead of coming to a conclusion about pre-existing particulars, moral reasoning in an incomplete world constitutes *inventing* the right rationale or qualification that will retroactively become the solution. Trollope's characters behave as if they are aware of this, and are plotting alongside their author to get out of (or get away with) the narrative conflict. This is an admittedly troubling view, potentially reducing ethical deliberation to arbitrary rhetorical puzzles like that over Gombroon's taxation. But just as for De Quincey, it might also be a hopeful view: always reserving the possibility that things might be better than you know.

THE SMALL HOUSE AT ALLINGTON

Although much has been said about the notion of Trollope's casuistry, either as a proposed model for his beliefs or on its validity as a philosophy in general, less attention has been given to the art of its narrative pleasures. In her classic study *Artist and Moralist*, apRoberts identified Trollope's casuistry as 'a more flexible morality' in which behaviour and judgement require 'the most careful, detailed consideration of the circumstances, even of a "crime"', rather than the reductive application of 'some theory, some precept, some generalisation [. . .] *any* precept or theory can be invalidated, by *some* case'.[43] Holding off premature judgement for a period of purposeful indecision, an attitude of 'benign unknowing', the depiction of this process in prose is one apRoberts finds not only ennobling (on which her critics tend to disagree) but also pleasurable:[44]

> The art of [casuistry] makes us see the uniqueness of character in circumstances, and the end of it is moral perception. It is a very satisfactory thing that the means to this end is so delightful that we can take the means for an end, and the end still achieves itself. [. . .] [Likewise,] One of the incidental pleasures of the novels is Trollope's positively virtuoso display of a variety of lawyers in action.[45]

ApRoberts comes close here to implying that, even if casuistry were not the effective philosophy she argues it to be, it could still have value as an aesthetic experience, like a 'virtuoso display of [. . .] lawyers in action' whatever they may be advocating. It is with such pleasures of performing deliberation that a typical Trollope narrative 'catches us [. . .] with a case in which the moral ambivalence is striking [. . .] carefully selected and significant cases constitute his content'.[46] Andrew H. Miller picks up her argument on this point, noting the narrative appeal of casuistry to the realist novel as a genre 'devoted to the display of consciousness'; by drawing attention to the processes of thought and perception, 'casuistry is a performance, for the casuist himself or herself first of all. We are receptive audiences for our own ethical dramas'.[47] We are evidently receptive, also, to the novel's performance of explanation about its own made-up situations, perhaps even preferring the virtuosity afforded by complex or ambiguous dilemmas – otherwise where would be the novel? – over clear-cut cases of right and wrong.

The clear danger in this aestheticisation of moral reasoning, in finding the performance of casuistry 'delightful' in itself, is that we might come to confuse narrative proficiency for moral clarity. This is the objection most commonly associated with the term 'casuistry', already widely recognised in the nineteenth century, as 'a quibbling or evasive way of dealing with difficult cases of duty; sophistry'.[48] As Kincaid argues in rebuttal to apRoberts, for all that Trollope admires a lawyer's consideration of the facts from every angle, he just as often portrays the speciousness of neutrality, such as in his unflattering portrait of the politician in *The Eustace Diamonds*: 'a large-minded man of the world, peculiarly conversant with the fact that every question has two sides, and that as much may often be said on one side as on the other [. . .] [who] sees there is an opening here or an opening there'.[49] Miller raises the similar case of Ferdinand Lopez in *The Prime Minister*, introduced in the novel as 'an accomplished linguist, and as a very clever fellow', who employs his rhetorical talents in the service of 'talking himself into pocketing money [. . .] reflecting and inclining and questioning and resolving, a process of casuistical ingenuity'.[50] In such examples of what Miller terms 'casuistry downward, as it were, ingenuity in the service of self-deception', more commonly represented in the nineteenth-century novel than 'where such deliberative reasoning is approved by the writer [. . .] as casuistry upward', the virtuosity which sustains narrative pleasure also convolutes moral judgement.[51] If casuists insist on keeping open a 'condition of possibility' in moral judgement, how do we reach a final moral conclusion? How do we avoid leaving room for further, potentially specious claims of leniency or exception, 'an opening here or an opening there'?

On the level of composition, I have proposed a deliberate artistry in the contrivance and artifice of Trollope's narratives; here, I reclaim the specious, the spurious, and the sophistic as morally useful qualities in his fiction. It is not so bad in Barsetshire to be clever about being good; while Trollope undeniably condemns self-deception and excuse-making in his villains, he also appreciates the fastness and looseness with which virtuous characters play difficult moral choices. These positive representations of evasiveness occur partly because apRoberts is right to identify Trollope's attraction to moral wriggle-rooms. It is also partly because fictional worlds operate on different rules to ours, including those of moral causation and explanation. If in life, casuistry can destabilise or manipulate the true facts or logic of the case, in fiction (especially in the unpremeditated plots of Trollope's novels), facts and logic are inherently unstable, constituted only by their consistent 'verbal expression' and reshapable *as truths* by creative reasoning. If casuistry assumes no moral precept can encompass the full complexity of possible situations, this is axiomatic to a world of radical incompleteness, where no determination can fully render a situation beyond qualification. The moral logic of Trollope's fiction, much like its narrative logic, is open to ingenious elaborations which would be disingenuous in life or history.

In this reading of *The Small House at Allington*, I examine Trollope's qualified support for a fictional or creative morality, by comparing two characters who allow themselves to perform actions they knew or thought to be wrong, but which they come after further reasoning to consider permissible, even morally desirable. Because the novel presents Mrs Dale and Adolphus Crosbie as morally poles apart – one arriving honestly at a just exemption, the other excusing himself into villainy – their strikingly similar processes of thought form a kind of meta-casuistry. What I propose separates narrative endorsement in the one case from condemnation in the other is not a difference of extenuating circumstance (as the non-fictional practice of casuistry would seek to reveal), but a difference only *in skill and success*. The logic of moral explanations in the novel is inextricable from the way Trollope's novels work themselves out as they go along – the mechanisms upon which their fictional realities operate – either successfully justifying the facts after the fact, or losing rhetorical control of the situation. Although she does not think of herself as such, Mrs Dale is simply a better improviser, self-advocate, or tactical player than Crosbie, contriving a more plausible story of justification than his collapsing account of inconsistent commitments.

Sophistry is an artificial logic, a view that moral reasons (like novels) are all made up, but it is not necessarily a moral nihilism. As this book argues, novel fictions possess different kinds of values and functions by virtue of its artifice than of mimetic representation. As historical individuals, we do not live in an incomplete world with indeterminate chains of causation, but by imagining that we do, we might see that our circumstances are often less determined than we think, and our moral options more flexible. The experience of Trollope's fictional world cultivates, if not exactly casuistry as apRoberts describes it, is nonetheless a 'more flexible morality' in which rightness is constituted not by the strictness of rules, but by the ability to account for one's actions within them – by morally getting away with it.[52] Through their artistry, Trollope's novels exhibit such ingenuity as a compositional process; through their characters, they propose its contentious value as a creative way to live.

The Case of Mrs Dale's Reneging

Rather than a casuistic flexibility, critical studies of *The Small House* have tended to emphasise an opposing theme of moral resolution or stubbornness – focussing particularly, but not exclusively, on the refusal of its heroine to marry another suitor after being jilted by her original choice. Matthew Sussman, for example, characterises Lily's continued love for Crosbie as 'an *ideé fixe* that she seems unable or unwilling to shake [...] an attachment that strikes her family as self-destructive and perverse'.[53] Dinah Birch similarly argues 'that the success of *The Small House at Allington* depended on the steadfastness of Lily Dale', and moreover that 'Lily's intransigence [...] forms part of a pattern that repeats itself throughout the novel', both within her family and among other characters.[54] Taking the novel as exemplary of Trollope's work more generally, Amanda Anderson has noted the distinctiveness of his 'recalcitrant psychologies', a state of individuals being 'obsessively dedicated to, or trapped by, their own psychological postures, which in themselves often express an excessive or unreflective relation to a position or principle that cannot be relinquished'.[55] Even a case where a character seems clearly to change her mind – Lily's sister Bell initially refuses, than accepts the proposal of Dr Crofts – is placed in the context of Bell's principled rejection of her other suitor, and in any case 'is not a genuine exception to the novel's dominant pattern of behaviour, for [...] Bell has committed herself to Dr Crofts from the very first, without fully understanding her own feelings' (*SH* xiv).

This critical emphasis on the fixity of Trollope's characterisation is fundamental to an interpretation of his narratives as hinged upon an a priori and diegetic logic of character. This formulation has been most strongly articulated by Stephen Wall, who has argued for the 'freedom [of Trollope's characters] to follow the emerging logic of his or her own nature', such that 'the circumstances being what they are and the protagonists being as they are', the novel's narrative follows naturalistically from 'the logical and psychological effect produced by the combination'.[56] In this model of the autonomic, emergent, or character-driven novel, the coherency of plot might therefore depend upon a style of characterisation which disproportionately favours the obsessive, the intransigent, and the recalcitrant, upon characters who act in accordance with a visible logic. This is particularly true of *The Small House*, which as Sussman has argued, is 'the first of Trollope's novels in which the plot is fully motivated by psychological characterisation', and also one thematically concerned with constancy.[57] In this argument, characters can surprise us, but only in ways that make 'sense' with what we already know of them – ideally, like Lily Dale, they do so with extraordinary perseverance in their existing positions – because characters whose rationales are inconsistent or obscure would threaten the meaningfulness of Trollope's narrative.

I want to offer a counterpoint to this model, an argument for greater indeterminacy in the novel's narrative and moral logic, through the example of a subplot whose motion cannot described as anything other than a prolonged backpedal. In a sequence of events that come to relatively little consequence, and occur in-between (sometimes literally sandwiched within passages about) the Dale sisters' respective, dramatic marriage plots, Mrs Dale decides to, and then decides not to, vacate the building of the novel's title: the Small House at Allington, which she and her daughters occupy by long-standing family arrangement with the squire of the Great House, Christopher Dale. This accommodation sours midway through the novel, not from misunderstanding or accident but because, as Hillis Miller puts it, 'Trollope's characters play their roles to the hilt'.[58] Because Bell rejects the squire's plans for her marriage and resents his presumption to make them for her, the Dale women feel increasingly uncomfortable about living off his patronage while refusing his paternalism: Bell reflects that 'in accepting his kindness, we ought to submit ourselves to him. If that be so, it is a conclusive reason for our going [...] it would be impossible to remain here' (*SH* 337); Mrs Dale similarly feels 'she now had no alternative. She could not now teach her daughters to obey their uncle's wishes [...] She had gone so far that she could not go back' (339). The decision is repeatedly framed as inevitable – the consequence of things and people being as they are – in addition to being charged with moral purpose, involving a sacrifice in social and living standards because they could not 'purchase those luxuries which they were about to abandon at the price which was asked for them' (340).

So it strikes the Dales themselves as somewhat ridiculous when, nineteen chapters later, their decision is categorically unmade. 'What geese everybody will think us!' (*SH* 513) Lily jokes, 'We shall look such fools!' (521). By this point, news of their move has passed from rumour to public knowledge, alternative lodgings have been acquired, and in a chapter entitled 'Preparations for Going', they have taken apart their home: 'they began it much sooner than was necessary, so that it became evident [...] that they would have to pass a dreadfully dull, stupid, uncomfortable week at last, among their boxes and cases, in all the confusion of dismantled furniture' (442). This uncomfortable period suggests both a pre-emptive over-commitment (they packed too early) and, at the same time, a symbolic suspension of fixed positions: Bell's engagement is comically settled with Dr Crofts 'seated in the middle of the room on an empty box', and her 'upon the lump of carpeting' (452). It is during this paradoxical combination of domestic arrangement and disassembly, the committed and the provisional, that Mrs Dale begins to invert her position: 'It was too late to abandon her project of moving and remain at the Small House, but she almost confessed to herself that she repented of what she was doing' (450). If this is consistent with her original regrets about the plan's circumstantial necessity, she now considers it in less circumstantial terms:

> 'Do you mean you repent?'
>
> Mrs Dale did not answer her daughter at once, fearing to commit herself by words which could not be retracted. 'Yes, Lily; I think I do repent. I think that it has not been well done'.
>
> 'Then let it be undone', said Lily. (481)

Mrs Dale's repentance matters less here than how the situation's inevitability has been reframed from that of *leaving* the Small House to *remaining* in it. Rather than the move having 'gone so far that she could not go back' (AS 339), it is now the decision to stay 'which could not be retracted' (481); where it was first 'settled among them [...] to quit the Small House' (338), it has now come 'to be the *fixed idea* [...] that they would abandon their plan of migrating' (513, emphasis added). The reversal of this subplot is not framed as their relenting, but the overtaking of one strong resolution by another; superficially vindicating the novel's reputation for fixity while in fact unfixing the motives of character. The aggregate pressure of personal resolve which made action so necessary in the first place becomes redeployed to present the opposite course of action as equally necessary: remaining in the Small House, paradoxically like leaving it, is suggested as the only psychologically and morally consistent option.

'The Fate of the Small House', as one chapter title terms it, forces us to reorient our understanding of the novel's fictional causation. Rather than the critical commonplace that Trollope's characters drive the narrative through adhering to 'an *ideé fixe*', characters in fact act by leaving themselves no choice, binding themselves down in order to exercise their agency, in a reflection of the compositional process by which the novel itself is plotted. While Mrs Dale is clearly changeable on the level of her 'idea', and not so apparently deadlocked by 'impossible' circumstances which allow of 'no alternative' (339), she remains attached in her thinking to an aesthetics or rhetoric of the 'fixed idea', fixated with projects 'too late to abandon' (450) or words 'which could not be retracted' (481), even as these refer to diametrically opposed courses of action. To take another example in a more obviously compromised character, Joseph Cradell explains his engagement to the beguiling Amelia Roper as having 'now gone too far for any alteration [...] nor would any mere earthly inducement suffice to change me' (529). The order in which he presents these two justifications strikes his friend Johnny Eames with grim amusement, and exemplifies the Sartrean bad faith with which Trollope's characters appear to follow their resolves: individuals who claim to be bound by their own decisions put these claims ahead of their capacities to decide.[59] Dissimilar in almost every other respect, Mrs Dale shares with Cradell this tendency to frame choices through (self-imposed) obligations: having reconciled with the squire, she announces to Lily that 'We may certainly unpack, for I have pledged myself to him' (521) to stay.

Trollope's characters do not have strong convictions, but rhetorical positions which they enforce in an illusion of moral will. They in fact distinctively *lack* conviction, because they behave almost entirely through making public commitments, never asserting their desires or preferences so much as protesting the apparently inevitable 'logic of his or her own nature'.[60] This mode of thought and behaviour is exemplified not only by the novel's subplots, but also by its central dilemma: compromised in a different way to Cradell, Lily rejects the possibility of a second engagement to Johnny because 'I should be disgraced in my own eyes if I admitted the love of another man, after – after –. It is to me almost as though I had married him' (*SH* 489). Framing her decision not as a decision but as a corollary of her previous commitment, her rejection also strikes others as producing an impasse: Johnny thinks it 'impossible that he should continue his suit after such a declaration' and Mrs Dale that 'words have been forced from Lily's lips, the speaking of which would never be forgotten by [Lily] herself' (489). All the while that the focus remains on this tactical deadlock, what exactly Lily continues to love about Crosbie is given short thrift, and her exact feelings on Johnny curiously elided as irrelevant or indeterminate. More than an obsessive constancy to a particular object, or even constancy as a virtue in the abstract, Lily is possessed by the facts of her previous admissions, 'declaration', and 'words'; that is, by the language through which she is in fact constructed as a fictional character. Anderson is right to describe this situation as that of an individual being 'trapped by [...] their own psychological postures', and Wall as Lily being 'caught in a trap of her own making, or which at least she could not stop herself making', but this metaphor of an autonomous thing constrained in a sense reverses the case: Mrs Dale, Cradell, and Lily are *made of their constraints*.[61] Their characterisation is the shape outlined by the trap.

They behave, in other words, like Mrs Proudie's heart condition: neither true nor false until its consequences become known. If, in the diegetic chain of causation, Lily's decision reveals the underlying logic that has determined that result from the start – as apRoberts puts it, Trollope 'will not let Lily Dale marry Johnny Eames because she wouldn't have' – from an extradiegetic perspective of the narrative as a progressive accumulation of fictional statements, her decision newly determines (partly through an interpretation of previous narrative facts) what that logic has been all along.[62] Trollope's own view, as James lamented, is a metaleptic straddling of the two in which the possible undoing of Lily's dilemma is a question of psychological artifice: now that she has said this, is there any way she can accept Johnny without contradicting herself? Is there a plausible account of her character or situation which could reconcile these positions? That Lily's engagement to Johnny persists so long as an optative possibility through the plots of two novels (*The Small House* and *The Last Chronicle*) speaks to a sense in which, as the De Quinceys knew, fictional facts are unlike real facts in that they are constituted by their 'verbal expression', and therefore infinitely vulnerable to reinterpretation or erratum which might at some point undo the force of the dilemma.

Undermining the internal reality or completeness of characters in this way, denying a predetermined or essential coherence from which external actions originate, would seem to realise the worst fears of casuistry's critics: the dissolution of principled into arbitrary action through *post hoc* justifications. By entertaining 'whether a particular act fits within an ethical paradigm and allow[ing] each – act and paradigm – to modify the other', we might arrive at a state of made-to-fit moral duties which can always be rendered less binding.[63] As Ratcliffe has pointed out, Trollope's respect for the personhood of characters is balanced by a sense of their subjection to the writing process: when he discovers that 'some young lady at the end of a story cannot be made to be quite perfect in her conduct, that vivid description of angelic purity with which you laid the first lines of her portrait should be slightly toned down' (*AA* 90).[64] This seems not only to constitute a qualification of character – as with the hidden heart of the female devil – but also a compromise of moral ideals, adjusting the standards of the angel to accommodate behaviour after the fact. Along these downward toning 'lines', Mrs Dale's original ultimatum between the sacrifice of luxury or principle is finally not to be decided, but adjusted in terms of its question so as to allow for no sacrifice after all; the novel succeeds at evading its own moral challenge.

The task of interpretation in such instances is, for one, not to give up the matter as fictional and arbitrary (all novels are fictional and arbitrary), but to appreciate the skill with which Trollope talks the plot out of its own premises – to acknowledge his specious art of narrative. As I have argued, opening 'not easily accessible' (*BT* 204) gaps in established states of affairs is characteristic of Trollope's narrative process. As Helena Michie has also pointed out, on the level of style, Trollope's prose is characterised by an '"internal revision", a process by which he uses one sentence to revise another, leaving the original sentence on the page [. . .] differences between sentences in Trollope [are] accretive – that is, slowly adding up over time'.[65] If the author's tendency in narrative problem-solving is 'to work the matter out when the pen is in my hand' (*AA* 145), his characters also perform their moral reasoning live, as it were, thinking about what they have already committed to the page, in a necessary parallel between the extradiegetic dynamics of writing and its representation of 'the process of thinking [. . .] the complicated and recursive logics through which people are said to "change their minds"'.[66]

For another, more difficult task, critical approaches must also evaluate how fiction's inherent open-endedness structures its moral perspective, and what ethical value the novel assigns to the kinds of flexible thinking it most readily represents. *The Small House* unambiguously endorses, has little more to even say about, Mrs Dale's rearrangement of the conditions by which her present course once appeared 'impossible'. Whether or not the subplot's self-deflation indicates one of those instances where incidents have been 'fabricated to fit my story as it goes on' (*AA* 266), the narrator and other characters clearly sanction Mrs Dale's reconsidering of circumstance. This is not always Trollope's judgement on such cases. The example of Mrs Dale bears comparison with others where characters are soundly reprimanded in and by the narrative for trying to adjust their commitments, particularly in the higher stakes of the engagement plot. Yet because the maligned vacillation of Trollope's jilts are – as I will show – formally indistinguishable from Mrs Dale's, I argue that what such examples recommend is more creative morals, not less; better revisions, rather than stronger resolutions.

The Case of Adolphus Crosbie's Jilting

The Small House and its immediate successor, *Can You Forgive Her?*, can be read together as a diptych of novels about engagements. Although both novels ostensibly present their heroines with a choice between two partners, this traditional question of the marriage plot is subordinated to the less binary problem of engagement, concerned with possibilities for agency given a seemingly foregone conclusion. Lily is engaged by chapter five of sixty, and Alice Vavasor from the novel's outset, but this is not all there is to say about their situations. As Sussman has argued, Trollope discovered a rich vein of narrative potential in the 'complex middle ground' between singlehood and marriage, 'where the technical commitment remains provisional but the moral barrier to exit is high'.[67] We have already seen this dynamic, even metaphorical language, at work in subplots which do not literally concern engagements: '*I have pledged myself to him*', Mrs Dale says of the squire, after reneging on a move she once thought to be irreversible, 'and he is to go into Guestwick himself and arrange about [i.e., to cancel] the lodgings' (*SH* 521, emphasis added). In form rather than as subject, engagements exemplify a category of social facts especially conducive to fictional narrative: which are neither truth nor falsity but an amenable 'verbal expression', a claim which is incompletely but also accumulatively established, increasingly set in stone as the practical arrangements accrue. Verbal but not yet legal, real but not yet actual, to be engaged to be *virtually* married, a plane of action which inherently parallels the incomplete worlds of fiction itself.

Abortive engagement plots such as the one at the centre of *The Small House*, between Lily and Crosbie, reflect this narrative interest of Trollope's in weakening or circumventing conclusions; a type of story peculiarly suited to his writing process but about which, as a mode of behaviour for characters, he also appears ambivalent. Like Mrs Dale's relocating subplot, *Can You Forgive Her?* shows the novel in the process of working out whether its heroine still has room to manoeuvre. Alice breaks her engagement to John Grey in favour of her cousin George, but rather than any affirmation about the value of either partner, the narrative focuses on the ever-narrowing possibilities of escape from the 'moral barriers' guarding commitment:

> She began to be aware that she was about to be guilty of a great iniquity, when it was too late for her to change her mind. She could not bring herself to resolve that she would, on the moment, change her mind. She believed that she could never pardon herself such weakness. But yet she felt herself to be aware that her purpose was wicked.[68]

The paragraph not only reproduces the novel in miniature – just as the story ultimately returns Alice to her original engagement with Grey, the fourth sentence here loops back onto the first with her dawning self-awareness – but also its toning down or subtle adjustment of the situation. The sentences do not exactly follow from each other, nor are they directly contradictory, but gradually reframe what exactly Alice is unable to do. In the first sentence, Alice cannot change her mind, because 'it is too late' to do so; in the second, she still cannot change her mind, but due to a lack of 'resolve' rather than practical possibility; her inability becomes entirely different in the third sentence, a hypothetical wherein she *has already* changed her mind but cannot 'pardon' herself for doing so. The wicked purpose of the fourth sentence becomes strongly ambiguous: referring either to the 'great iniquity' of jilting Grey, of which Alice 'began to be aware' in the first sentence, or to another guilty consciousness, developing through the free indirect discourse of the paragraph, by which she is already edging her way back.

At the same time, it is exactly this process of 'casuistic ingenuity', escaping the dilemma by small extenuations, which Trollope indicts in Alice as her moral failing. *Can You Forgive Her?* is a title which explicitly mounts this as a casuistic challenge, both reprimanding and redeeming Alice for the habits of thought by which she both talks herself out of the right conclusion and then back into it. *The Small House* poses the same question less leniently with the figure of the male jilt, for whom the indictment is absolute.[69] With more implied culpability than Alice, Adolphus Crosbie creatively talks himself out of his engagement to Lily because he is tempted by a self-serving alliance with the aristocratic De Courcy family:

> He had said to himself a dozen times during that week that he never could be happy with Lily Dale, and that he never could make her happy. *And then he had used the old sophistry in his endeavour to teach himself that it was right to do that which he wished to do* [...] He had discussed the matter in this way within his own breast, till he had almost *taught himself to believe that it was his duty* to break off his engagement with Lily; and he had also almost taught himself to believe that a marriage with a daughter of the house of Courcy would satisfy his ambition[.] (*SH* 203–4, emphasis added)

Unlike for either Mrs Dale or Alice, the narration passes a harsh and explicit judgement on Crosbie for employing 'the old sophistry' which underlies the behaviour of *all* Trollope's characters. In an exemplification of casuistic self-deception, Crosbie teaches himself to disguise 'that which he wished to do' as that which 'was right to do' – closely following this dishonest adjustment, the narration provides what Wall describes as 'a full account of [Crosbie's] drift into perfidy [...] a study of the ways in which a man may persuade himself to revise his intentions'.[70] But on what basis is this account distinguishable, for one, from Mrs Dale; and for another, from the disingenuous logic of the narrative itself, thinking in lockstep with Alice about how to turn her situation around?

Although *The Small House* gestures towards a moral dichotomy between Crosbie's inconstancy and the Dales' collective 'steadfastness', on the level of their construction as fictions, the two are not so easy to separate. If we might appreciate Trollope's virtuosity at writing his characters into and out of tight corners, to think of an engagement as a logic puzzle about navigating barriers to exit is to take the perspective of the novel's proclaimed villain. Appallingly, Mrs Dale who 'almost confessed to herself that she repented of what she was doing' performs a style of thinking almost exactly like that of a man whom she believes to have caused harm and suffering to her family. They are at one point syntactically identical:

> [Self-promotion] was the line of life into which he had fallen, and he confessed inwardly that the struggle to extricate himself would be too much for him [...] He had *almost acknowledged to himself that he repented his engagement* with Lilian Dale, but he still was resolved that he would fulfil it. He was bound in honour [...] Yes; he would sacrifice himself. As he had been induced to pledge his word, he would not go back from it. (*SH* 159, emphasis added)

For Crosbie as (disturbingly) for Mrs Dale, the first step to unsettling the force of commitment is to acknowledge it as a necessity rather than a choice; for Trollope, restriction is only a prompt to creative agency. Here, both the commitment which binds him to Lily and the nature which would lead him to abandon her are too strong 'to extricate himself': so pledged that 'he would not go back' on the engagement, yet also 'too late now to remedy the ill effects of an early education' (159) that has shaped his character. As Sussman also notes of this passage, Crosbie 'alienate[s] his agency when he wishes to distance himself from decisions',[71] but this is clearly not an exclusive character trait in Trollope's narrative world; Lily's rejection of Johnny is a similar non-decision, a calculus of apparently inevitable conditions ('I should be disgraced [...] if I admitted', *SH* 498). Such statements would also not be out of place in *An Autobiography*, catching an imaginative freedom between what one's nature makes 'necessary' and an act of 'binding myself down' (*AA* 33).

Like his author, Crosbie constructs his situation as a set of conditions; like the novel, a more flexible narrative arises out of the apparently inevitable. It does not take long for the initial formulation of his dilemma to invert into its opposite – that he has already determined to abandon Lily and has only to follow it through, exactly as he had previously determined to follow through with the engagement. On having been led to declare his love for Alexandrina De Courcy, Crosbie returns to his room again to contemplate another unalterable situation:

> [N]ow that he had told Lady Alexandrina he loved her [...] he was obliged to confess to himself that the die was cast.
> As he thought of all this, there was not wanting to him some of the satisfaction of an escape. Soon after making that declaration of love at Allington he had begun to feel that in making it he had cut his throat. He had endeavoured to persuade himself that he could live comfortably with his throat cut in that way [...] But the self-immolation had not been completed, and he now began to think that he could save himself [...] he acknowledged at this moment, as he rose from his seat to dress himself, that the die was cast, and that it was open to him now to say what he pleased to Lady Alexandrina (*SH* 205).

Crosbie's various convictions move in different directions in this passage – even as he admits not to be so 'bound in honour' (159) to Lily after all, and achieves 'some of the satisfaction of an escape' from a provisional situation that after all 'had not been completed', he conversely commits to the belief about his character (the apparent inevitability of his unhappiness with Lily) and to a sense 'that the die was cast' on this new decision: 'there was the fact, and he found himself unable to contend against it' (204). Even as his hyperbolic metaphors of escaping 'self-immolation', 'suicide', and having 'his throat cut' reveal the 'sacrifice' (159) of marrying Lily to be not so irreversible after all, Crosbie is unable to acknowledge the agency he has already exercised in changing his mind. When his mind changes yet again – or on realising his mistake – he returns more literally to 'thoughts of self-destruction as the only means of escape' (222), describing his self-made trap as that of 'marry[ing] Lady Alexandrina; – that is, if I do not cut the whole concern, and my own throat into the bargain' (225).

Crosbie does not kill himself, but that he continually resorts to imagining this as his 'only means of escape' becomes emblematic of his case as a singular one in which, for once, a character is finally unable to extricate himself from a fixed situation. And it is on this basis of his *inflexibility*, rather than a continuing 'drift' of position, which seals his fate as the irredeemable villain of the novel; he cannot invent another explanation of his own actions, and the narrator will not collude with him (as they do with Alice or Mrs Dale) to do so. As he realises when his marriage to Alexandrina is finalised, 'The course was now before him, and he had no choice but to walk in it' (409). All Trollope's characters protest their powerlessness before circumstance, but only Crosbie manages so badly to trap himself beyond redemption.

The charges of Crosbie's 'perfidy', in these terms, is not sophistry but a failure at sophistry. If Trollope's 'internal revision' advances subtle adjustments which impose a new logic on established facts, as he himself admits, this is a performance which is not always successful, a danger which Crosbie embodies as a moral failure. Like many characters, Crosbie revises his intentions with new interpretations, 'contradicting one argument by another over and over again [...] teaching himself to think that this engagement of his was a misfortune' (*SH* 159), but unlike others, his public statements are too visibly contradictory: for instance, he struggles to reconcile the fact 'It had been already settled that he was to spend his Christmas at Courcy; as it had been also settled that he was to spend it at Allington' (221). He repeatedly attempts to edit the past, wishing first to 'have blotted out that visit to Courcy Castle from the past facts of his experience' (220), then retroactively claiming that he had been 'already half engaged' (224) to Alexandrina before his proposal to Lily. As the narrator intrudes to point out, 'The reader, however, will understand that this half-engagement was a fiction' (224), and implicitly, a more incompetent fiction than the unblotted and still agile narrative of the novel itself. Overcommitted to and overstretched between incompatible positions, unable to delete or convincingly revise past facts in the narrative, Crosbie fails precisely at De Quincey's evasive demurring or at Trollope's art of fiction, having 'rushed at the work as a rider rushes at a fence which he does not see [...] [and] encountered what, in hunting language, we call a cropper' (*AA* 111). What these metatextual metaphors identify as Crosbie's real crime is not the making of excuses in itself, but the inability to make better excuses, having compromised himself beyond the possibility for reinvention.

Trollope's novels continually evaluate, as the narrative unfolds, whether it is still possible to construct a workable explanation of the characters' actions. Both the narrative and its characters are actively engaged in making excuses as they go along, fashioning a coherent rationale for their behaviour after surprising narrative turns which leave them in difficult situations. This is the reverse of how casuistry, and its manifestation through the realist novel, is ideally supposed to work in their shared aims at perspicuity: casuists rely 'on the expansive descriptive powers native to realistic narrative [...] the thought that the everyday needs careful study if its true nature and value are to be revealed', and through this careful empiricism, question 'whether that description is all that is relevantly true of me and my situation, or if it is, whether it should continue to be true of me [. . .] as it unfolds an assessment of my past and my future'.[72] But this is a model of realism's functions which has its alternative in the novel as fiction, whose native powers are not 'descriptive' but creative, interested in inventing realities rather than its 'careful study'. The casuistic questions which guide this mode of thinking may be, instead: what *can* be true of me or my situation? How can I reimagine the necessary facts of my past to fit a better vision of my future? What are the acceptable limits of my agency? How do I morally get away with it?

These questions about living well by living skilfully, about creative action rather than accurate knowledge, is an ethical perspective the novel can offer precisely because of its difference from history. If real causation and circumstances are not as flexible as fiction, we can nonetheless usefully respond to them as if they were. 'For Trollope', Ratcliffe argues, literary practices like editing are 'more than a career – it is also a habit of mind [. . .] an alternative understanding of how individuals might exist in time, and of the ways in which selves might resolve their contradictory urges'.[73] *An Autobiography* recurrently demonstrates a sophist's creativity with small details to be Trollope's characteristic mode of self-narrativisation. When the publishers of *The Cornhill* required *Framley Parsonage* to begin serialisation before the novel had been completed, Trollope invented a caveat to a 'principle with me in my art, that no part of a novel should be published till the entire story was completed [. . .] But such a principle becomes a tyrant if it cannot be superseded on a just occasion [. . .] I can say, however, that I have never broken it since' (*AA* 90–91). Readers, however, should understand this final claim as a fiction; textual evidence proves at least four other novels – *Orley Farm*, *The Small House*, *Can You Forgive Her?*, and *The Belton Estate* – to have been written during their serial runs.[74] But much as principles might casuistically give way 'on a just occasion', the facts of the case might bend to accommodate the better story of a lone exception. Trollope had contrived this account of himself, but in doing so, demonstrates the value of fiction to producing a more malleable perspective on the world: not being the whole truth, the account nonetheless captures the significant features of the dilemma; without being an outright lie, it also expresses something about how he aspires to have acted. To 'live with' fiction in this way imagines life's events not merely as they were, but as they are still possible.

CHAPTER 4

Continuation, Attachment, and William Makepeace Thackeray

'Thackeray wallowed in it; Anthony Trollope lived on it'.[1] The practice of writing new novels about old characters, G. K. Chesterton argued, betrays a lack of artistic and emotional discipline. Chesterton's study of Dickens distinguishes the novelist from his contemporaries such as Trollope and Thackeray because unlike them, Dickens demonstrates a serious commitment to form: he upholds 'the separation and unity of a work of art' and refuses the temptation of 'putting, as it were, after-words and appendices to [...] already finished portraits'.[2] Dickens is further to be praised for a willingness to kill his darlings, because 'although his heart must have often yearned backwards to the children of his fancy whose tale was already told [...] [characters] were dead for him after he had done the book; if he loved them as children, it was as dead and sanctified children'.[3] For Chesterton, this restraint on both structural and personal fronts from revisiting former subjects meant Dickens 'never did yield at all to exactly that indiscretion or act of sentimentalism [...] Or rather he never did yield to it except here in this one case; the case of *Master Humphrey's Clock*".[4] The familiar friends of Mr Pickwick and Sam Weller, last seen when *The Pickwick Papers* ended in 1837, returned three years later to further adventures in Dickens's new periodical. Novel-writing, as we have seen, is often an art of exceptions.

Yet if Pickwick's return in 1840 was a lapse in Dickens's exception from an unfortunate contemporary practice ('everybody else did yield to it'), this case can be more simply restated: *Master Humphrey's Clock* typifies a broader trend in the mid-Victorian novel of 'introduc[ing] old characters into new stories'.[5] James similarly alludes to Trollope's 'practice of carrying certain actors from one story to another', and moreover, constructs a genealogy of this literary habit 'which he may be said to have inherited from Thackeray, as Thackeray may have said to have borrowed it from Balzac'.[6] In his study of Balzac, James again makes this connection:

All [society] in Balzac's hands becomes an organic whole; it moves together; it has a pervasive life; the blood circulates through it; its parts are connected by sinuous arteries. We have seen in English literature, in two cases, a limited attempt to create a permanent stock, a standing fund, of characters. Thackeray has led a few of his admirable figures from one novel to another, and Mr. Trollope has deepened illusion for us by his repeated evocations of Bishop Proudie and Archdeacon Grantly.[7]

The biology of Chesterton's language, Trollope's living against Dickens's dead, becomes in James's the 'pervasive life' of characters who outstay the individual novel. But James's account also suggests a 'pervasive life' to novel practices, as authors borrow and pass on their habits much as 'the blood circulates' through a fictional society 'connected by sinuous arteries'. If, as Tillotson puts it, Thackeray 'takes pains to link his novels by the consanguinity of the personages' in series of long works which 'hang together like a dynasty',[8] this is something Thackeray 'inherited' from Balzac's 'permanent stock', both in the commercial property sense implied by 'a standing fund' and also in the sense of 'a line of descent [. . .] a family or race'.[9] In other words, the liveliness of characters in an organic world of relations is a family resemblance of the novel, a hereditary feature genetic to the form.

At the same time, 'life' represents another characteristic of fiction towards which the novel and its tradition bears a strongly ambivalent attitude. '*The Newcomes* has life, as *Les Trois Mousquetaires*, as Tolstoi's *Peace and War*, have it', James writes in his preface to *The Tragic Muse*, 'There is life and life'.[10] In this passage, Thackeray's *The Newcomes* comes infamously to exemplify the 'large, loose, baggy monsters' of the nineteenth-century novel, possessing a pervasive liveliness which both characterises the novel and threatens its monstrous growth.[11] Chesterton, too, singles out Thackeray's attachment to fictional lives as violating the novel's 'separation and unity', deforming the proper boundaries between his individual texts:

> The habit of revising old characters is so strong in Thackeray that *Vanity Fair*, *Pendennis*, *The Newcomes*, and *Philip* are in one sense all one novel. Certainly the reader sometimes forgets which one of them he is reading [. . .] he cannot remember whether his favourite dialogue between Mr. and Mrs. Pendennis occurred in *The Newcomes*, or in *Philip*. Whenever two Thackeray characters in two Thackeray novels could by any possibility have been contemporary, Thackeray delights to connect them. He makes Major Pendennis nod to Dr. Firmin, and Colonel Newcome ask Major Dobbin to dinner.[12]

106 Continuation, Attachment, and William Makepeace Thackeray

Tillotson similarly notes how, although each of Thackeray's works has 'its own FINIS', we nonetheless 'cease to be much aware of differences, ceasing to attend to the chronology of the novels'.[13] The habit of Thackeray's characters all to dine together, to sprawl out their social lives across multiple (each individually baggy) novels, exemplifies the 'organic whole' which James praised in Balzac as a feature of realist fiction. But such characters might therefore collapse the literary structure in which they reside, breaking down the novel form into a shapeless mass of homogenous experience.

This chapter reassesses the virtual lives of characters, the 'deepened illusion' of their persistence between and beyond individual texts, as a function of the novel's capacity for fictional worlds.[14] In doing so, I defend 'wallow[ing]' and 'liv[ing] on' as legitimate modes of literary response, as well as critically useful methods of participatory interpretation. They provide another example of how Victorian novels produce meaning and pleasure through other means than as representations of life or finished artworks; and another instance of how these alternative uses of the form have been undervalued in criticism, but can be recovered as deliberate practices through their unembarrassed exemplifications in play. I develop Chesterton's and James's critiques while reversing their evaluative judgements: contextualising their observations about the appeal of fictional lives with Thackeray's own critical reflections, the reception history of serials and sequels, as well as autobiographical accounts from De Quincey, Brontë, and Trollope about the difficulty of leaving imaginary worlds. These perspectives together articulate the experience of attachment to fictions, what media psychologists describe as the development of a *parasocial* bond, as an alternative and underexamined sense of the what the novel is good for. In addition to providing vicarious experiences of power and possibility, and at odds with its other literary aims, the novel acts to sustain the imagined companionship of characters; a version of which is embryonic in, and can be more clearly understood through comparison to, the practice and narratives of the paracosm.

The Newcomes is my exemplary text for considering the novel's divided loyalties between its double roles as a literary and virtual object, affording two sometimes conflictual, sometimes cooperative forms of pleasure and interpretation. As critics have argued, the novel's narrative explores the lasting emotional effects of past relationships, refracting a central experience of loss and entanglement through multiple plots of widows, first loves, and second marriages. As I argue, however, the novel's fictional world also continually includes Thackeray's former characters from *Vanity*

Fair and *The History of Pendennis*, embodying *as a reading experience* the inability to let go of finished relationships, or as Chesterton puts it, to bury 'dead and sanctified children'.[15] The narrative's progress towards formal closure and thematic resolution, therefore, conversely intensifies the fictional experience of separation from a set of relationships cultivated through the long course of the serial text. Through this disjunction, Thackeray makes visible a tension between a literary work and its fictionality; opening a critical distinction which reveals other ways of using and valuing novels of this period.

Novels for Life

In an article for *Fraser's Magazine* in 1846, facetiously addressed to Alexandre Dumas, Thackeray pitched a half-parodic, half-wishful set of 'Proposals for a Continuation of *Ivanhoe*'. Dumas would be right to reopen Walter Scott's historical novel, Thackeray argues, because Ivanhoe had in his opinion married the wrong heroine, choosing 'that icy, faultless, prim, niminy-piminy' Rowena over 'the tender and beautiful' Rebecca – but also because Scott had ended the original prematurely:

> I, for my part, am one of the warmest admirers of the new system which you [Dumas] pursue in France with so much success – of the twenty-volume-novel system. I like continuations [...] and was never more delighted after getting through a dozen volumes of the *Three Musketeers*, than when Mr. Rolandi furnished me with another dozen of the continued history of the same heroes under the title of *Vingt ans après* [*Twenty Years After*]; and if one could get the lives of Athos, Porthos, and Aramis until they were 120 years old, I am sure we should all read with pleasure.[16]

The presumption and infeasibility of these 'Proposals' is of course their deliberate comedic conceit, but they articulate a real (if wishful) form of literary response. While Thackeray is joking about his expectations, he is *not* feigning his earnest desire for an endless novel series, nor wrong to intuit Dumas's penchant for 'continuations'. In 1849, Thackeray wrote from Paris with 'intense delight' – perhaps more intense than when he 'was never more delighted' – about 'a novel called *Le Vicomte de Bragelonne*, a continuation of the famous *Mousquetaires* and just as interesting, keeping one panting from volume to volume, and longing for more'.[17] Dumas's new novel, which carries the subtitle *Dix ans plus tard* (*Ten Years Later*) and ends with the death of two out of three musketeers, seems improbably to have vindicated Thackeray's earlier demand to 'get the lives of Athos, Porthos, and Aramis' in wholesale blocks of time. That he accidentally presaged this newest continuation, years before its appearance in print, suggests how his fantasies of Dumas were rooted in the objective qualities and narrative desires of the existing novels. 'I am sure we should all read with pleasure', Thackeray writes, in an evidently perceptive appraisal of what those pleasures are.[18]

The 'Proposals' are a flippant but honest expression about the powerful appeal of novel fictions – and the inevitable disappointment of novel texts. The publication of *Dix ans plus tard* exceeded Thackeray's expectations, but it could not exceed his fantasy. That his 'panting' through the new volumes (emphasising again the material size of the book) concludes with the open-endedness of his still 'longing for more' suggests how the desire for fiction is ultimately not exhaustible by the literary objects that spark them. Although a whole market of unauthorised D'Artagnan sequels emerged at the turn of the century, further justifying Thackeray's assessment of their givenness to continuation, no 'more' was forthcoming from Dumas himself. The impossible standards of the 'Proposals', only partially met by an already fortuitous reality, also anticipates this dissatisfaction: if the premise of the article is to extend Scott's *Ivanhoe* into something like Dumas's exemplarily long works, it quickly comes to desire an extension of the exemplar itself, with *The Three Musketeers* continued in batches of 'a dozen volumes' until its heroes 'were 120 years old'. This scheme, which presumably sextuples the original 'twenty-volume-novel system', embodies a more general dissatisfaction than with any specific novel or ending.[19] The 'Proposals' present a fantasy not yet realised in any precedent, not even those that surprise us with another (but still insufficient) *dix ans*.

What Thackeray wants from novels, and what novels cannot realistically provide, are their fictional 'lives'. Not the aesthetic arrangement of those lives, nor their meaningful explication, nor even their further adventures or dramas – he makes few demands to any of these – only their 'continued history'. Rather than any usual literary function, the 'Proposals' imagine using the novel primarily as a medium for staying in touch with its characters and world, for what Chesterton discerningly terms 'wallow [ing]' in fiction: 'To remain plunged in [. . .] sensuality, degraded habits', but also 'to be immersed or engrossed'.[20] Such a desire is unreasonable, but hardly unusual: Gaskell makes a similarly formless and contentless appeal in her 'wish [that] Mr Trollope would go on writing *Framley Parsonage* for ever';[21] James's character Theodora 'should like [*Daniel Deronda*] to continue indefinitely, to keep coming out always, to be one of the regular things of life';[22] Tennyson has a strong 'dislike [for] beginning a new novel. I should like to have a novel to read in a million volumes, to last me my life'.[23] Samuel Taylor Coleridge, deploring this kind of vacant absorption, refuses to 'compliment their *pass-time*, or rather *kill-time*, with the name of *reading*', comparing it instead to 'swinging, or swaying on a chair or gate; spitting over a bridge; smoking; snuff-taking; tête-à-tête quarrels after dinner between husband and wife [...] &c. &c. &c'.[24] If '*reading*' implies a process of narrative attention, aesthetic judgement, critical interpretation, etc., 'readers' like Thackeray, Gaskell, Theodora, and Tennyson are engaged in different forms of relation to the literary object, which may indeed include passing or spending time in fiction. Or in another way of putting 'kill-time': living with the novel.

Practically, of course, novels cannot *only* provide the continued experience of their fictional worlds, but must also necessarily perform their more usual functions of telling a story, making expression, reflecting the real, or even fitting into a book, most of which contribute in some way to the appeal of that world in the first place. The novel may be the most available nineteenth-century cultural medium with which to – and the most inspiring of a longing to – 'live in a world altogether outside the world of my own material life' (*AA* 33), especially by offering lives and worlds peculiarly compatible with those of its readers, and as we will see, by imaginatively sustaining them through the serial. Yet those testimonies which draw explicit attention to this feature of the form are also inherently expressions of disappointment: *Ivanhoe*, *Daniel Deronda*, and *Framley Parsonage* do not go on for 'a million volumes', even as they might recommend themselves to do so. If the novel is dependent on the printed volume or number as a medium for its reading experience, in their shared fantasies for a more impractical novel, readers like Thackeray make visible the *disjunction* as well as *affordance* between the novel's virtuality and its material or literary form. At stake in feeling the disappointment of novels for ourselves is a keener critical perception of what their contemporary readers and authors 'proposed' the form could do.

Perhaps the best, culminating case for exploring this disjunction is that of John Ruskin, who in a more earnest version of Thackeray's article, petitioned the novelist Henrietta Stannard for a kind of text she was clearly unable to deliver.[25] In a public letter to *The Daily Telegraph* in 1888, entitled 'Novels and their Endings', Ruskin laid out his vision for a novel he could live with:

> [O]ne of the increasing discomforts of my old age, [is] never being allowed by novelists to stay long enough with people I like, after I once get acquainted with them [...] I felt this acutely the other day, when the author answered my quite tearful supplication to her, that Mignon and

> Lucy might not vanish in an instant into the regions of Praeterita and leave me desolate, by saying that [...] the public of to-day would never permit insistence on one conception beyond the conventionally established limits. To which distrust I would answer – and ask you [the *Telegraph*'s editor], as the interpreter of widest public opinion, to confirm me in answering – that for readers even of our own impatient time [...] the highest praises of invention are in the recognised and natural growth of one living creation; and neither in shifting the scenes of fate as if they were lantern slides, nor in tearing down the trellises of our affections that we may train the branches elsewhere.[26]

The novel, Ruskin argues, requires recognition for its appeal in sustaining the 'natural growth of one living creation', a formulation which echoes the 'pervasive life' and 'organic whole' James similarly identifies in Balzac's narrative world, but which is also metaleptically entangled with the life of the reader.[27] It is not only the fiction that grows in this passage but also 'the trellises of our affections' with it, as well as the reader himself in his 'old age', both of which derive a sense of structure in the presence of fictions (as branches on a trellis), and are violently discomforted by their withdrawal at the end of the novel, stopping 'in an instant' what Tennyson (also in his final years) wishes 'to last me my life'.[28] As Auyoung has similarly noted, readers can desire more of a novel 'not because of what happens in the narrative but because of the social separation imposed by its termination'.[29] Again without any suggestions of narrative content or aesthetic intention, the desire simply to '*stay* long enough with' fictions, not to be left stranded outside the imaginary 'regions' opened by the novel, is meaningful (even life-affirming) in itself.

What can we learn from looking at individuals' fantasies of novels – at satirical proposals, earnest supplications, and uncritical yearnings for continuation – rather than actual novels? For one: the alternative uses of the novel as a fictional world, occasioning real and meaningful experiences of the text without reference to its content or form. Ruskin helps to point out a conflict between alternative criteria for the novel, between what Stannard believes 'the public [...] would never permit' and what 'widest public opinion' (*NE* 605) might in fact support – as I have argued, this is a critical disagreement about the function and value of the form in which its fictionality has long been sidelined. As F. R. Leavis summarily appraised them in *The Great Tradition*, in Thackeray's novels 'the essential substance of interest [is] so limited that (though, of course, he provides incident and plot) for the reader it is merely a matter of going on and on [...] that time has been killed (which seems to be all that even some academic critics demand of a novel)'.[30] Literary responses such as Ruskin's, Tennyson's, or Thackeray's own, by emphasising the novel's accompaniment to life, give examples for reassessing the significance and particularity of what fiction offers through its presence in time – as well as what criticism might (not quite so simply) demand from it on that score.

For another: we learn how a fictional world can deform its medium. Ultimately, Ruskin's attachment to certain fictional friends produced a strange distortion of the literary works in which they featured as characters. Only five months after his letter to *The Telegraph*, Stannard published *Bootles' Children*, a continuation of her three existing novels about the life of the foundling girl Mignon (*Bootles' Baby* in 1885, *Mignon's Secret* in 1886, and *Mignon's Husband* in 1887). In her preface to the new novel, Stannard acknowledges the necessity 'for me to give some word of explanation that, after bidding farewell to *Bootles' Baby*, I should continue the story', by responding almost directly to 'Novels and their Endings':

> The truth is this – I received many letters asking me to show something of Mignon's later life, all of which made me wish with regret that I had not closed that page, as I thought, forever. But when my dear and honoured friend, Mr. Ruskin, said to me that he also would like to know more of Mignon, I felt that there was no more to be said, but that when the spirit moved me to do it, Mignon must go on the stage again.
> There is not much about Mignon in this story, but there is a little that I hope will interest those who love her; and if there are some who are a little tired of her, well, I hope they will bear with her when they remember that this story was written in the hope of giving an hour's pleasure to one whose whole life has been to give delight and help wherever the English language is spoken.[31]

The language of resistance and obligation recurs throughout this passage, which is riven with Stannard's self-consciousness about breaching 'the conventionally established limits' (*NE* 605) she had first protested to Ruskin. It is 'necessary' to explain herself to readers who will hopefully 'bear with her', but she has been 'moved [. . .] to do it' by Ruskin's request (other readers also make her 'wish with regret', but are insufficient to persuade her). At the same time, Stannard's preface is also apologetic to those who *wanted* the continuation: as there is really 'no more to be said' about Mignon's life, the novel produced specifically to say more about her finally has 'not much about Mignon' after all. Caught between bad form and readerly disappointment, Stannard's dilemma suggests how fictional objects can disrupt works of art, distending formal boundaries and unpicking narrative closures in order to 'stay long enough with people I like' (*NE* 605); and even in so doing, achieve not so much the 'natural growth of one living creation' (605) as the uncomfortable extension of an exhausted subject.

This is a more conflictual picture of the relationship between forms and fictionality than John Plotz presents in his survey of current criticism on the 'persistent features of Victorian-era worldmaking projects [...] larger than any single book'.[32] As Plotz observes, reformulating and updating James's Theodora, literary studies on continuation are strongly grounded in the book or media history of serial formats:

> This sensation of iterativeness, of repetition bound up with everydayness – and both bound up with the format in which many Victorian novels first appeared – was long slighted in critical accounts of the 'age of the novel' [...] It's been a welcome development of recent times that scholars have drawn our attention to the role that such serialization played then – and its affinities to some of the roles that TV plays now. The everydayness and indefinite continuation of narrative (its non-evadable all-over aspect) pervasively shapes recent critical accounts[.][33]

A critical account of Thackeray's 'Proposals' or Ruskin's 'tearful supplication' cannot but pervasively notice the Victorian desire for fiction 'to continue indefinitely, to keep coming out always, to be one of the regular things of life'.[34] Yet neither can it avoid their sense of frustration or disappointment with how 'the format in which many Victorian novels first appeared' in fact failed to accommodate this desire.[35] If such readers felt their wishes for 'indefinite continuation' to be 'bound up' with format, they seem less likely to think of this boundedness in Plotz's intended sense of *delivered through* the serial format than *restricted by* material forms in general, as a set of 'established limits' (*NE* 605) which (to their dismay) puts practical brakes on the experience they want. To further distinguish the specificity of fictional experience, and its ambivalent place within the mixed purposes of the literary work, we need to examine how the novel's material forms *attempt but fail* to realise readers' desires for continuation.

'Bound Up with the Format'

Plotz's argument is informed by book history and media studies, specifically by their emphasis on the material shape and experience of the text as it arrived in the hands of historical readers. The particular advantage of this emphasis for studying serial works is that it recovers the physical divisions of parts, numbers, and instalments, and their attendant narrative rhythms and breaks over time – otherwise lost in their subsequent assimilation into a completed edition – which critics have argued as sustaining a distinctive reading experience. Holly Furneaux has suggested how 'the approaches recommended by book history, attentive to the conditions of publication' help critics to perceive a 'serial form in which linear, teleological reading is structurally discouraged and closure is only ever a temporary cessation'.[36] For Ben Winyard, reconstructing the 'original format and rhythms of publication brings us closer to the work's initial modes, cadences, and temporalities [. . .] [and] gives us formal spaces or gaps in between instalments that encourage the proliferation of imaginative surpluses'.[37]

The disadvantage of this focus on real, material texts is its occlusion of what historical readers may have found still incomplete or disappointing about literary objects. Theodora, whom Plotz quotes in epigraph, is wilfully blind to material conditions when she envisions her ideal *Daniel Deronda* as a hypothetically infinite version of Eliot's novel. Her wishful comments – like Tennyson's, Thackeray's, Gaskell's, or Ruskin's – are antitheses of book history, representing an approach of deliberate inattentiveness to the realities and exigencies of publication in their collective demands for the impossible: for million-volume novels, 120-year-old protagonists, and fictions without end. The insufficiency of any reading experience, including that of the serial (although it may go further than others), to realising the ongoing fictional life such readers desired is reflected in the variety of material formats in their accounts, all of which they can imagine expanding into continuations, from the expensive triple-decker of *Ivanhoe*, to the serialised D'Artagnan novels (which Thackeray read in collected volumes), and the single-volume Mignon novels (published annually). Yet such wishes clearly attend to something with real effects: Thackeray's unfeasible wish accurately anticipated *Le Vicomte de Bragelonne*, Ruskin's directly produced *Bootles' Children*, and Theodora's fantasy is reflected by the many unauthorised *Daniel Deronda* sequels that came to infuriate Eliot.[38] That none of these cases really created an infinite novel (often creating very bad novels instead) does not mean they were not historically shaped by the optative, the historically unrealised version of themselves; the object in hand may be both a completed novel in itself and only a partial satisfaction of something else.

If, as book historians suggest, the serial format encouraged its readers 'to imagine more' than the sum of its parts, another way of putting this may be as a discrepancy between the material text and its imagined world.[39] As we have seen with Trollope, a discontent with closure and the readiness of 'space or gaps' are not exclusive to the experience of the serial, but inherent to the novel's projection of an ever-growing fictional reality.[40] As George Levine argues, 'realism, in its antiliterary preoccupation with the real', struggles to represent 'the monstrously shapeless and unattainable nature of ordinary reality' within any given literary work.[41] D. A. Miller observes how '"reality", or the realist text, unmoors [...] the anchors of traditional narrative' which conventionally maintain 'a well-policed periphery, where narratable potentialities are either nullified, reined in, or denied importance'.[42] Whether it is an overflow of 'ordinary reality' or 'narratable potentialities', such critics agree that the novel can have divided loyalties between a tendency to experiential profusion and a commitment to other goals (aesthetic, moral, narrative, or commercial). If the novel's fictional experience is 'bound up' within its material conditions, this relationship may be one of bad fit, the imaginative potential of one chafing the necessary limits of the other.

Investigating the novel's 'everydayness' requires looking beyond seriality or continuation as material experiences of format, to the inherent capacity of fictional worlds to accumulate and engross. This experience and appeal of fiction, separate from (or even straining) narrative or form, is present even in those works Plotz cautions as the '*non*-serial novel', works whose continuousness should not (he argues) be overstated above 'a distinctive formal disposition to center around one plot, one set of linked outcomes that are arrayed in a determinable relationship with one another and pegged towards the resolution'.[43] Yet a reader's perverse desire to *stay* in a novel, even after the work is finished, can outweigh better judgements of form and meaning. John M. Picker, for instance, highlights the many unauthorised continuations to *Daniel Deronda*, realisations of Theodora's fantasy which as 'a sequel to an Eliot novel, in its very status as a sequel, misrepresents Eliot's aesthetic of realism'.[44] Such presumptuous reader-responses almost unanimously reconvert Deronda back to Christianity, clearly misconstruing the narrative and moral values of Eliot's original text. But they also identify a different kind of value in the fictional lives of its characters, caring enough to continue them while leaving much else (more ostensibly significant) about the work behind.

Brontë's novels, with their original three-volume format and narrow focus, similarly reveal themselves to contain expansive fantasies of continuous fiction, a pervasive life which threatens to break out of narrative. As Elisha Cohn has argued, in Brontë's *Villette*, Lucy Snowe's recurrent daydreaming 'misrepresents and distracts from the plotted – that is, moralized – experience', pausing the development towards resolution to offer a 'moment of non-closure, projecting the pleasure of suspended animation outward toward the reader'.[45] For Cohn, these moments of 'still life' represent instances of lyrical reflection embedded within novelistic narrative, but the imaginative practices of Brontë's protagonists are often not so much still as agitated, turning circles in one spot or 'swaying on a chair or gate'.[46] Unwilling to seek adventure, Lucy claims to 'hold two lives – the life of thought, and that of reality', each bespeaking not so much reflection as sustenance, not still life but pass-time: 'the former was nourished with a sufficiency of the strange necromantic joys of fancy [...] the latter might remain limited to daily bread, hourly work, and a roof of shelter'.[47] Newly arrived and restless at Thornfield, Jane finds it a relief to pace the third storey 'and, best of all, to open my inward ear to a tale that was never ended – a tale my imagination created, and narrated continuously; quickened with all of incident, life, fire, feeling, that I desired and had not in my actual existence' (*JE* 132). What the young Jane narrates internally is a distraction from the *bildungsroman* being narrated by the older Jane, a continuous provision of imagined experience rather than the plotted course of the novel. In sharp contrast to the tale of her 'actual existence', which progresses teleologically from childhood towards marriage, Jane walks 'backwards and forwards' (132) along the corridor while imagining her 'quickened' and 'never ended' story. Speeding continuously towards no destination, Brontë's protagonists enact serial desires within their distinctively non-serial narratives, imagining fictions which fill up the empty time of their lives.

All realist novels contain the desire or potential to continue – whatever their material format or narrative appropriateness – because they imagine fictional worlds, and worlds are not read, nor communicated, nor published but inhabited, departed from, and ongoing. Brontë's mise-en-abymes express these forms of relation in the midst of a material medium both suited and unsuited to them, but also gestures to the biographical practice where such experiences took precedent over writing's other uses – in play. The continuous narrative of 'incident, life, fire, feeling' (*JE* 132) with which Jane amuses herself is an exact characterisation of the sprawling narratives of the Brontë juvenilia. As Brown puts it, 'the Angrian plot is "never-ending": contingent rather than causal, episodic rather than progressive, without impediment to desire and without principle of closure'.[48] I argued earlier that the world of the juvenilia is a space for fictional wish-fulfilment, where desires about fictions can be realised without the constraints or responsibilities of the professional novelist. Here, it becomes a space for realising the desire for fictional living – the lives of characters can occupy their creators for decades of play, because they are exempt from such exigencies as literary meaning, material format, and commercial pressure.

The fantasy which Thackeray and Ruskin struggled to make real, stretching the 'conventionally established limits' (*NE* 605) of the adult literary market, finds an ideal format in the impossible, unreasonable, and childish world of the paracosm. Social scientists such as Cohen, MacKeith, and Root-Bernstein emphasise the distinctiveness of imaginative play which involves 'the consistent return [...] to a specific scenario, as evidenced by the naming of place and characters or the elaboration of a continuous narrative'.[49] Nineteenth-century accounts too stress the pleasure and significance of this persistence, even to the point of apprehensiveness, about how long children (and eventually, adults) go on imagining one creation. As we have seen, Jameson's play lasted 'from ten years old to fourteen or fifteen',[50] while Trollope carried on developing the same tale 'for six or seven years before I went to the Post Office, and was by no means abandoned when I commenced my work' (*AA* 33). Derwent Coleridge writes of Hartley that 'if the early age in which this power was exercised be remarkable, the late period to which it was continued was not less so. I have reason to believe that he continued the habit mentally, from time to time, after he left school' (*HC* xlv). As Shuttleworth observes, the underlying anxiety in these accounts – that paracosmic play went on too long, extending inappropriately into adulthood and professional life – disturbed nineteenth-century psychologists as a potential 'disturbance of natural rhythms'.[51] We will encounter more of such cultural-medical anxieties in the next chapter, particularly around the case of Hartley, in order to theorise the period's debates about the psychological nature of fictions.

Here, however, what play again enables us to understand about the novel is its distinctive pleasures and qualities as a medium for fiction, which we might otherwise evaluate as aspects of its materiality or literariness. Play reveals the burgeoning fictional world inside of and discontenting the literary work, modelling the intense attachments and relations such worlds cultivate in tension with aims of artistic separateness or ethical disinterest. Can these divided goals be reconciled? How can we perceive the novel as a form of compromise? As I argue, these are questions authors themselves confront on the borders between fiction and literature. By investigating instances of fiction's explicit discontinuation, I examine what it means to cut off the worlds of play and the novel – what novelists such as Brontë, Trollope, and Thackeray found both necessary and painful about such departures, and how a longing for the fictional world registers in their writings of closure as a formal distention or lingering.

Farewell to Angria

Children are often articulate about the importance of their possessions, and particularly of their creations; the unwillingness of play to surrender an entire imaginary world is an extravagant example of this tendency. As Root-Bernstein argues, worldplay requires 'that the child value the play highly [...] the paracosm had to satisfy certain emotional or intellectual needs; it had to "matter"'.[52] As we have seen, De Quincey's commitment to the persistence of imaginary worlds extended even to those of others, leading him to imagine the state of things in Ejuxria after Hartley Coleridge's death. For himself, sustaining the reality of Gombroon mattered to the point of transforming the relationship between creator and creation into a set of 'contracted obligations [...] submitting my conscience to a yoke' (*AS* 47), even when the game turned sour from repeated assaults by his older brother:

> Still there was one resource: if I 'didn't like it', meaning the state of things in Gombroon, I might 'abdicate'. Yes, I knew *that*. I might abdicate; and, once having cut the connection between myself and the poor abject islanders, I might seem to have no further interest in the degradation that affected them [...] but this connection with my poor subjects had grown up so slowly and so genially, in the midst of struggles so constant against the encroachments of my brother and his rascally people; we had suffered so much together; and the filaments connecting them with my heart were so aerially fine and fantastic, but for that reason so inseverable, that I abated nothing my anxiety on their account[.] (53)

It would be more appropriate to characterise De Quincey's play as a *need* for continuation rather than a *desire*, as the affective attachment between him and his own fictions – the 'obligations' of care, the 'yoke' (47) on his conscience – becomes coercive or masochistic in its hold. Maintaining 'further interest' (53) in his defeated peoples only further perpetuates his and their abjection in a game he cannot nonetheless give up, in an example of what Lauren Berlant has called 'cruel optimism', 'a relation of attachment to compromised conditions of possibility [...] whatever the *content* of the attachment', a more dispiriting version of Root-Bernstein's sense that paracosms 'satisfy certain emotional or intellectual needs'.[53]

Without suggesting that all (or even most) attachments to play's fictions are cruel in this way, De Quincey's account is a useful model for the bonds between fiction and reader that drive the desire for continuation. In the novel, something like De Quincey's 'connection' to his islanders clearly underlies Ruskin's explicit emotional need to 'stay long enough with people I like' (*NE* 605), where longer is never enough. His resistance to changing one fiction for another 'as if they were lantern slides' (605), as well as Tennyson's to 'beginning a new novel',[54] flinches from the kind of separation De Quincey avoids in refusing to 'cut the connection' (*AS* 53) between himself and the paracosm (and presumably, start anew with less harrowed characters). The concept of 'Praeterita', the 'regions' (*NE* 605) into which Ruskin imagines characters receding after the narrative, explicitly imagines the fiction as a world from which one has become 'inseverable' (*AS* 53). Like the serial reader, the paracosmic player too deploys the metaphor of the organic tie, a sense of form for which interruption entails pain: for De Quincey, the 'filaments connecting [Gombroon] with my heart'; for Ruskin, the 'natural growth of one living creation' supported by and entwined with 'the trellises of our affection' (*NE* 605). This connection is an effect of time, of having 'grown up so slowly and so genially' (*AS* 53) or become 'acquainted' (*NE* 605), but is now also the living structure which keeps it growing 'beyond the conventionally established limits' (605), supplanting literary form or publication format as the ideal structuring principle of the novel. Like Theodora – wishing for fiction to be 'part of one's life; one lives in it, or alongside of it' – they petition for novel fictions which ornament, structure, and fill in the gaps of actual life, for a relationship where 'the continuity of its form provides something of the continuity of the subject's sense of what it means *to keep on living on*'.[55]

In using the novel as a medium or habitat (as a vine does a trellis), fictional worlds produce literary effects and distortions precisely through their distinction from the literary text. Defending Pickwick's reappearance in *Master Humphrey's Clock*, Dickens argued that he 'revived Mr Pickwick and his humble friends; not with any intention of reopening an exhausted and abandoned mine, but to connect them in the thoughts of those whose favourites they had been, with the tranquil enjoyments of Master Humphrey'.[56] The deceptively simple infinitive clause combines two actions of socialisation – *connecting* Humphrey and Pickwick as fellow members of a storytelling club, a relationship in the narrative world, and Pickwick *having been* a favourite of readers, a metaleptic relationship – in the service of creating a new loyalty between readers and 'the tranquil enjoyments of Master Humphrey'. It is of course disingenuous to imply that a scheme to familiarise old readers with a new periodical is not also economically motivated, but as Holly Furneaux points out, such a strategy is both 'conceptually coherent as well as commercially astute', designed to imbue the new narrative with 'a sense of continuation, as characters, never wholly tied to the text in which they (first) appear, have an ongoing imaginative currency for regular readers [...] eager to foster relationships of long gestation through many instalments by incorporating fictional characters into their own social circle'.[57] Dickens's comments implicitly acknowledge that the logical flipside to this 'sense of continuation' is a resistance to discontinuation – as Ruskin observes, to the unnatural act of suddenly exchanging one set of acquaintances for another – which can only be overcome by strenuously connecting the old with the new. Yet as Dickens's defensiveness shows – *not* 'reopening an exhausted and abandoned mine' – and as Chesterton subsequently argues, familiarity is at once a draw for readers and a literary failing. For Stannard, likewise, a consolatory reunion with Mignon is an infringement on the public responsibilities of authorship, requiring justification for those 'who are a little tired of her'.[58]

Such guilt about returning to the imagined world, yet the pain of leaving it behind, models the inherent conflict between the novel's fictional and literary functions. In 1839, after thirteen years of playing and writing her imaginary world, but still eight years before the publication of *Jane Eyre*, Brontë encountered this conflict as a point of transition between two biographical phases of her authorship. In the untitled autobiographical fragment which critics evocatively call 'Farewell to Angria', Brontë claims to 'have now written a great many books, & for a long time I have dwelt on the same characters & scenes & subjects'.[59] In its first paragraph, Brontë describes a creative exhaustion radically at odds with our canonical sense of where her literary career begins:

> I have shewn my landscapes in every variety of shade & light which morning, noon & evening – the rising, the meridian & the setting sun – can bestow upon them [...] So it is with persons – my readers have been habituated to one set of features, which they have seen now in profile now in full-face [...] with the round outline of childhood, the beauty & fullness of youth, the strength of manhood & the furrow of thoughtful decline. But we must change, for the eye is tired of the picture so oft recurring & now so familiar. (*FA* 314)

Cyclical and developmental time combine in this descriptive time-lapse, running both the 'familiar' face of the character through the linear progression of age and the Angrian environment through 'recurring' daily and seasonal changes, the two terminating together with the need for 'change'. The dual timescales suggest perhaps how the indefinite accumulations of successive Angrian plots ('a great many books') have finally become repetitive iterations of each other, like Jane Eyre walking 'backwards and forwards' in her daydream of 'a tale that was never ended – a tale my imagination created, and narrated continuously' (*JE* 132). It may also reflect how the increasing inevitability of change ultimately builds up to an arbitrary point of termination – the juvenilia having no overarching plot or structure for closure, it seemingly ends midway (in a circle, every point is midway).

Yet if the first paragraph of 'Farewell to Angria' expresses a tiredness of paracosmic subject and practice, a development from the solipsistic never-ending tale towards the published three-decker novel, the second paragraph acknowledges the difficulty of such a move. The same temporal force that exhausts a fiction also creates its familiarity and attachment:

> Yet do not urge me too fast reader – it is no easy thing to dismiss from my imagination the images which have filled it so long. They were my friends & my intimate acquaintances & I could with little labour describe to you the faces, the voices, the actions, of those who peopled my thoughts by day & not seldom stole strangely even into my dreams by night. When I depart from these I feel almost as if I stood on the threshold of a home & were bidding farewell to its inmates. When I but strive to conjure up new inmates, I feel as if I had got into a distant country where every face was unknown & the character of all the population an enigma which it would take much study to comprehend & much talent to expound. (*FA* 314)

A different kind of time overtakes this second paragraph, transforming the unstoppable natural progressions of ageing and the sun to the more malleable speeds of human effort, reluctance, and urging. Associations of exhaustion reverse, turning the 'tired' subjects of the previous paragraph into ones which also require 'little labour' compared with new subjects which conversely 'would take much study'; not continuing the paracosm is a departure from an imagined space both 'familiar' and 'a home', a parting with characters too 'recurring' but also 'my friends & my intimate acquaintances' (314). Brontë's 'Yet' is not simply feeble protest but an argumentative turn, revealing the same reasons which make new fictions necessary as also those that make the discontinuation of old fictions difficult.

'Farewell to Angria' is the antithesis to Thackeray's speculations about literary continuation, not only because it gives up one set of fictions for another, marking the end of continuation rather than a hypothetical start, but also because it is apologetic about the very desires the 'Proposals' express. Autobiographically, 'Farewell' represents a point at which Brontë was seriously considering how to transition from play to work, or how to harness her already voluminous writing into a professional practice and into literary products. Whereas Thackeray's article suggests to us what the novel could be (for one, materially impossible) if it were fully to realise its fictional potential, Brontë's note identifies the painful distancing from fiction necessary for there to be a material novel.

Such apologetics exemplify a broader anxiety among Victorian novelists about the limited allowances of the form (and their grave discomfort with this limitation) for the desire 'to deepen ties to [an] imagined world'.[60] In 1867, Trollope published *The Last Chronicle of Barset*, the final of a six-novel series that began with *The Warden* in 1855. After twelve years of writing about the same county – albeit switching his focus between an ever expanding network of characters each time – the end of this novel is also the end of a long relationship:

> And now, if the reader will allow me to seize him affectionately by the arm, we will together take our last farewell of Barset and of the towers of Barchester. I may not venture to say to him that, in this country, he and I together have wandered often through the country lanes [...] I may not boast that any beside myself have so realised the place, and the people, and the facts, as to make such reminiscences possible as those which I should attempt to evoke by an appeal to perfect fellowship. But to me Barset has been a real county, and its city a real city, and the spires and towers have been before my eyes, and the voices of the people are known to my ears, and the pavement of the city ways are familiar to my footsteps. To them all I now say farewell. That I have been induced to wander among them too long by my love of old friendships, and by the sweetness of old faces, is a fault for which I may perhaps be more readily forgiven, when I repeat, with some solemnity of assurance, the promise made in my title, that this shall be the last chronicle of Barset. (*LCB* 727–28)

Trollope's 'last farewell' is concerned throughout with what he may or 'may not' do, or what he supposes the reader will or will not allow him. Although the passage begins with a positive request to 'seize [the reader] affectionately by the arm', Trollope imagines that the reader *has not* 'wandered often through' Barsetshire, and *has not* 'so realised the place, and the people [...] as to make reminiscences possible' (727) – but might forgive *him* for having done so. Like Brontë, who also assumes that her reader is urging her from her imaginary country, from 'the faces, the voices, the actions' (*FA* 314) of her characters, Trollope apologises for how 'the voices of the people are known to my ears', for how 'old friendships, and [...] the sweetness of old faces' has perhaps led him 'to wander among them too long' (*LCB* 728). Both writers seem conscious of having committed a 'fault', of having indulged a selfish love of their own characters over their relationship with the reader. Trollope seems to feel he has dragged us somewhere only he expects to be able to go: '*But to me* Barset has been a real county' (728) – to us, presumably, it has only been a literary setting. The recurrent language of permission and apology in these farewells, and the 'promise' to take responsibility and write an ending at last, suggests finally that disjunction between public expectation and private desire, between the novel and its fictions, also visible in photo-negative form in proposals and supplications for continuation.

The arm that we may or may not have linked with Trollope's raises the question of whether fiction's intimate attachments and familiarities, its friendships and its homeliness, are shareable through a professional literary work. Is the desire to continually spend time with certain characters inherently at odds with the form and function of the nineteenth-century novel? If so, how is the novel shaped (or distorted) by the competing demands of its fictionality with its literariness? The next section investigates these questions through Thackeray's own novels, which attempt to reconcile the sensation of indefinite ongoingness with the production of realist narratives. In writing *The Adventures of Philip*, he privately admitted that 'I can repeat old things in a pleasant way, but I have nothing fresh to say', conceding to the imagined indictment which agonised Brontë, Trollope, and Stannard.[61] In *The Newcomes*, he deliberately evokes these dual experiences of staleness and freshness as contending thematic forces in a novel sequel about past relationships, finished adventures, and 'old things'. Engaged in the same, contradictory quest to produce literary works and to stay in fictional worlds, Thackeray's continuation can be read as an extended version of his 'Proposals': a practical experiment on how far our desires for fiction can be feasibly met by the novel.

THE NEWCOMES

In 1912, the editor and critic Amy Barter arranged and produced a volume entitled *Stories of Pendennis and the Charterhouse from Thackeray*. Barter's book contributed to a series published by George G. Harrap and Company that repackaged canonical narratives for young readers – alongside titles like J. Walker McSpadden's *Stories from Chaucer* (1907) and Thomas Carter's *Shakespeare's Stories of the English Kings* (1912), Barter also later produced *Stories from George Eliot* (1913). Her instalment on Thackeray, however, is distinctive for being an anthology rather than an abridgement, departing from the series' convention of retelling or summarising plot, character, and appropriate moral in favour of a more thematic, even geographical, focus in its material. Potentially because Thackeray's novels are simply too expansive to retell, or in order to appeal to its school-going audience, *Stories of Pendennis* extracts only those chapters from *The History of Pendennis*, *The Newcomes*, and *The Adventures of Philip* which prominently feature Grey Friars, the central London public school attended by the protagonists of all three novels. The first four chapters of the book excerpt the schooldays of four characters in order of their matriculation: 'Thomas Newcome', 'Arthur Pendennis', 'Clive Newcome', and 'Philip Firmin'; the fifth chapter, 'Old Boys', takes two passages from *The Newcomes* in which alumni encounter each other in the world and reminisce about the school; and the sixth chapter, 'The Poor Brother', extracts Colonel Thomas Newcome's return to the school as a hospital pensioner, and his eventual death there.[62] As much as Barter's arrangement hints at the publication order of the novels, it also reshuffles them (*The Newcomes* in particular) to more closely follow the fictional timeline of the narratives, and to form a thematic progression from schoolboy to alumnus to pensioner. The profusion of plots and characters excluded by this selective focus (most significantly, the novels' women) are relegated to the endnotes, which briefly explain the relation of characters to each novel and to each other.

Barter's selection and rearrangement of the novels model a radical alternative to reading them as individual literary works, prioritising a bond to location and homosocial tradition over narrative or interpretation. The excerpts are prefaced by an introduction in which Barter provides both a meticulous history of the real Charterhouse School on which the fictional Grey Friars is based, and a narrativised account of Thackeray's schooldays there, drawn from autobiographical and contemporary sources. This introduction is analogous to the excerpts themselves, especially in the context of Barter's habit to treat the real Charterhouse interchangeably with the fictional Grey Friars, as if Thackeray were himself one of his protagonists and his biographical experiences one more excerpt among the fictional ones that follow. The structure of Barter's anthology not only suggests the lifecycle in which Thackeray and his protagonists enter, leave, and return to Grey Friars but also how the reader returns, with increasingly familiarity, to a known and knowable location over time and across multiple novels. Moreover, the premise of her anthology itself suggests how these fictional visits can be isolated for enjoyment from the chaotic background of other plots, pleasures, and functions also active in a literary work. If, as Leah Price has argued, anthologies represent a view of the novel as 'islands of lyric or didactic or sententious collectibles bobbing up occasionally from a sea of dispensable narrative', what Barter fishes out from the vast ocean of Thackeray's novels are neither moral nor aesthetic but nostalgic and personal, the souvenirs of a set of relationships between Thackeray, his protagonists, his readers, and a (semi-fictional) school.[63]

Gathered together and freed from their functional role as *bildungsroman* backdrop, the prose 'collectibles' of Grey Friars create a sense of the school's independent fictionality as a setting, of its broader existence and autonomous future beyond literary representation. In a lengthy passage at the end of her introduction, Barter dispenses not only with the narratives and characters outside the school but with Thackeray's novels *altogether*, loosening the already attenuated connection between anthology and text to depart, wholly and imaginatively, into continuation:

> We are sure that Arthur Pendennis, Clive Newcome, and Philip Firmin kept up the custom which had long prevailed in their families of 'sending their sons from generation to generation to the old school'. We are confident that Clive's son, Tommy, went there, and was a big boy and a monitor when little Arthur Pendennis arrived [. . .] that Tommy patronised and protected Arthur, and had much joy in thus reversing the relative positions held by a Newcome and a Pendennis a generation before; that Arthur, in his turn, patronised his own small brothers, who soon began to appear, one by one, at the bottom of the school, and tried to patronise a flaxen-haired, chubby little boy, who came with, let us say, the third Pendennis, and was named Philip Firmin [. . .] Further, by the help of the last paragraph of 'The Adventures of Philip' (in which Mr Pendennis tells of 'the great gathering the other day at Roehampton, at house of our friend Clive Newcome, whose tall boy, my wife says, was very attentive to our Helen'), we can see pupils of yet another generation, sons of a Newcome and a Pendennis, within the walls of the old school.[64]

If Barter's excerpts reorganise Thackeray's novels into a series of pleasurable return visits to Grey Friars, this passage engineers that pleasure to be pervasively self-replicating beyond even the end of his final novel, *Philip*. The children of the three protagonists enter the school in switched positions and recombinations, endlessly 'reversing the relative positions' and reappearing 'one by one, at the bottom of the school' in new generations of old characters. (Even the names repeat: besides Arthur junior and Philip the second, Helen is named after Pendennis's mother, and Tommy after Colonel Newcome.) Barter's repeated assurances that 'We are sure [...] We are confident' ward off and reveal the unspoken anxiety about finally leaving the familiar fictional space within the enclosed 'walls of the old school' – the type of space Brontë calls 'a home' shared with 'intimate acquaintances', or more troublingly, with 'inmates' (*FA* 314). Barter's turn to futurity represents Grey Friars' final emancipation as a fiction from the contexts of narrative and novel. On the other hand, its new, independent unreality (its free-standing *virtuality*) seems to realise Trollope's fear that the reality and 'old friendships' of such places are sustained only by the retreading of old ground (*LCB* 728).

Barter's continuation takes clear cues from Thackeray's texts, responding to inherent desires in his fiction, much as Thackeray himself once responded to similar qualities in Dumas. *Stories of Pendennis* explicitly spins out a future from 'the custom which had long prevailed' in the novels and 'by the help' of direct quotations from them.[65] It is surprising, in fact, that Barter does not mention how the final paragraph of *Philip* from which she quotes also jokes that 'The mothers in Philip's household and mine [Pendennis's] have already made a match between our children', suggesting not only Barter's speculative Newcome-Pendennis heir but also a future Firmin-Pendennis, and moreover, how the party 'having been educated at the same school [...] sat ever so long at dessert, telling old stories'; both reflections on Thackeray's creative tendencies that pre-empt Barter's later response.[66] Her liberation of Grey Friars into its own, sovereign paracosm reflects how Thackeray's novels lend themselves to a paradoxical experience of fictional nostalgia and continuation, to a form of literary appreciation where satisfaction accrues onto 'old things' through the course of ever more familiar relationships, and finally, to a sense that these relationships and things outgrow the narrative text. Accounting for our evolving attachments to characters or settings is significant both because they arise from novels, prompting questions of how textual mechanisms encourage real relationships to fictional objects, and because they so often work against the more strictly literary (formal, narrative, moral, and practical) goals of the novel.

This section uses Thackeray's *The Newcomes* to examine this conflict between affective attachments to fictions and literary commitments to convention and form. I foreground *The Newcomes* over the three other novels that share its characters, history, and world – *Vanity Fair*, *Pendennis*, and *Philip* – first because it most exemplifies the features of continuation that run throughout the series, making the most intertextual connections *to* Thackeray's oeuvre of any work *in* his oeuvre. Secondly, the nature and experience of attachment is a central theme of *The Newcomes*, which (as its title suggests) models its multiple yet closely entangled plots after the estranged but inescapably related branches of the Newcome family. Finally, *The Newcomes* occupies an emblematic position within the critical history of the novel form, now perhaps best known for its reputation as the original English example of James's nineteenth-century 'baggy monsters' – alongside Tolstoy's *War and Peace* and (what would have delighted Thackeray) Dumas's *The Three Musketeers*. This account of the novel enables a reassessment of its formal bagginess as a function of its narrative and reading experience – both concerned with the weight of emotional baggage – and suggests a new analysis of form in general as part of the concretised experience of fiction. By investigating *The Newcomes* as a site of contestation between fiction and form, I seek to describe their competing demands in terms of physical tension, and more specifically, of elasticity: how they pull, distend, and resist each other, how they cling, stretch – and snap.

Clinginess in the Family Network

The Newcomes, family and novel, begins with an originary Thomas Newcome whose two marriages form the root of the narrative's elaborate family tree, plot structure, and thematic pattern. Arriving in London 'on a wagon, which landed him and some bales of cloth, all his fortune, in Bishopsgate Street', this ancestral Newcome makes his fortune in a cloth and banking business, and marries twice.[67] First, his penniless betrothed from his native village, who dies giving birth to (the later Colonel) Thomas Newcome Jr.; and 'en secondes noces' (*NC* 18), his employer's wealthy daughter, who bears him the twin sons Hobson and Brian Newcome ('called after their uncle and late grandfather, whose name and rank they were destined to perpetuate', 26). The Colonel himself comes to have two love-affairs: with his French tutor's daughter Mademoiselle du Blois, who is forced into a more convenient marriage, the heartbreak of which alienates him from his family and drives him to India; and then with the widow Emma Honeyman, who dies after marrying the Colonel and giving birth to Clive Newcome, the novel's protagonist. The twins produce a number of step-cousins for Clive, most of whom only occasionally surface in the novel, but Brian in particular (married into the aristocracy) begets Ethel and Barnes Newcome, the heroine and villain respectively.

Stripping the novel down to this abstract (and not too enthralling) genealogy reveals, even in the pre-narrative, its preoccupation with patterns of moral behaviour that replicate through generations of characters. Nicholas Dames has noted, after the contemporary reviewer James Hannay, that the original Thomas Newcome's marriages are 'neatly allegorical, one a love match (which produces the Colonel) and one a money match (which produces the novel's least morally admirable characters)'.[68] Characters throughout the novel, especially but not only the Newcome offspring, are recurrently presented with the same choice between a difficult marriage of love and a more indifferent marriage of convenience: Clive chooses between his beloved Ethel and the merely pleasant Rosie, Ethel between struggling painter Clive and a host of aristocratic suitors, Barnes between a villager he has impregnated and the respectable Lady Clara Pulleyn, Clara between her impoverished sweetheart Belsize and the wealthy but abusive Barnes – among other examples. As Juliet McMaster has also argued, 'the repetition of the mercenary marriage between various couples and its outcome is a unifying structural principle [. . .] *The Newcomes* is a set of variations on this theme'.[69]

But this often-noted structuring principle extends its logic beyond the consistent moral dichotomy of marriage choice. For instance, Clive, his father, and his grandfather share not only a doubling of partners but also the early deaths of their wives (who often themselves have chosen between, or survived to have, two husbands), just as Hobson and Brian's names, ranks, and even destinies explicitly echo forebears from their maternal line. As these relationship patterns replicate down the generations, the central plot of the novel can also be seen as a series of horizontal rearrangements – as the potential match between Ethel and Clive rises and recedes in probability over their lives, as they meet and separate, fight and reconcile, engage or marry others and break off or are widowed, the branches of the Newcome family they represent also oscillate between intimacy, estrangement, and outright hostility. *The Newcomes* can therefore be characterised as an intersection of three narrative directions: the generational reproduction of an ancestral marriage plot, which increasingly divides and splinters the family tree; the novel's particular and focal marriage plot between its protagonists, which seeks to reintegrate the branches; and the picaresque chronicling of what Dames calls the novel's 'minutiae', the fine-grained experience of which hides the 'thematic architecture' of an at-once expansive and detailed novel behind the characters' day-to-day lives.[70]

Such a reading of the novel borrows its method from Caroline Levine's recent, 'new formalist' reading of *Bleak House* as 'using narrative form to work through the dynamic unfolding of kinship networks over time' – as apt a description of *The Newcomes* as any – but with a characteristically Thackerayan focus on time as a regulator (rather than facilitator) of connection.[71] Taking *Bleak House*'s thrice-married Mrs Badger as an example, Levine argues:

> As anyone who has ever tried to make a genealogical chart will know, the family is never graspable as a whole. It stretches indefinitely across time and space. Distant branches connect ever outwards, as marriages creates links to other families, old generations stretch back into the past indefinitely, and generations yet to come will continue to add nodes. And as Mrs. Badger suggests, the nodes of the family network are best figured as positions that can be endlessly emptied and refilled: new people supplant previous husbands and wives [...] nodes repeatedly replace themselves, and in doing so replicate the network in ways that stretch the institution of the family itself across time.[72]

The Newcomes' textual version of the genealogical chart, and Barter's later elaboration of its logic, both amply demonstrate a sympathy to this view of the family as network, but Thackeray's novel also requires us to modify Levine's model in two major respects. For one, Levine emphasises the way Dickens's detective mystery withholds knowledge of how characters are unsuspectingly networked through social and material systems, only gradually connecting the dots through suspense to create a narrative experience of 'indefinitely expanding processes of interconnectedness [...] [which] can never be grasped all at once'.[73] While *The Newcomes* involves some (slipshod) detective work – Ethel's accidental discovery of a lost will, slipped between the pages of an old book, reshuffles the legal lines of inheritance between the branches – almost every connection between the characters, however tangential, is laid out from their introductions and can be deciphered with a little readerly mental labour. In periods of particular estrangement, members of the Newcome family are even irritated by an awareness of (and social necessity of acknowledging) their ties to each other, the exact opposite problem to the secret familial connection between Esther and Lady Dedlock. As Dames points out, in absolute antithesis to 'plotted suspense', the novel's 'lack of forward-directed plot' in fact led critics to complain of Thackeray's 'loitering, be it ever so humorously, philosophically, picturesquely' in the webbing of his character's intersecting lives.[74]

For another, if Levine identifies Dickens's key interest in the 'replaceability' of abstract family positions, marital 'nodes' in Thackeray's novels *cannot* be 'endlessly emptied and refilled' but replaced precisely once, and only with significant emotional consequence.[75] Unlike Mrs Badger (many Thackerayan characters remarry, but none marry three times) and unlike 'Esther's two husbands, one of whom replaces himself and his house with another husband and another house in one of [*Bleak House*'s] most unsettling moments',[76] *The Newcomes*' significant marriages are always explicitly unsettled, either by the failure of a first love, the death of a previous spouse, or already-present (if unnoticed) signs of illness; characters either marry in conditions of compromise, or share love in conditions that compromise their ability to love again. Much as the original Thomas Newcome returns to his village to marry his first wife after her 'pale face [. . .] had grown older and paler with long waiting' (*NC* 18), as George Levine has argued, Thackeray's characters only ever marry after 'it is too late for passion':

> The narratives carefully enfold passion in layers of irony and of time that diminish passion and transform it into self-consciousness [. . .] In [Thackeray's] four best novels, Dobbin gets Amelia only when he has discovered the vanity of her selfishness; Esmond gets not the beautiful and sexually vital Beatrix, but her mature mother; Pen gets neither Fotheringay, nor Blanche, but a saccharine Laura [. . .] and we bestow Ethel on Clive only after she has outgrown her youthful energy, and he has gone through the embittering experience of a loveless marriage.[77]

Where for Dickens the effect of time on networks seems to be one of indefinite expansion, creating or revealing new connections to increasingly far-flung people and places, for Thackeray time *degrades* connectivity, beginning with a more or less fully available picture of social ties before tapering or sealing off the ability of individuals to make new relations. Read this way, the choice between two partners that confronts each character in *The Newcomes* is difficult not only as a moral choice between love and convenience but also because of the inevitable wear-and-tear in replacing one relationship with another – all of the new generation have problems detaching from previous partners even after they have been married to others, which in Clara's case eventuates in actual infidelity with Belsize. In Thackeray's novel, it is not only *how* the world is networked (the variety, quantity, or reach of our social ties) that is being represented and scrutinised, but also how it *feels* to be connected to others, an experience far from the clean slotting together of compatible connections and nodes.

Indiscretion or Sentimentalism

If a central motif of *The Newcomes* is the way in which characters are stuck with each other, unable to let go of their past connections, the novel also uses the social network of these characters to obsessively retrace its connections with an *intertextual* past. As almost all of Thackeray's critics have noted, one of the consistent habits of his oeuvre is what Chesterton deplored as an 'act of sentimentalism': the revisiting of old characters in new novels. Familiar names and faces from previous novels not only reappear, but are revealed as tangentially connected to the social world of the new work, as mutual friends or schoolmates or distant relatives: Lawrence Zygmunt, who traces the practice back to Thackeray's early journalistic career, describes the 'extraordinary tangle of bickering, overlapping links among his fictional works [...] Thackeray piles up interconnected characters and plots to produce a messy, confusing, picaresque narrative expanse'.[78] For example, Arthur Pendennis is both an active character and the narrator of *The Newcomes* (both a friend of the family and its chronicler), whose continued life from *The History of Pendennis* takes place in the margins of this novel and in the later *Adventures of Philip*. At a party thrown by the Colonel (where Pen is also present), an initially unnamed gentleman strikes up a conversation with Clive:

> 'I knew your father in India', said the gentleman to [Clive]; 'there is not a more gallant or respected officer in that service. I have a boy too, a stepson, who has just gone into the army; he is older than you, he was born at the end of the Waterloo year, and so was a great friend of his and mine, who was at your school, Sir Rawdon Crawley'.
> 'He was in Gown Boys, I know', says the boy; 'succeeded his uncle Pitt, fourth Baronet. I don't know how his mother – her who wrote the hymns, you know, and goes to Mr. Honeyman's chapel – comes to be Rebecca, Lady Crawley. His father, Colonel Rawdon Crawley, died at Coventry Island, in August, 182-, and his uncle, Sir Pitt, not till September here. I remember, we used to talk about it at Grey Friars[.]' (*NC* 172–73)

'How d'you do, Dobbin?' (174) the Colonel later greets him, providing a redundant confirmation of recognition, given the extent and exactness to which Clive and Dobbin's conversation has mapped out every other major character of *Vanity Fair*. But redundancy is also very much the point of the passage, designed for both characters and readers to reminisce ('I remember, we used to talk about it'), specifically invoking both *Vanity Fair*'s critically lauded Waterloo chapter and the continued pretensions of Thackeray's 'famous little Becky Puppet'.[79] If *Middlemarch*'s famous check on its own favouritism – 'but why always Dorothea?' – is for Gage McWeeny 'an Eliotic version of the question posed by any realist novel intent on broad social description', the Thackerayan version of this question – why Becky, again? – is the antithesis of both Eliot and Dickens's concerns, evoking not a 'broad' but narrow world in which everybody knows the same old people.[80]

The novel's fictional social network extends beyond the borders of the individual text; at the same time, its connections withdraw and fixate on the familiar, on first loves and former protagonists. Such episodes of intertextual reminiscence therefore reproduce, on the level of literary experience and form (reviving characters, revisiting locations, retelling narratives), the social experience being described on the level of plot (first loves, second marriages, widowhood). Rather than Chesterton's sense that such references damage the original work by attaching unnecessary 'after-words and appendices', or Zygmunt's argument that they represent 'isolated vignettes [which] seem largely an indulgence in characters of whom Thackeray was fond, allowable chiefly because loyal readers will recognize them', the novel evokes readerly fondness, loyalty, and recognition to simulate the feeling of being entangled in the same attachments as its characters.[81]

For the character of Mrs Mackenzie, a lively Scottish widow with a young, unmarried daughter, there is especially little difference between what Zygmunt terms the 'practical' narratives of the novel's plot and the 'Extraneous' anecdotes of continuation.[82] In 'setting her cap' at Clive and the Colonel, seemingly unconcerned in which combination their families are joined – 'Should you like a stepmother, Mr. Clive', one friend teases, 'or should you prefer a wife?' (*NC* 285) – Mrs Mackenzie ultimately secures a match by pushing Rosie to win over the Colonel's fatherly love, who in turn persuades Clive to marry his chosen daughter-in-law. This circuitous solution comes after Mrs Mackenzie's abortive attempts to persuade Clive through Rosie alone, and (the novel implies) trying for the Colonel herself. 'If she tried she failed', writes Pendennis, recounting her private impressions to him:

> She said to me, 'Colonel Newcome has had some great passion, once upon a time, I am sure of that, and has no more heart to give away [...] You see

tragedies in some people's faces. I recollect when we were in Coventry Island – there was a chaplain there – a very good man – a Mr. Bell, and married to a pretty little woman who died. The first day I saw him I said, 'I know that man has had a great grief in life. I am sure he left his heart in England[']. (286)

Modelled by Thackeray's own admission from his 'she-devil of a mother-in-law', Mrs Mackenzie is not often portrayed with much sympathy in the novel.[83] In this passage, however, *Pendennis* allows her a lengthy testimony that speaks to her effectiveness in the role of (as the novel calls her) 'the Campaigner' (741), a satirical title with an implicit significance given the parallel plot in which Barnes loses his campaign for parliamentary re-election. While Barnes takes voters' loyalties for granted, and is disastrously accused of not recognising his own illegitimate children, 'the Campaigner' accurately intuits what readers already know as the Colonel's backstory (his failed relationship with Mademoiselle du Blois) and cannily reroutes her strategy through his abundant love for children, and Clive's love for him, to marry off Rosie. Where Barnes's failure arises from his blindness to the ties that organise society and the novel, Mrs Mackenzie's success at achieving her ends (whatever we may think of them) is rooted in a keen perception of their dynamics.

More than simple social aptitude, however, the widow's canny acuity for navigating the Newcomes' family network also has an uncanny, intertextual dimension. For example, she is again accurate in ascertaining that the chaplain 'Mr. Bell [...] has had a great grief in life' lingering from his life in England, over and above his marriage to the 'pretty little woman who died' (*NC* 286) in the colonial outpost of Coventry Island. These not at all straightforward conjectures about the history of Mr Bell in fact retell the pre-narrative to *The History of Pendennis*: Bell shared a doomed first love with Pendennis's mother, who agrees to raise his daughter after his own early death. (Mrs Mackenzie seems unaware that Pendennis, to whom she tells this story, grew up with and is now married to Laura Bell.) In another recollection from Coventry Island, she also recalls 'poor dear Sir Rawdon Crawley', Becky's husband-in-exile, and continues to follow their family narrative as 'I saw his dear boy [Becky's son] was gazetted to a lieutenant-colonelcy in the Guards last week' (283). Much as the challenge of 'why always Dorothea?' evokes the counterfactual possibility of 'a novel with a nearly unbounded factual field of characters [...] a vast shadow *Middlemarch*', George Levine has argued that Thackeray's 'constant allusions to and introductions of characters from other novels [...] imply both the artificial closure of any single narrative, and the proximity of other equally important novels while any particular narrative is going on'.[84] What Thackeray might share with other realist novelists is a dissatisfaction with the limits of the novel form for a full representation of the social; where they differ is in the scope and aim of representation.

If Mrs Mackenzie embodies this dissatisfaction by habitually wandering away from the central plot of *The Newcomes* and into the physical 'proximity' of other lives and stories, it is always Thackeray's previous fictions that are revealed as skirting the boundaries of the present narrative. Rather than a realist and socially inclusive ambition to democratise the scope of representation, *The Newcomes* opens up its narrative for a certain social exclusivity, to let in an alumni's club of fictional characters. Put otherwise, intertextuality for Mrs Mackenzie is not so much about all the 'equally important novels' (that is, all the unrepresented life stories) *out there* as those like Dobbin, Bell, Rawdon, and Pen who are awkwardly *still here*:

> You gentlemen who write books, Mr. Pendennis, and stop at the third volume, know very well that the real story often begins afterwards. My third volume ended when I was sixteen, and was married to my poor husband. Do you think all our adventures ended then, and that we lived happily ever after? (*NC* 286)

Her speech, continuing from her analysis of men who have 'no more heart to give away' (286), moves from unknowingly intertextual examples of lost or disappointed love to an analogy of intertextuality *as* the experience of married life or widowhood. Like Dobbin, Becky, or Pen, Thackeray's widows and widowers insist on continuing as characters beyond the conventional limits of the marriage plot, and analogously, on being emotionally welded to particular partners even after the relationship's end. Just as she understands the Colonel's story as having occurred 'once upon a time' (286), Mrs Mackenzie's (somewhat) continued loyalty to her former spouse and her (metaphorically) intertextual life after 'my third volume ended when I was sixteen' resists both social and literary forms of living 'happily ever after'. Directing her comments towards Pen as the representative of a professional class, she is unaware of his purported authorship of *The Newcomes* itself, and of her own place as a character within it – nevertheless, Mrs Mackenzie instinctively represents her life and those of others as fictions that outgrow the boundaries of their texts.

The messy, extraneous, seemingly redundant references that connect together Thackeray's long novels embody an experience of fiction as being more persistent than the novel form allows, if nonetheless dependent on the novel as a medium. Much the same way, Thackeray's characters cling determinedly and often tragically to lost persons and pasts. *The Newcomes*, a novel which draws this analogy explicitly through Mrs Mackenzie and implicitly throughout, is morally pitched against the heartlessness of 'replaceability': Clive, trying to love his second choice; Clara and Ethel's families, negotiating their affections on the marriage market; Mrs Mackenzie, happy to be either widow or wife, stepmother or mother-in-law; and the novel form, occasionally demanding we exchange one set of characters for another. In Ruskin's (admittedly melodramatic) view, the innocuous act of finishing a novel and beginning a new one is a deeply unnatural and Mrs Badger-like act of exchanging one set of emotional investments for another. As Thackeray's 'Proposals' protest on the insensitivity of the marriage plot, 'Do we take leave of our friends, or cease to have an interest in them, the moment they drive off in the chaise and the wedding-*déjeûné* is over?'[85] Similarly, as Ruskin argues, novelists inflict a type of emotional violence on readers with their endings, by 'shifting the scenes of fate as if they were lantern slides' (*NE* 605). If relationships do sometimes come to satisfying conclusions, Thackeray and Ruskin point out that this other sense of closure rarely synchronises with 'the conventionally established limits', where the pages of the novel run out; the continued attachment of our fictional 'interest' or 'affections' forms an alternative structure that (like widowhood in the marriage market) fit poorly into form and format.

Closing Lines

This sense of bad fit is most visible in *The Newcomes*'s ending, where the narrative must self-consciously cut off while the lives it depicts continue. As James famously argued in the preface to *Roderick Hudson*, relations and narratives structure each other: in his elegant formulation, 'relations stop nowhere, and the exquisite problem of the artist is eternally but to draw, by a geometry of his own, the circle within which they shall happily *appear* to do so'.[86] Novels like *The Newcomes* demonstrate how this circle is not only shaped by the internal structure of relations between characters, or the narrative form that rounds them off, but also acted upon by the inelegant pull of metaleptic relations – for example – by the demand to 'stay long enough with people I like' (*NE* 605), or as Chesterton terms it, by an inexcusable 'sentimentalism'.[87] Yet even as such forces drag out the Jamesian circle into a looser and baggier shape, as Caroline Levine points out, the form of the network ultimately 'runs up against the limits of [the novel's] capacity for representation',[88] a capacity limit to which Thackeray draws emphatic attention in his abrupt conclusion to *The Newcomes*:

> Two years ago, walking with my children in some pleasant fields, near to Berne in Switzerland, I strayed from them into a little wood; and, coming out of it presently, told them how the story had been revealed to me somehow, which for three-and-twenty months the reader has been pleased to follow. As I write the last line with a rather sad heart, Pendennis and Laura, and Ethel and Clive, fade away into Fable-land. I hardly know whether they are not true: whether they do not live near us somewhere. They were alive, and I heard their voices, but five minutes since was touched by their grief. And have we parted with them here on a sudden, and without so much as a shake of the hand? Is yonder line (– –) which I drew with my own pen, a barrier between me and Hades as it were, across which I can see those figures retreating and only dimly glimmering? (*NC* 1007)

Three lines mark the end of the novel: the 'last line' of narrative text Thackeray writes (describing the Colonel's death), the printed 'line (– –)' that Thackeray draws (and then miniaturises in parentheses) to separate Pendennis's narration from his direct authorial voice, and finally the 'barrier' between reality and the 'Fable-land' or 'Hades' (1007) of fiction. Media scholars Keren Eyal and Jonathan Cohen have used the term 'parasocial breakup' to refer to 'the termination of imaginary relationships' in their study of viewer reactions to the end of the decade-long television serial *Friends*, an event they theorise as compatible with 'premises regarding relational dissolution' with real individuals.[89] Thackeray's ending seems to register a similar phenomenon, conflating a 'sudden' narratological discontinuity with an emotional break from the 'grief' of living characters, contrasting the 'three-and-twenty months' of serialisation with the difference 'five minutes' makes. Even for a novel where characters like Pendennis and Mrs Mackenzie make a point of surviving beyond their 'third volume', such an ending deliberately cuts off the inter- and extratextual relationships the novel so carefully maintained, emblematised by the refusal of a final gesture of metaleptic social connection – a handshake between author and character.

Thackeray could not help but be aware, as Brontë and Trollope were, of how literary works eventually demand an end to fiction. Just over a year before his death, in a touching essay entitled 'De Finibus (On Endings)', Thackeray would return to the moment of breakup after the finish of a novel, describing in a striking echo of both his ending to *The Newcomes* and Brontë's hesitation at the 'threshold' of Angria: 'Those people who were alive half an hour since, Pendennis, Clive Newcome [...] What an odd, pleasant, humorous, melancholy feeling it is to sit in the study, alone and quiet, now all these people are gone who have been boarding and lodging with me for twenty months!'[90] Much as Brontë reminisces of 'the voices, the actions, of those who peopled my thoughts by day & not seldom stole strangely even into my dreams by night' (*FA* 314), Thackeray recalls in mock frustration how characters have 'interrupted my rest [...] thrust themselves upon me when I was ill, or wished to be idle'.[91] Just as Trollope asserts how 'the voices of the people [of Barset] are known to my ears' (*LCB* 728), Thackeray claims 'with respect to the personages introduced into your humble servant's fables, I know the people utterly – I know the sound of their voices'.[92] The reality and force of Thackeray's relationship with his own fictions lead him even to the psychological, to suspect that as 'Madmen, you know, see visions, hold conversations with, even draw the likeness of, people invisible to you and me. Is this making of people out of fancy madness? and are novel-writers at all entitled to straitwaistcoats?'[93] Yet it is not the potential madness of fiction-making (about which he is largely facetious) which necessitates its end, but the much more banal objections of literary convention and criticism. 'My good friends', Thackeray writes, speaking to Pendennis, Clive, and Philip, 'some folks are utterly tired of you, and say',

> 'What a poverty of friends the man has! He is always asking us to meet those Pendennises, Newcomes, and so forth. Why does he not introduce us to some new characters?[']'[94]

Through the imagined critic, Thackeray puts into explicit words the habit for which Brontë and Trollope also apologised, for staying among one set of characters 'too long by my love of old friendships' (*LCB* 728). But perhaps more revealing than the criticism Thackeray imagines for himself is the sense in which he conceives of the novel as a meeting between character, author, and reader as mutual 'friends' – such that a staleness in subject becomes a matter of bad social etiquette, always reintroducing us to his favourite families.

Readers like Barter are proof that, even if Thackeray were repeating a contemporary perception of his work, his novels nonetheless appeal to the appetite for a persistent fictional world. Representations of characters who 'vanish in an instant into the regions of Praeterita' (*NE* 605), or 'fade away into Fable-land' (*NC* 1007), or readers who go 'into a distant country' (*FA* 314) or must 'take our last farewell of Barset' (*LCB* 727), express the traumatic separation that awaits at the borders of literary form, where character and reader must part; but they also identify the origins of fictional character in the realm of the subjective imaginary. Maia McAleavey has noted that Coventry Island, a colonial outpost without a real-world referent which Thackeray's novels continually reference but never depict, exemplifies Edward Said's characterisation of the colonies in major Victorian novels as 'territories [...] available for use, at will, at the novelist's discretion, usually for relatively simple purposes such as immigration, fortune, or exile'.[95] Notoriously, soon after their removal there, an unspecified 'island fever' kills off any character Thackeray needs dead, like Rawdon Crawley and Arthur Bell, news of whom return to the novel as distant correspondence months after the fact. Mrs Mackenzie, however, uses the island as a nexus of connections to *Vanity Fair* and *Pendennis*; rather than a dumping ground of plot, Coventry Island could be redescribed as a unified storage space for fictions that no longer fit within the limits of representation or the literary work, or as a shared afterlife for Thackeray's finished narratives. Its availability throughout Thackeray's novels helps not only to dispose of narratives but also tie them together, drawing old and new characters closer to each other even as a distant reference point. Coventry Island undeniably represents a kind of narratological imperialism, an imagined space carved out to be 'available for use, at will, at the novelist's discretion', but its usefulness – like that of all fictional 'territories' – accommodates a range of authorial desires besides narrative and ideological convenience, including that longing for continuation which Chesterton dismissed as a novelist's '*in*discretion'.[96]

Locations such as Grey Friars and Coventry Island, where threads from across Thackeray's multiple novels converge and characters seem to exist in continual, intertextual simultaneity, envision within the narrative an ideal of fiction's survival beyond the literary work. In a rare moment of distinction between the historical and fictional schools of her anthology, Barter's introduction admits that 'In 1872 the Charterhouse school was, for sanitary and other reasons, removed to Godalming. But for readers of Thackeray the old Grey Friars will always stand 'in the heart of London city' [...] and will always be peopled by the creations of his brain'.[97] Thackeray's novels very deliberately provide familiar spaces that survive each individual text, which can 'be peopled' by characters one may want to keep imagining after the story's end. 'I hardly know [...] whether they do not live near us somewhere', he writes of Ethel and Clive, Laura and Pendennis – who for Barter could be as close as central London – and ultimately ends his afterword to *The Newcomes* by detaching the fictional from the literary, by gesturing to the greater 'Fable-land' lying beyond literature:

> But for you, dear friend, it is as you like. You may settle your Fable-land in your own fashion. Anything you like happens in Fable-land [...] Friendly reader! may you and the author meet there on some future day. He hopes so; as he yet keeps a lingering hold of your hand, and bids you farewell with a kind heart. (*NC* 1007)

The 'lingering hold' which the author keeps on his reader, a gentler parting than Ethel and Clive's disappearance 'without so much as a shake of the hand', ultimately reintroduces the malleable force of reluctance and longing to the brutal 'line (– –)' (1007) with which the afterword first opens to cut off the fictional world.[98] Like Brontë pausing at 'the threshold of a home' (*FA* 314), or Trollope seizing the reader 'affectionately by the arm' (*LCB* 727), these gestures acknowledge the allowances for human feeling that the aesthetic work ought to make (however apologetically) as an object which generates real experiences of familiar attachment. That we in fact exit the novel by an afterword – the kind of 'appendices' to finished work Chesterton disdained – exemplifies the lines of form stretching to meet these needs for fiction.

At the same time, Thackeray also reveals fiction to be a domain of subjective wish-fulfilment after all, where the inherent disappointment of novels can nonetheless be made 'as you like' (*NC* 1007). As with the sophist or the Chief Genii, this does not represent a pessimism about its reality or importance, but an exercise of its resources as a pretence to satisfy what seems materially impossible. The literary text must necessarily finish, closing out the fictional world which burgeons from within it, but it can also provide – through the examples of Grey Friars and Coventry Island – an imaginative conceit of its continuation: a fantasy that its fictions are still 'out there', living on beyond sight of narrative. To acknowledge this fantasy as it simultaneously vitalises and outlives the text is to understand the novel not only as a material and literary work, but as a tool in the wider imaginative practice of fiction. Making such distinctions between the literary and the fictional offers a new perspective on the novel as a medium for fictional worlds, one which enables a critical reassessment of its value and uses in that capacity.

CHAPTER 5

Description, Projection, and Charles Dickens

George Henry Lewes's essay 'Dickens in Relation to Criticism', published in the *Fortnightly Review* in 1872, enters midway into what he himself describes as a 'digression': an anecdote about 'a patient who believed he had transformed into a bear'.[1] In a rhetorical move we may now recognise from other ambivalent critical encounters – from Gaskell, James, and Chesterton – Lewes takes a sideways approach to an alternative understanding of the novel. Rather than a material text, an aesthetic work, or a faithful picture of the world, his anecdote reclasses Dickens's novels as *imagined experiences*, albeit by means of a dangerous comparison:

> [T]hat abnormal condition in which a man hears voices, and sees objects, with the distinctness of direct perception, although silence and darkness are without him; these *revived* impressions, revived by an internal cause, have precisely the same force and clearness which the impressions originally had when produced by an external cause. In the same degree of vividness are the images *constructed* by his mind [...] with the distinctness of objective reality; when [the patient] imagines that he himself has been transformed into a bear, his hands are seen by him as paws.[2]

'Returning from this digression', Lewes continues, 'To [Dickens] also *revived* images have the vividness of sensations; to him also *created* images have the coercive force of realities [...] When he imagined a street, a house, a room, a figure, he saw it not in the vague schematic way of ordinary imagination, but in the sharp definition of actual perception, all the salient details obtruding themselves on his attention'.[3] As his essay acknowledges, the association between literary genius and madness is not a new one, but Lewes uses the specific psychology of hallucinatory madness to articulate a particular sensory feature of Dickens's creativity: much as the mad patient sees the image of his bear paws 'with the distinctness of objective reality',[4] the novelist is allegedly capable of envisioning fictional scenes and objects with 'the sharp definition of actual perception'. By emphasising 'vividness' and 'clearness', 'details' and 'distinctness' – particularly in opposition to the 'vague' and 'schematic' – Lewes characterises Dickens with what modern photography might term a *high definition* imagination.

For the man who introduced the word 'realism' into English literary criticism as a principle about 'the representation of Reality, i.e., of Truth', with this digression, Lewes reframes much of his own criteria for 'realistic' art. The essay appears generally disparaging, assuming 'a series of positions' which Tyson Michael Stolte argues 'have come to represent standard ways of attacking [Dickens]', but it also acknowledges the extent to which such criticisms miss the point of their objects, requiring a turn to other (for instance, psychological) ways of understanding.[5] As many of Dickens's critics have found, the novelist's characters strike Lewes as 'caricatures and distortions of human nature [. . .] moving like pieces of a simple mechanism'; a critique similarly formulated by James in 1865, describing the cast of *Our Mutual Friend* as 'lifeless, forced, mechanical [. . .] animated by no principle of nature whatever'.[6] Yet, as Lewes goes on to point out, these clunky machines have nonetheless 'established themselves in the public mind like personal experiences', so engrained that 'Against such power criticism was nearly idle. In vain critical reflection showed these figures to be merely masks [. . .] these unreal figures affected the uncritical reader with the force of reality'.[7] This is not only a condescension on 'the uncritical reader', but the recognition of a different kind of realist power which 'critical reflection' has failed to acknowledge: the production of unreal objects and experiences with 'the force of reality', rather than as 'the representation of Reality'. Just as Lewes finds his patient 'willing to admit that the idea of such a transformation was utterly at variance with all experience', but still 'remained fixed in his mind [on] the image of himself under a bear's form', novel readers already know that Dickens's characters are not real (nor even realistic), but remain 'affected' by them, weeping over the death of Little Nell as if it had or even could have happened.[8] 'There is no power of effacing such conviction by argument', Lewes writes of his ursine patient, and likewise, a critique of the novel's artifice offers no purchase on its explicitly artificial, but nonetheless impactfully real, experience.[9]

'Dickens in Relation to Criticism' therefore moves to assume a different critical function than insisting in 'vain' why certain novels ought or not to feel real, turning instead to the psychology of hallucinations to model how fictions project their own reality. By opening a theoretical distinction between the novel's persuasiveness (as plausible, accurate, or faithful representations of the world) and its experiential force (as 'constructed' or 'created' images), perhaps even by offering the latter as an alternative realism, Lewes's essay is more sympathetic to Dickens than what Rosemarie Bodenheimer, for instance, has perceived as 'a long and predictable attack on Dickens's "incorrect" and "false" depictions of human character [...] couched in the authoritative language of the mental sciences'.[10] Lewes takes the incorrectness for granted – useless to protest the actual absurdity of bear paws – to attend to the concreteness of the image. Rather than authority, what the mental sciences offer Lewes and (as we will see) his contemporaries are relevant, if often dangerous analogies for real-but-not-actual experiences: in memory, daydreaming, and hallucination, individuals similarly conjure and take pleasure in objects not materially present, nor subject to the standards of material reality. Victorian scientists and critics generally stop short of endorsing a literary function which bears comparison to examples of mental illness, but theorisations such as Lewes's essay suggest an escape from the binary upon which Dickens's fictions are judged to be either true to life or fatally unrealistic – and at the potential of the science behind hallucination to articulate a category of the real, but unrealistic; the palpable, but non-material. By comparing novel fiction to the imagined objects of diseased minds, these writers speculated about its virtuality.

Taking its cue from Lewes's essay, this chapter reconstructs a nineteenth-century debate over the vividness, palpability, or concreteness of fictions – a historical theory of virtual experience – as an intervention into our presently diminished sense of these qualities. In the period, Lewes contributed to a wider cultural discourse with strong anxieties about experiencing absent or imagined things: 'seeing' a room described by a novel, 'talking' to imaginary people, or 'believing' in the actions of play. Such anxieties collected particularly around the case of Hartley Coleridge, whom critics and doctors claimed to have experienced hallucinatory sensations and delusional beliefs about his imaginary world. (Although Hartley's life, as we will see, reveals no evidence of such symptoms – only a practice of virtual play.) At the same time, critics also acknowledged the experiential vividness of characters or scenes as an inherent appeal of literature, and commonly suggested the skill of conveying vividness to depend on the author's own 'belief' in their creations: that Dickens 'seeing [his fiction] vividly, made us also see it; and believing in its reality however fantastic, he communicated something of his belief to us [...] that even while knowing it was false we could not help, for a moment, being affected, as it were, by his hallucination'.[11] Both sides of this historical debate about the sense experience of fiction, both as a literary power *and* a psychological hazard, appear hopelessly quaint today – few in the world of modern cinema, VR headsets, or cultural fantasies of the hologram are concerned about the hallucinatory reality of novels.

Yet these accounts are useful because, precisely in their now expired anxieties, they recover a perspective on the novel as an experience of imaginary objects and environments – which, if not at all scientifically or medically accurate, nonetheless enables us to reassess a real and underexamined literary function. As this book has argued throughout, current approaches to the Victorian novel neglect its value and uses as a medium for artificial realities, an inherent capacity which their contemporary readers and writers consciously avoided or exploited. I have proposed the different kinds of pleasure and meaning to living vicariously in fictional worlds, as distinct from the novel's representational, aesthetic, or narrative value. In what follows, I argue that the period's concerns about the vivid perceptibility of fictions suggest (or exaggerate into anxiety) what Lowe has described as the 'sensuous-imaginative function, which, though it is a function of all fiction to a greater or lesser extent, has been undertheorized'.[12] Like Lewes, we need a criticism that accounts for how novels provide 'personal experiences' of their imagined-material worlds, and what they offer through this mode of engagement. By examining what Victorians feared the novel could do, but which we have since ceased to apprehend, I suggest what the novel *can* do through the felt reality of its places and things.

The Luxury of Fictional Objects

'In June 1828', Brontë recounted a year later, 'we erected a school on a fictitious island' (*EW* 22). This record of play and writing exercise, entitled 'A Description of Vision Island',[13] employs the prose equivalent of what architects call a *fly-through sequence*: the depiction (usually simulated) of a designed space 'as if captured on film by a roving camera'.[14] A floating point of view descends to show us around the imagined domain, sweeping over its geographical area, '[more] like the region of enchantment or a beautiful fiction than sober reality [...] made terribly sublime by mighty rocks, rushing streams and roaring cataracts' (22); then the school's grounds, where 'clear lakes [...] seemed the crystal, emerald-framed mirrors of some huge giant' (23); then its building, 'a magnificent [*sic*] palace of pure white marble, whose elegant and finely wrought pillars and majestic turrets seem the work of mighty genii and not of feeble men' (23); then the entrance, accessed by 'a flight of marble steps [...] which leads into a hall surrounded by Corinthian pillars of white marble' (23);

and then a detailed inventory of the furnishings, moving progressively through the halls and rooms:

> From this hall you pass onto another splendid and spacious apartment all hung with rich, deep, crimson velvet; and from the grand dome is suspended a magnificent lustre of fine gold, the drops of [which] are pure crystal. The whole length of the room run long sofas covered also with crimson velvet. At each end are chimney-pieces of dove-coloured Italian marble, the pillars of which are of the Corinthian order, fluted and wreathed with gold. From this we pass into a smaller but very elegant room, the sofas of which are covered with light blue, velvet flowers with silver and surrounds [*sic*] with small, white marble columns. (23–24)

Nothing happens in the 'Description'. The narration never coalesces around an embodied perspective from which a story might emerge, following no perceptible narrative logic except the exhibition of an open house: from the surroundings to the grounds, exterior to interior, room 'pass[ing] onto' room. Nor does much more happen on 'Vision Island' hereafter. At the end of a narrative written four months later ('The School Rebellion'), the only tale to be set on the island and whose action never enters the palace, the siblings 'becoming tired of it, sent the children off to their own homes and now only fairies dwell in the Island of a Dream' (104). The juvenilia never return to this location.

As is often the case, paracosmic fiction baffles our usual modes of approach, investing its efforts to other ends or at cross-purposes to what interpretation ordinarily seeks to 'get out' of a text. Vision Island and its riches exemplify what Brontë would later repudiate, in her preface to *The Professor*, as 'the ornamented and redundant in composition' (*TP* 3), offering three sets of Corinthian pillars where there could be one (or just as well, none), each separately accounted for in colour, size, and fluting, appearing to support no greater object beyond themselves. Brontë points out the wastefulness of her early work, its elaboration of material specifics which ultimately serve no narrative function; yet wasteful is not the same as useless. She criticises its functional redundancy, but in the same instant acknowledges an explicit function – to ornament – implicitly discounted as a legitimate purpose of fiction. The 'Description' is clearly satisfying, and at the same time critically confounding, because it indulges in imagining material excess, or even further, in constructing and decorating a fantasised domain with all the gold and marble a twelve-year-old can think to demand. It is not as if Brontë no longer recalls these motives of her juvenilia, but that they no longer suffice for – are in fact antipathetic to – the purposes of writing as a novelist. The 'Description' embodies as a whole those stray 'notations' of the realist novel Barthes declares as 'scandalous (from the point of view of structure), or, what is even more disturbing [...] a kind of narrative *luxury*, lavish to the point of offering many "futile" details and thereby increasing the cost of narrative information'.[15] If it is exactly the gratuitousness of fiction which most appeals to the child – capable of every luxury at zero cost – Brontë and Barthes conversely suggest that nothing comes free in the novel, where the textual economy demands repayment with certain prescribed forms of literary value.

    The development of the realist novel, biographically for Brontë as historically for Barthes, involves a new and contradictory set of demands for functional and 'objective' detail. Attempting to define the form – one to theorise, the other to practice – from other, preceding kinds of writing, both identify the changing value of description for meeting the needs of a new verisimilitude; but in so doing, I argue, write off the concrete and experiential as aspects of the novel. In 'The Reality Effect', Barthes notes two classical typologies for description allegedly left behind by realism: 'ecphrasis, the detachable set-piece (thus having its end in itself, independent of any general function), whose object was to describe places, times, people, or works of art'; and '*hypotyposis*, whose function was to 'put things before the hearer's eyes', [...] by imparting to representation all the lustre of desire'.[16] As he looks 'ahead to Flaubert', such motives are overtaken by the new imperatives of a 'realistic description [which] avoids being reduced to fantasmatic activity'.[17] The structural analysis of description by these standards must look either for narrative signification – a character's piano acting 'as an indication of its owner's bourgeois standing' – or else for the production of a 'reality effect', a backdrop of nominal particulars codifying (an illusion of) the narrative's objectivity.[18] These rationales, rather than the goals of classical description, constitute Barthes's explanation for the characteristic clutter of novel worlds, the bric-a-brac of material information which seems to exceed structure and yet 'forms the aesthetic of all the standard works of modernity'.[19] As James Wood puts in summation, 'Nineteenth-century realism, from Balzac on, creates such an abundance of detail that the modern reader has come to expect [...] a certain superfluity, a built-in redundancy, that [narrative] will *carry more detail than it needs*'.[20] By rejecting the fantasmatic for a new division between the necessary and the redundant, however 'built-in', Brontë's reassessment of her juvenilia exhibits (or appears to exhibit) her gradual assumption of 'realist' demands.[21]

The Luxury of Fictional Objects 145

Yet 'waste', as James wrote of the baggy monsters, 'is only life sacrificed and thereby prevented from "counting"', a calculation to which he too applied his own metrics of value.[22] This book argues for an expansion of what 'counts' in the novel, specifically to include the disparaged value – not exactly aesthetic, nor directly moralising, and certainly not historical – of the form as a medium for artificial experience. On Vision Island, nobody finally sits on either the crimson or light blue velvet sofas, but to read about their placement is to feel how it might nonetheless be satisfying to *have* them there – or entangled with this sense of possession, to describe and perceive them as being there. What Lowe has described as the 'virtual presence of sensual particularities' represents a mode of relation to fictions clearly distinct from their metaphorical or metonymic interpretation, and also more subtly distinct from their aesthetic expression in language.[23] The details of Brontë's upholstery are pleasurable beyond prose because they derive their value as concrete qualities of the object imagined by description, rather than as verbal qualities of the description itself. Moreover, instead of the objectivity signalled by a reality effect, the 'Description' repeatedly evokes the power to bring subjective realities into virtual being: from the very space itself, explicitly 'a fictitious island' (*EW* 22) but evidently firm enough to build on, to natural features which more slyly 'seemed' the playthings 'of some huge giant', to architecture which suggest 'the work of mighty genii and not of feeble men' (23). The young Brontë writes not only to compose a literary text, but to craft and place fictional objects, investing care and quality into their immaterial construction and arrangement: 'At each end are chimney-pieces of dove-coloured Italian marble, the pillars of which are of the Corinthian order, fluted and wreathed with gold' (23). Such objects ask not to understood, nor believed in, nor read aloud (the subclause on the pillars is particularly awkward), but imagined as the homemade artefacts of a godlike author. By this alternative criteria, their abundance of detail is not more than they need, but as much as they want.

The gratuitous luxuries of the 'Description', precisely by their 'scandalous' indifference to traditional functions, incite us to imagine other motives for realism's fixation with material details; ones closer to the 'lustre of desire' with which Barthes's rhetoricians conjured through language just what they wanted to see. '*Middlemarch* is a treasure-house of details', James wrote in his 1873 review, 'Its diffuseness [...] makes it too copious a dose of pure fiction'.[24] Perhaps the most extravagant vision the 'Description' might put before our eyes is that of the novel as exactly this kind of repository for 'pure fiction', providing like the 'fictitious island' a ground on which imagined objects can be placed, sustained, and valued for the vicarious experience of their details. Though 'of course, [the novelist] provides incident and plot', as Leavis deprecated of Thackeray, satirising the incidental nature of these components in his later novels, something else is being offered by the concreteness of the bodies and objects involved which Leavis can register only as a waste of text and time.[25] Davis protests of the concreteness itself that 'When we "see" a house in a novel, there is really nothing "there", and, worse, there is really no "there" for a "there" to be. The house we "see" in our mind is [. . .] a cultural phenomenon with recognizable signs to tell us what kind of a house, what class, whose taste, and so on'.[26] There is indeed no 'there', but what else than 'plot' or 'signs' might we see in the novel if we *pretend* that 'there' is? How might a participatory experience of explicitly fictional objects subvert, or differently fulfil, a novel's narrative or cultural aims?

Play's anomalousness can help to reorient criticism towards such questions of alternative function and value, enabling us to perceive other uses for the novel's distinctive fictions of reality. Such is the argument and methodology of this book, but also a historical statement about a general capacity, because play performed a similar function for the nineteenth century's own critics in *their* engagements with contemporary theories of subjective realities and imagined experiences. Before turning to Dickens's *Little Dorrit* and the novel's uses for its fictional objects, I want to register the role of play and (by cautionary association) hallucination in providing literary critics of this period with a heuristic for the 'real but not actual'. Influenced both by older concepts of poetic imagination and new psychologies of perception, such critics were engaged in a similar task of revealing the sensuous or fantasmatic functions of fiction as I have attempted to show through Brontë's 'Description'. Moreover, they do so by drawing on similar examples from paracosmic play – as we will see, especially from the case of Hartley Coleridge. Yet the stakes of this historical criticism are also directly inverse to ours: whereas after the twentieth century such functions have been obscured by the easy dismissal of subjective illusions ('there is really nothing "there"'), nineteenth-century accounts of 'seeing' fictional objects are produced by acute anxieties about the potential for hallucination (that individuals might lose consciousness of what is really 'here').[27] Recovering these alarmist perspectives offers a strong corrective to our partial and disenchanted view of fiction's capacities, as well as a cultural concept of the virtual as it was forming embryonically in debates about perceiving fiction's non-existent things. By this digression we might relearn a criticism that 'sees things' (perhaps too much) in literature, so as to approach the novel from a more credulous vantage.

'The Spurious Resemblance'

So how to see an object which is not there? In the associationist school of epistemological philosophy which dominated psychological study in late eighteenth- and early nineteenth-century Britain, there is a crucial distinction between the *sensation* and the *idea* of an object. Philosophers such as 'John Locke, David Hume, and David Hartley' – Hartley Coleridge is named after the last – proposed 'that humans develop rational consciousness by the accretion and mental combination of sense experiences', foundational to which was an explanation of how sense experiences last beyond the moment of immediate experiencing; in other words, how the sight of an object sticks around in the mind to accrete and combine after the object has gone out of sight.[28] 'It is a known part of our constitution', James Mill writes in 1829, 'that when our sensations cease, by the absence of their objects, something remains. After I have seen the sun, and by shutting my eyes see him no longer, I can still think of him'.[29] In blocking out the sight of the sun, Mill's mind still carries its remnant, and the difference between them is the difference between 'two classes of feelings; one, that which exists when the object of sense is present; another, that which exists after the object of sense has ceased to be present. The one class of feelings I call *sensations*; the other class of feelings I call *ideas*'.[30] Sue Zemka's reading of Mill rightly emphasises 'the temporal premise of this model', a story of before and after-thought, but Mill's definition here also draws another, more static distinction between two types of access to an object in its material presence and absence.[31] In his footnote on Mill's text, Alexander Bain goes on to make this additional point:

> Another distinction between the Sensation and the Idea, is of the most vital importance. To the Sensation belongs Objective Reality; the Idea is purely Subjective. This distinction lies at the root of the question of an External World; but on every view of that question, objectivity is connected with the Sensation; in contrast to which the Idea is an element exclusively mental or subjective.[32]

Mill's thought experiment with the sun, in terms of this distinction, produces not only a progression forward in time but a switch between worlds or realities. Sensations are produced by objects of the world outside, and the idea is an object of the world inside – the world that appears when we close our eyes.

This conceptual component of associationism provided a logical structure for succeeding writers to theorise about other kinds of non-material sense experiences.[33] The most sensational of these was 'the maniacal hallucination', which James Cowles Prichard defined in his 1822 *Treatise on the Diseases of the Nervous System* as a condition which 'represents unreal objects as actually present [...] the creations of reverie or imagination, are presented to the mind in such vivid colours as to produce a similar effect to actual perceptions', in some cases 'so intense in its operation as to carry [the patient] away from the influence of his external perceptions, and to environ him with visions of unreal scenes'.[34] Hallucination, for medical psychologists throughout the century, would be so understood as a disorder of the relation between sensation and idea, complicated by the imagination's ability to create ideas without original objects of sense; for instance, Robert MacNish's 1834 work *The Philosophy of Sleep* describes a state of 'perception, independently of the usual cause [that is] the presence of external bodies [...] the result is a series of false images or sounds, which are often so vivid as to be mistaken for realities'.[35] Such accounts emphasise the intrasubjective nature of the hallucinatory object, having no external material presence or cause even in the malfunction of sensory organs. As John Abercrombie's *Inquiries Concerning the Intellectual Powers* argues in 1849, 'the hallucination of mind, or a belief of the real existence of the object [...] [does] not consist on false impressions on the senses, but depend upon the mind mistaking its own conceptions for real and present existences'.[36] The apparent 'struggle [...] betwixt illusive and real sensations', according to Henry Holland in his 1852 *Chapters on Mental Physiology*, made hallucination so clear-cut a psychological phenomenon that it represented a paradigmatic mental illness: 'If it were an object to obtain a description of insanity, which might apply to the greatest cases of such disorder, I believe this would be found [...] [in] the loss, partial or complete, of power to distinguish between unreal images created within the sensorium and the actual perceptions drawn from the external senses, thereby giving to the former the semblance and influence of realities'.[37]

Literary critics, moreover, identified another striking analogy for these liminal or metaleptic experiences – objects which transgress between inner and outer worlds – in the fictions of play, that which De Quincey would come to describe as the psychic hardening of a 'shadow into a rigor of reality far denser than the material realities of brass or granite' (*AS* 47). Such critics found their most prominent example in 1851, two years after Hartley Coleridge's death (from bronchitis), when Derwent's publication of his brother's *Poems* and biography brought imaginary worlds into public scrutiny as semi-literary instances of 'unreal objects [...] actually present'.[38] Derwent's account of Hartley's play became the focus of the *Poems*' reviews in the press, especially his suggestion that the world of Ejuxria 'became for [Hartley] more real and important than the matter-of-fact world in which he had to live' (*HC* xl–xli). On Hartley's 'shadowy (but to him most actual) realm', a language which recalls De Quincey's *Sketches*, the reviewer at *Bentley's Miscellany* presented the portrait of a child 'believing in his own tale [...] he had hardly become conscious of the difference between fact and fiction'.[39] *Fraser's Magazine* similarly suggested Hartley to be 'a most firm believer in his own inventions, and continued to inhabit his ideal world so long, that it assumed in his mind an equal consistency with the real, till at last he became quite incapable of distinguishing truth from fiction'.[40] *The Gentleman's Magazine* considered the account 'well worth recording for the consideration of psychologists', noting that while 'in ordinary cases these brain-creations [...] pass like the day-dreams of maturer age in swift succession, having no coherency, and leaving no trace', Hartley's exceptional case led him to 'preserve the outward form of the fiction from its natural dissolution'.[41] *The Christian Remembrancer*, more generally admiring about 'the fairy land of this young genius', is nevertheless troubled by 'the strength of the illusion which seemed to possess him, and his unwillingness to believe it a dream [...] he seemed not to be able to distinguish between reality and pretence'.[42]

It is important to clarify, at this point as I argue elsewhere, that such interpretations in fact mistake the nature of 'belief' in play and fiction. There is no evidence, only continual restatements of Derwent's impression, that Hartley or other children lost the double consciousness intrinsic to pretence, the virtual, and the novel as 'believable stories that did not solicit belief'.[43] This growing misdiagnosis of Hartley's practices reveals, for one, the still incomplete availability of a concept of non-material concreteness; and for another, the recapitulation of Platonic arguments on fiction through the new idiom of psychology. 'By the 1850s', Shuttleworth observes, 'Hartley became a definitive model of a ruined childhood: indulged by his parents in his imaginative passion for creating alternative lands, he had been trapped for ever in an unhealthy childhood, hindered from making the necessary progression into adulthood'.[44] Compounding these stakes in 1860, the psychologist James Crichton-Browne's lecture and essay 'Psychical Diseases of Early Life' cited Hartley's case as part of his argument on child insanity:

> [I]n childhood, [delusions] are frequently induced by castle-building, and we would here take an opportunity of denouncing that most pleasant but pernicious practice. Impressions, created by the ever fertile imagination of a child [...] are soon believed in as realities, and become a part of the child's psychical existence. They become, in fact, actual delusions. Such delusions are formed with facility, but eradicated with difficulty [...] [children] ought to be allowed little opportunity to 'Give to airy nothings a local habitation and a name'.[45]

A long excerpt from Derwent's memoir immediately follows this passage, as well as from Jameson's essay 'A Revelation of Childhood', which had similarly been singled out by reviews of her 1855 *Common-Place Book* as being 'the most interesting passages in the book [...] valuable from its psychological character' and of 'affording [...] excellent cautions of sound practical quality and real psychological moment'.[46] The inclusion of these cases in Crichton-Browne's work represents the accumulative consensus of literary critics who repeatedly referred this group of paracosmic biographies 'for the consideration of psychologists'; even as such critics originally interpreted them through scientific (mis)conceptions of fictional experience as shades of diseased belief.[47]

The problem at hand, in this medical-literary feedback loop and its reductive drive towards diagnosis, is the danger of a comparison which overshoots its analytical usefulness. This is particularly evident in 'Psychical Diseases', for one, in its failure to address the implications of identifying Hartley and Jameson as examples of 'delusional insanity' in children, when both survived to be (by fairly public account) more or less sane adults. Despite his alcoholism and career disappointments, Hartley was never suspected of hallucinatory madness during his lifetime – did not, for instance, claim to others that he had bear claws for hands – and Jameson, a well-respected art and literary writer, even less so. For another, Crichton-Browne also raises, by oblique reference, the problem of theatrical illusion as an analogous but more ambivalently pathological form of unreality. By warning against the 'airy nothings' of play, he quotes from the final act of *Midsummer Night's Dream*, from Theseus's speech that 'The lunatic, the lover, and the poet/ Are of imagination all compact' (5.1.4–5):

> THESEUS   And as imagination bodies forth
> The forms of things unknown, the poet's pen
> Turns them to shapes, and gives to airy nothing
> A local habitation and a name.
>
>   (5.1.14–17)

The allusion is especially appropriate for articulating anxieties with the 'shapes', 'forms', and 'bodies' of the paracosm as a 'local habitation': the delusion of a '"there" for a "there" to be'.[48] But it is also one whose significance in the play – an ambiguity between the illusions of madness, love, and poetry – attaches implicatively onto its usage as a caution against 'actual delusions'. Crichton-Browne's determination of play as psychologically dangerous, with a clear prescription for abstinence, is complicated first by the (symptomatically speaking) unspectacular lives of its alleged sufferers, and second, by a broader range of concrete but subjective experiences beyond hallucination. If the logic of madness offers a conceptual handle on such experiences, allowing critics to identify and refer to something of 'real psychological moment', it is also unhelpfully loaded with the social and medical baggage of real disease.[49]

A similar problem of slippery pathologisation also troubled equivalent investigations on fictional experience. Given the overextension to which hallucination has already been taken as a comparison for imaginative experience, Lewes is being somewhat optimistic by assuming in 1872 that 'Psychologists will understand *both the extent and the limitation* of the remark, when I say that in no other perfectly sane mind [than Dickens] [...] have I observed vividness of imagination approaching so closely to hallucination'.[50] More cautiously than the use of this same comparison by Crichton-Browne, the analogy of the 'perfectly sane' Dickens to the explicitly insane bear-patient jostles back and forth within the tentative limits Lewes sets on his argument, a space he takes (and has) great trouble demarcating:

> I am very far indeed from wishing to imply any agreement in the common notion that 'great wits to madness nearly are allied;' on the contrary, my studies have led to the conviction that nothing is less like genius than insanity, although some men of genius have had occasional attacks; and further, that I have never observed any trace of the insane temperament in Dickens's works, or life, they being singularly free even from the eccentricities which often accompany exceptional powers; nevertheless, with all due limitations, it is true that there is considerable light shed upon his works by the action of the imagination in hallucination.[51]

The proliferating conjunctions and subclauses of this single sentence – confirming, denying, and conceding at every turn – mark out the thin line upon which Lewes's argument must walk between defending Dickens's sanity and advancing a literary theory *modelled on* a paradigmatic form of insanity. Genius is not 'allied' to madness but 'on the contrary', 'very far' from it and 'nothing is less like', 'although' they sometimes occur together; in any case, Dickens 'never' manifests any actual insanity, not 'even [...] the eccentricities which often accompany' genius; 'nevertheless, with all due limitations', that mental illness which is claimed to be both the antithesis of genius and its frequent accompaniment will shed 'considerable light' on the work of an author for whom Lewes has already denied 'any trace' of illness. This frenetic, see-sawing passage attempts to capitalise on the likeness of imagination to hallucination while actively avoiding the diagnostic or prescriptive implications of their equivalence, overcorrecting its trajectory as the argument oscillates between the insights and dangers of comparison.

At stake in this account is not the history of intellectual transmission between literary and medical theory, nor the ways they in fact distort each other, but a sense of the more difficult task Lewes is attempting in this essay: to work obliquely at an unknown object with an imperfect tool; to produce knowledge through 'digression'. P. R. Marland, in his reading of 'Dickens in Relation to Criticism', argues:

> I do not think making a pathology of genius – that is, in slightly less loaded terms, the capacity for producing verbal prodigies – is very helpful or accurate. To imply that Dickens wrote so well because he suffered from a benign madness is not just wrong but impertinent, both misunderstanding and deprecating the writing. Yet literary practice, certainly fictional practice, demands 'seeing things' at an illusory, if not hallucinatory, level.[52]

The track of Lewes's argument is not so different, I would argue, from the 'Yet' on which Marland's own objection turns. Reaching for the nearest thing to a contemporary understanding of the virtual, Lewes's reference to hallucination aims not at 'a pathology of genius' but at an investigation of how we experience the imaginary. In this, he succeeds and echoes Charles Lamb's 1826 essay 'The Sanity of True Genius', which argued that the common fallacy of seeing genius as 'allied to madness' arises because poetry produces 'a condition of exultation, to which [men] have no parallel in their own experience, besides the spurious resemblance of it in dreams and fevers'.[53] However imaginative experience might resemble the basic operations of hallucination by enabling the perception of objects which are not present or existent, the distinction between genuine madness and its semblance would have been an especially clear and significant one for Lamb, as Adam Phillips points out, given his intensely personal experience of family psychosis.[54]

Otherworldly Encounters

Hallucination is a heuristic – as we have seen with Brontë, much like the analogy of magic – for fiction's power to conjure non-material realities. Putting aside the necessary qualifications, the positive potential of this analogy is to articulate a literary criticism of fictional experience. For Lamb as later for Lewes, the concept (but not diagnosis) of hallucination helps to distinguish between the 'real' as content and quality, as well as to characterise a distinctive type of genius. Much like Lewes's view of Dickens, Lamb's sane 'True Genius' is characterised by the power to represent mental creations with the distinctness or detail of external objects, conferring 'to the wildest dreams [...] the sobrieties of every day occurrences', where the hack would give an ostensibly realistic narrative of 'Bath and Bond-street – a more bewildering dreaminess [...] [than] all the fairy grounds of Spenser'.[55] As the critic Taylor Stoehr has put it, 'two kinds of verisimilitude can be seen lurking in the theoretic background: that which appeals to our *judgment* of the correspondence between a fiction and life, and that which appeals to our *impression* of the lifelikeness of a fiction [...] scarcely a matter of fidelity at all, but rather one of appearance or effect'.[56] The literary critical questions Lamb and Lewes raise through (as they themselves acknowledge) the tenuous and hazardous analogy of 'the action of the imagination in hallucination' concern this distinction between two types of realism, and moreover, how to assess a non-correspondent verisimilitude as an unorthodox literary power.[57]

Play, too, provided a heuristic for theorising an alternative criteria of literary 'genius' founded on the felt reality of fictions. In one useful and less cautionary interpretation of Hartley's play, the resituating of his example in the context of other paracosmic cases prompted a reassessment from his anonymous reviewer in *Bentley's Miscellany*, who returned to the topic with a signed essay for the same periodical in 1866. Francis Jacox's 'About Ejuxria and Gombroon: Glimpses of Day-Dreamland', which includes a speculative canon of 'quasi-Ejuxria or Gombroon' from fiction and biographies (not unlike the first chapter of this book), comes to an explicit conclusion about this form of play as 'an apprenticeship in the author's craft'.[58] In Jacox's reconsidered view, the problem of Hartley 'believing in his own tale' is reconfigured into the author's 'passionate belief in the reality of his every character and incident':

> For genius, when it takes to writing fiction, will more or less vividly, 'realise' to itself the ideal beings it summons into existence. It is not free and happy in its creations, unless it in some sort believe in them [...] The practical

importance is obvious of a certain intensity of belief, on the author's part, in the reality of his creations. If void of such belief himself, he will hardly succeed in impressing a conviction of it on his readers. In proportion to the liveliness of his belief in his characters as real people [...] will greatly depend the degree of interest he can expect to excite in his readers.[59]

Like for Lewes, there is something besides accurate representation, social critique, moralised narrative, or compositional aesthetics which Jacox identifies here as a capacity and goal of fiction (for him, particularly of novel fiction) through the practices of 'Day-Dreamland'. Examples of imaginary worlds enable him to evaluate literature by the 'certain intensity' of what we might again substitute 'experience' instead of 'belief' as a more helpful term; or vividness, concreteness, the 'force of reality'. One need not subscribe to his view about the processes of the authorial mind to recognise, for one, its inversion of hallucinatory logic into literary skill, 'the mind mistaking its own conceptions for real and present existences'; and for another, its according of literary value to the production of such existences.[60]

Through such geniuses – or genii – we return to Vision Island, and to criticism today in its need to recuperate alternative models of literary value. Albeit advancing from significantly different premises, the nineteenth century's pseudo-hallucinatory criticism of fiction presages, and can help to inform, Lowe and Marland's recent work on rehabilitating 'seeing things' as a function of realist fiction which (according to Barthes) ought to have outgrown it. Reading the opening of *Bleak House*, for instance, Marland notes 'how fanatically, fantasmatically visual the passage is – it is, if nothing else, a "vigorous ocular demonstration" [...] caking an impasto as thick as the "crust upon crust of mud"'; or as he otherwise explains it, how the narrator 'mentally rolls [the description] around the tongue of the mind (underneath the eyes of the mind)'.[61] The passage – and the reading – is not only visual but gustatory and somatic, emphasising the sensuous-imaginative function of description apart from its 'structural purpose' in producing a reality effect and 'to sound the theme that will be developed throughout the novel'.[62] Similarly, examples of what Lowe examines and calls 'feminine fiction', a realism attentive to the texture and experience of the everyday, invite the reader to 'enter a realm of sensual and experiential pleasure, a "phantom", as [Charlotte] Brontë calls it, of real experience'.[63] The examples of *hypotyposis* foregrounded by these critics resist Barthes's suggestion that the richly ornamented worlds of realism abstract either into symbolic meaning or into a connotative 'category of "the real" (and not its contingent contents)'.[64] Within the period itself, the capacity for conjuring literary realities (theorised by Lamb, de Vere, Jacox, and Lewes), or the mind's susceptibility to its own illusions (repudiated by other critics and psychologists), exemplify polar opposite views of fiction which both lack any kind of structuralist disenchantment. Rather, such potentials for vision captured the critical imagination with horror or with qualified approval, locating the spectral (but really vicarious) experience of 'seeing things' at the heart of imaginative literature.

What do Victorian novels offer by way of 'detachable set-piece[s]' – through the sensuous-imaginative experience of their fictional spaces and objects?[65] Equipped with the critical perspectives of hallucination and 'hypotyposis', we return from these digressions to the value and uses of the virtual, especially as they deviate from more usual literary functions. Marie-Laure Ryan points out the attractions inherent to what she calls the 'diluted narrative' (a term which James also uses to describe *Middlemarch*), particularly characteristic in nineteenth-century realist novels:

> [T]he plot of diluted narrative competes for attention with nonnarrative elements such as extended description, metanarrative comments, digressions [. . .] the text of diluted narrativity invites [the reader] to linger on the scene, to step outside narrative time. The reader is less concerned with finding out how the story ends than visualising the setting, experiencing its atmosphere, and achieving intimacy with the minds of characters.[66]

There are of course a host of other concerns which, as Leavis remarked, readers ought to 'demand of a novel' – through various forms of more 'critical' reading – than wallowing diffusively in the fictional world or narrowly following the story. Yet as Lowe too suggests, there is something more to be gained by reimagining Eliot's *Scenes of Clerical Life* as a fairground ride or fly-through sequence, allowing the reader or critic a turn at the various domestic comforts on offer: 'You are invited imaginatively, phantom-sensuously, to join Tina in playing with the medicine bottle [. . .] in strolling in the garden [. . .] [with] sensuous participation; we can choose the easiness of chair, the peculiar flavour of tobacco, the very physical attitude of the vicar'.[67]

These fantasmatic sideshows of narrative can distract, 'compet[ing] for attention' with the novel's purpose to communicate something significant or representative about the world; but as we have seen again and again, the experience of vicariously being 'in' or 'with' the virtual realities of fiction can have its own distinctive uses.[68] 'Think of what this implies!' Lewes concludes about his theory of Dickens. 'Think how little the mass of men are given to reflect on their impressions, and how their minds are for the most part occupied with sensations rather than ideas, and you will see why Dickens held an undisputed sway'.[69] Bodenheimer and Stolte are right to point out this 'implication' as a patronising judgement on Dickens and his readers, followed and exacerbated by a return to the language of mechanism and artifice. But Lewes's terms of deprecation also articulate the particularity, even advantages, of the artificial:

> Give a child a wooden horse, with hair for mane and tail, and wafer-spots for colouring, he will never be disturbed by the fact that this horse does not move its legs, but runs on wheels – the general suggestion suffices for his belief; and this wooden horse, which he can handle and draw, is believed in more than a pictured horse by a Wouvermanns or an Ansdell. It may be said of Dickens's human figures that they too are wooden, and run on wheels [...] Just as the wooden horse is brought within the range of the child's emotions, and dramatizing tendencies, when he can handle and draw it, so Dickens's figures are brought within the range of the reader's interests[.][70]

As this book argues, play is not an analogy for a naïve or immature way of reading, but an alternative approach to fiction alive to both its distinction from reality and the usefulness of that distinction. On the one hand, Lewes appears to use the toy horse as an analogy for Dickens's 'wooden' figures in the idiomatic, deprecating sense of 'Lacking grace, liveliness', 'Mentally dull', or 'Of inferior character'; and to use the playing child to show up an uncritical reader's lowered sufficiency for 'belief'.[71] On the other hand, his comparison also implies some of the advantages of the vivid but unrealistic toy: that the horse 'runs on wheels' allows the child to 'handle and draw it' (an interactivity which Lewes repeatedly emphasises) in a way that a more realistically 'pictured horse', or in fact a real horse, cannot.

Woodenness and wheels, in this sense, signify not dullness and limitation but materiality and functionality. Analogously, Dickens's fictions mobilise 'the reader's interests' and their 'dramatizing tendencies' in ways an accurate but less tangible realism might not, thereby offering an experience of the real more easily handled (and more rewarding) in miniature. In the following reading of *Little Dorrit*, I explore the experience and functionality of fictions as objects through Dickens's own novel of hallucination. In this text, characters recurrently fail to understand their implication in the moralised or thematic patterns of the novel, because they are distracted by 'that most pleasant but pernicious practice' of 'castle-building'.[72] They do not see disasters approaching in their life-stories because they are busy visualising the details of a mental construction, often about their future lives, whose imagined concreteness is already so absorbing that it forecloses the possibility (or blinds them to the impossibility) of its material realisation. The symbolic culmination of this theme is in fact represented by a mental breakdown, where the elderly Mr Dorrit loses all consciousness of his material surroundings to the vision of an imagined environment.

Little Dorrit has therefore been read as Dickens's most Foucauldian text, in which the private retreats of subjectivity always belie and abet one's incarceration within larger formal structures. But as I have been arguing, being fooled or interpolated are not the only uses of fantasy, and as Lewes is right to point out in spite of his ambivalences, the abstract and schematic are not the right rubrics for assessing Dickens's fiction. Although the novel appears to replicate both modern and historical fears about the entrapments of subjective illusion, it is also a novel which is insistently and sensuously detailed, realising its and its characters' fictions with extensive specificity. Besides Mr Dorrit, other characters also take hope or refuge in imagined environments – particularly buildings and interiors – which accompany and help them to manage their experiences of actual circumstance. The emotional usefulness of such projections for Amy Dorrit and Young John Chivery, like the analogous experience of the novel itself, depend on their acknowledged status as concretely sensible but explicitly fictitious objects; real but not actual. Mr Dorrit might choose a toy over a Wouvermanns because he has become unable to tell which is more like a real horse; but others may do so because they know which kind of object affords more fantasmatic solidity, pleasure, and resources for survival.

LITTLE DORRIT

In the opening scene of Dickens's *Little Dorrit*, the prisoner John Baptist Cavalletto projects the geography of southern Europe onto the floor of his cell. Drawn with his finger (and no ink), the invisible map is both expansive ('Spain over there, Algiers over *there*') and improbably precise, apparently capable even of representing the cell itself:

> 'How can I say? I always know what the hour is, and where I am [...] See here, my master! Civita Vecchia, Leghorn, Porto Fino, Genoa, Cornice, Off Nice (which is in there), Marseilles, you and me. The apartment of the jailer and his keys is where I put this thumb; and here at my wrist they keep the national razor in its case – the guillotine locked up.'[73]

The play of scales in this opening, integrating the cramped locality of the cell within the wider world beyond, seems to offer a metaphor for the novel's structure of the novel. Cavalletto's top-down representation of his own imprisonment within a massive, abstract design strikingly presages what Philip Collins has determined as 'not merely a critical commonplace but the obvious main approach to the novel', most prominently advanced by Lionel Trilling, that *Little Dorrit* is 'marked not so much by its powers of particularization as by its powers of generalization and abstraction [...] under the dominion of a great articulated idea'.[74] The subject of the novel is 'borne in upon us by the informing symbol, or emblem, of the book, which is the prison' as it manifests literally (in the case of Cavalletto, the Dorrits, and later Arthur Clennam) and metaphorically through 'persons and classes being imprisoned by their notions of predestined fate or of religious duty, or by their occupations, their life-schemes, their ideas of themselves, their very habits of language'.[75] Edmund Wilson similarly argues that 'the fable is [...] of imprisoning states of mind as much as [...] of oppressive institutions'; as does Hillis Miller after him, that the prison has 'a religious or metaphysical meaning for Dickens as well as a psychological or social one [...] linking physical imprisonment and imprisoning states of the soul'.[76]

The contention I want now to take up is not with this interpretation,[77] but with the systematic legibility it makes of the novel as a 'great articulated idea'. There seems little which the novel invites us (or at least, critics) to 'see' in its fictions than their thematic connection to each other and collective subordination to a grand design; little of what James and Ryan call diffuseness, or Barthes 'the irreducible residues of functional analysis'.[78] In its polemic against bureaucratic redundancy and red-tape, the novel appears itself almost utilitarian about its components: John Holloway marvels that 'in the end, there are no gaps left in [the novel's] pattern: everything is related to everything else', an economical tightness which Collins points out as an explicit authorial intention, expressed in Dickens's letters to John Forster, to make the subplots of 'Society, the Circumlocution Office, and Mr Gowan [...] three parts of the one idea and design', and of 'making the introduced story [of Miss Wade] fit into surroundings impossible of separation from the main story'.[79] In his manuscript plans, Dickens wrote and double-underlined the note '*Parallel Imprisonments*', almost overdetermining the critical case.[80] The curious effect of this visible workmanship is that, much as the characters are physically or psychologically locked up, they also seem trapped in a rigid narrative scheme and lacking, as Trilling notes, the 'autonomous life' of the typical Dickensian fiction, appearing 'to be the fruit of conscious intention rather than of free creation'.[81] Cavalletto's map, as an analogy of the novel, is the antithesis of George Orwell's aphorism that Dickens is 'all fragments, all details – rotten architecture, but wonderful gargoyles'; rather, the picture it suggests of *Little Dorrit* is that of a meticulous prison floorplan.[82]

But Cavalletto's map is also something else, not meticulous but excessive, unplanned but perhaps inevitable: a virtual object in the local scene of the cell. In a kind of metaleptic encounter between representational and represented space, Cavalletto discovers while drawing that 'there's no room for Naples [...] he had got to the wall by this time' (*LD* 6). Itself taking up 'room', the abstract map exerts its own concreteness by bumping up against the (itself fictional) cell, and its creator's resignation that 'it's all one; it's in there!' (6) only highlights the imperfect fit of a mental object into their specified physical space. If maps and blueprints encourage a top-down, structural view, Cavalletto's map brings us jarringly back into a cramped locality, vicariously stubbing our finger. Moreover, with Cavalletto's fellow prisoner Rigaud, who he repeatedly exhorts to 'See here [...] See here, my master!' the map's presence on the floor also passes into an intersubjective reality:

> Cavalletto sat down on the pavement, holding one of his ankles in each hand, and smoking peacefully. There seemed to be some uncomfortable attraction of Monsieur Rigaud's eyes to the immediate neighbourhood of that part of the pavement where the thumb had been in the plan. They were so drawn in that direction, that the Italian more than once followed them to and back from the pavement in some surprise. (9)

Cavalletto is comically surprised by the fact that, having emphatically made Rigaud look at his creation, the other prisoner continues to see – for his own reasons, attaching his own significance to – something which Cavalletto himself has stopped imagining. The narration too takes this perspective of someone for whom there is no longer anything to see, only 'the immediate neighbourhood of that part of the pavement where the thumb had been in the plan' (9); for Rigaud, however, the spot evidently continues to mark out the location of 'the jailer and his keys' (6). The trouble is again that the map is more present, more concrete, and more distracting than its original function requires, transforming from a design into a miniature, an object invested vicariously with Rigaud's desire for freedom.

The characters of *Little Dorrit* are recurrently side-tracked by designs which turn into fictions, by abstract conjectures or plans which materialise in the present as fantasy. They prefer or tend to experience such imaginary objects as external and concrete – sometimes pathologically, sometimes not – in a different and more perverse engagement with fictions than the structural or the symbolic, and I suggest this to be an alternative perspective on the fictions of the novel itself. The opening chapter, for instance, calls to be interpreted as narrative foreshadowing for the series of literal and metaphorical prisons that follow in the novel (including, in the next chapter, the quarantine barracks); and as a schematisation of the prison or of 'imprisoning states of the soul'. In Rigaud and Cavalletto's cell, imprisonment is abstract and universal, applicable to anything and available anywhere:

> The imprisoned air, the imprisoned light, the imprisoned damps, the imprisoned men, were all deteriorated by confinement. [...] Like a well, like a vault, like a tomb, the prison had no knowledge of the brightness outside, and would have kept its polluted atmosphere intact in one of the spice islands of the Indian ocean. (*LD* 2–5)

This is the mode of deterioration the novel would again reveal through Mrs Clennam in her sickroom, Amy and Mr Dorrit in the Marshalsea, Miss Wade in her mental self-torment, and so on, through different but interchangeable contexts 'Like a well, like a vault, like a tomb'. Imprisonment in this collective sense is a social or spiritual state, to be subject to something like 'the diagram of a mechanism of power reduced to its ideal form [...] a pure architectural and optical system [...] a figure of political technology that may and must be detached from any specific use'.[83] Just as Foucault sees the formal structure of Bentham's Panopticon at work in hospitals, schools, and society at large, Dickens extrapolates the degradations of the Marseille prison all over; as the Leavises puts it, 'The prison is the world of 'the mind-forg'd manacles' [...] it is Society with a big S'.[84]

But like Rigaud with Cavalletto's map, we can be distracted from an intentional design by its details; by imagining these prisons individually through the material specificities which the novel's realism provides in excess of its abstract, signifying functions. The Marseille cell is not only filled with 'imprisoned air' and a 'polluted atmosphere' (*LD* 2), with the nebulous stuff of a carceral relation replicated universally, but with signs of life (however degraded): 'a draught-board rudely hacked upon [a bench] with a knife, a set of draughts, made of old buttons and soup bones, a set of dominoes, two mats, and two or three wine bottles' (2). Rigaud has been sleeping on 'a broad strong ledge of stone [...] three or four feet above the ground' under a grated window, and Cavalletto on the other side of the cell 'on the stone floor, covered with a coarse brown coat' (2). These are not exactly the domestic comforts Eliot invites us to imagine in the vicar's armchair and tobacco, but it is nonetheless a vivid insistence on the fictional lives of these characters as they have lived in this specific fictional place, with their needs for sustenance, entertainment, and places to lean and lie. In 'Seeing' his characters, George Gissing wrote, Dickens 'saw the house in which they lived, the table at which they ate, and all the little habits of their day-to-day life'.[85] If these 'little habits' tend not to matter in the narrative and social system which will unfold from this initial cell, for Cavalletto himself, they are worth vicariously and sensuously imagining:

> Perhaps [Cavalletto] glanced at the Lyons sausage, and perhaps he glanced at the veal in savoury jelly, but they were not there long, to make his mouth water; Monsieur Rigaud soon dispatched them [...] and proceeded to suck his fingers as clean as he could, and to wipe them on his vine leaves. Then, as he paused in his drink to contemplate his fellow-prisoner, his moustache went up, and his nose came down.
> 'How do you find the bread?'
> 'A little dry, but I have my old sauce here', returned John Baptist, holding up his knife.
> 'How sauce?'
> 'I can cut my bread so – like a melon. Or so – like an omelette. Or so – like a fried fish. Or so – like Lyons sausage', said John Baptist, demonstrating the various cuts on the bread he held, and soberly chewing what he had in his mouth. (8)

These fantasmatic pleasures are poor substitutes for Rigaud's meal, just as the invisible miniature of a jailer's key stands in poorly for the actual key, but they matter for extending the severely limited scope of these characters' experiences. Life, Cavalletto suggests, requires imaginative complement or sustenance, a sauce to go with the 'daily bread' allotted by the larger systems which govern material existence.[86] Moreover, Cavalletto's feast and map are doubles for the novel's own practice of creating imaginary things – for the reader's encounter with its 'sausage of Lyons, veal in savoury jelly, white bread, strachino choose, and good wine' (6) – which affords not only sober chewing but vicarious responses of perception and appetite.

At stake in recognising the 'autonomous life' of fictional spaces, lives, and objects, as they assert themselves through unnecessarily sensuous details, is what the novel has to offer in addition to a representation or scrutiny of life: a reparative extension thereof. If the 'conscious intention' of Dickens's novel is continually to reveal the barrenness of its world as a system of oppressive relations, in the *richness* with which it represents this world, the experience of the novel itself is anything but barren. Criticism of the Victorian novel requires more emphatic attention to this kind of conflict between the interpretation of the novel as literature and its experience as fiction, because the latter affords a practical, alternative use of the form as a tool of imaginative living. What the opening chapter of the Marseille prison represents thematically, as the first of many prisons in the narrative, or representationally as a reflection of society, is complicated by its specificity and concreteness as a fictional space containing fictional objects. Visualising this space, tasting its food, or feeling the hardness of its mats might be all 'beside the point', pulling us temporarily 'outside narrative time' and logic, but the novel also draws attention to such distractions through suggestive examples of its characters' own imaginative practices.[87] As we will see in the similar but more extensive case of Mr Dorrit, Dickens can be ambivalent about the value of such practices, but also recognises it as an alternative capacity of the novel – to enrich the real through the fantasmatic – from its systematic prosecution of a social critique.

Mr Dorrit and the Castle in the Air

The pair of consecutive chapters which narrate the final days of *Little Dorrit*'s tragic father figure, William Dorrit, are titled after an intangible, spatial metaphor which, as Barbara Hardy has argued, forms 'a local structure for his death-scene'.[88] In 'A Castle in the Air' and 'The Storming of the Castle in the Air', freed from decades of imprisonment in debtors' prison with a newfound wealth and position, Mr Dorrit travels from London to Rome absorbed in this figurative activity:

> On again by the heavy French roads for Paris [...] Mr Dorrit, in his snug corner, fell to castle-building as he rode along. It was evident that he had a very large castle in hand. All day long he was running towers up, taking towers down, adding a wing here, putting on a battlement there, looking to the walls, strengthening the defences, giving ornamental touches to the interior, making in all respects a superb castle of it [...]
> Building away with all his might, but reserving the plans of his castle exclusively for his own eye, Mr Dorrit posted away for Marseilles. Building on, building on, busily, busily, from morning to night. Falling asleep, and leaving great blocks of building materials dangling in the air; waking again, to resume work and get them into their places. (*LD* 614, 616)

Building a castle in the air – alongside variants like *in the clouds, in the sky, in Spain*, or its simple contraction into *castle-building* – has been idiomatic since the sixteenth century for the act of imagining a 'visionary project or scheme, day-dream, idle fancy'.[89] The extended use of the expression in 'A Castle in the Air' certainly conforms to this meaning in its suggestion that Mr Dorrit is preoccupied with planning the social transformation and future of his family, and more specifically, with a proposal to the snobbish Mrs General: during his stopover in Paris, Mr Dorrit interrupts his journey to purchase two pieces of jewellery – a 'love-gift' and a 'nuptial offering' – which 'plainly got up his castle now to a loftier altitude than the two square towers of Notre Dame' (616).

In a novel with multiple plots involving disastrous speculations, the expression's connotations of unrealistic fantasy bodes ill for this projected marriage plot. As a *narrative* 'structure', the castle embodies the narrative expectations precariously set up by Mr Dorrit himself, unendorsed by the narrator, in what Ryan would describe as a deviation of the 'text actual world' – the real plot as it will unfold – from its versions in the 'dreams, fictions, and fantasies conceived or told by characters [...] plans, passive projections, desires, beliefs'.[90] Hardy argues such projections and deviations to be characteristic of the novel as a whole:

> Dickens concentrates on acts of forecast and fantasy, both conscious and unconscious, as micro-narratives in a subtle cellular structure composed on inner anticipations and retrospects [...] Like all good novelists he does two things at the same time: he prefigures future action in what Henry James in the Preface to *The Tragic Muse* called the art of preparations, and he also imagines individual imaginations as his characters look ahead realistically or fancifully [...] [with] subtle and unpredictable continuities and discontinuities.[91]

But this emphasis on imaginative lives as part of the 'cellular structure' of a narrative design, another means by which characters are 'imprisoned by their notions of predestined fate [...] their life-schemes, their ideas of themselves', overlooks another sense in which Mr Dorrit becomes imprisoned by his castle as it transforms into a literal vision of the past.[92] As well as explicitly representing Mr Dorrit's expectations and implicitly preparing him for a fall – so, in fact, doing three things at once – 'The Storming of the Castle in the Air' also evokes the expression's new, nineteenth-century associations with a 'most pleasant but pernicious practice', a precursor to hallucination.[93]

As an *architectural* 'structure', the danger of Mr Dorrit's fantasy is ultimately not the unrealism of forecast but of mental misperception and breakdown. Like Cavalletto's map, the plans abstractly represented by the aerial castle begin to assert a material presence in the fictional space of the scene, to more serious consequences than Rigaud's 'uncomfortable attention' to an invisible map. On the way to a high society dinner at a Roman villa, Mr Dorrit is found 'at his building work again'; midway through the meal, this work unexpectedly culminates in a persistent image of the Marshalsea debtors' prison which overtakes his awareness of the (fictionally) real surroundings. Mentally transforming dinner guests into fellow prisoners and 'The broad stairs of his Roman palace' into 'the narrow stairs of his London prison', this eventually fatal episode echoes contemporary cautionary narratives about 'seeing things' through the imagination. Just as Prichard warned in 1822, over-dwelling on mental images has 'carr[ied] him away from the influence of his external perceptions, and [...] environed him with visions of unreal scenes'.[94] Mr Dorrit is imprisoned within his own delusional creation until his death, when the device of the castle and the prison are conflated and dispensed with in symbolic and grammatical parallel: as the inescapable past and the unrealisable future disappear together with his passing, 'Quietly, quietly, all the lines of the plan of the great Castle melted one after another [...] Quietly, quietly, the reflected marks of the prison bars and of the zig-zag iron on the wall-top, faded away' (*LD* 631). The wrapping-up of this episode, mirroring and reversing its initial construct of Mr Dorrit 'Building on, building on, busily, busily' (616), morphs the cultural idiom and local motif of the castle into the novel's central image of the prison, integrating the lines and zig-zags of 'a local structure' back into the greater, overarching plotline.[95]

But it is necessary to untidy this virtuosic handling of a motif, in its multiple meanings of unrealistic forecast, narrative foreshadowing, and psychological symptom – *because at no point does Mr Dorrit ever literally picture a castle*. The neatness of the disappearing 'lines' disguises a snag in the symbolic 'plan' of these chapters: Mr Dorrit's vision of the Marshalsea, even as it is absent in a British expatriate's dining room in Rome, is not the same as – not even unreal in the same way as – his castle in the air, a figure of speech for his idealism. Mr Dorrit's plans for the future, as they are implied through narrative clues, do not appear to involve construction of any kind. That the narrative builds up an extensive catalogue of 'towers', 'wing', 'battlement', 'walls', 'defences', and 'ornamental touches' (614), expanding, materialising, and visualising the figurative castle in the air, in fact diverts attention away from the character's actual thoughts while metaphorising his mental processes; besides a nominal comparison between the two gifts and 'the two square towers of Notre Dame' (616), it hardly seems likely that each architectural component specified has some direct correspondent in Mr Dorrit's scheme for social climbing. Yet the language insists on appealing to the proprioceptive and kinaesthetic – senses of space, direction, and weight – encouraging an experience of the castle not as a moralising idiom but as imagined object and area, running 'up' and 'down', 'here' and 'there', consisting of an 'interior', and even 'dangling in the air' (616). This overdetermined detailing of the aerial castle as a thing in itself, especially as it foreshadows the misperception in the following chapter, obscures the fact that it is constructed not in the diegetic reality (including within diegetic minds) but alongside it, within the mind of the reader.

When we think of the castle in the air as an imagined space like the hallucinated prison, as the novel's prose prompts us to do, we become implicated in our own episode of 'seeing things' which Mr Dorrit does not in fact share (he is busy considering remarriage), but which offers a sympathetic perspective on his later breakdown (narrated largely from the outside). Readerly fantasy can itself be discontinuous with the narrative proper, distracted or misled not only by the dreams of characters but by our own excessively sensuous imagination, our own creative energy blurring the distinctions between realities even of abstract figures of speech. As Stoehr argues, Dickens's figurative language derives a 'dream-like, hallucinatory, super-real' quality when it crosses metaleptically from the world of the novel into the different fictional world of the extended metaphor:

> The completeness and inner consistency of the metaphor, as it is extended and expanded to constitute a world in itself, seem to lift the figure out of the realm of metaphor altogether. We believe in the metaphor as though it were not a metaphor at all [...] figures have transcended metaphor to become dreamlike amalgams of object and feeling.[96]

Stoehr's argument revolves around the 'storming' of another prison – the Bastille in *A Tale of Two Cities* – but his account of metaphors 'extended and expanded' into worlds is particularly apt for describing *Little Dorrit*'s transformation of the castle in the air from colloquial figure into the kind of three-dimensional, perceivable space that Mr Dorrit experiences through madness.[97] Much as in the novel's opening chapter, Dickens brings the imaginative practices of his characters into analogy with the experience of the novel, for better or worse, by juxtaposing levels of imagined concreteness: the invisible map bumps into the fictional cell, the figurative castle morphs into the hallucinatory prison. Far from the 'powers of generalization and abstraction' Trilling perceives in the novel, Dickens recurrently demonstrates the ways in which the imagination (literary or non-literary) is drawn almost inevitably to making spaces and solids concrete.[98]

The organisation of these chapters around a figure of speech – the castle in the air – suggests language's particular role in this tendency to make experiential 'sense' of meaning. While characters within the novel draw, sculpt, and daydream their fictional objects, the novel's own exemplary transformation of the abstract into the concrete is embodied through an expression which seems inherently given to this process. The expression most likely originated from a sermon by Augustine which, as Auerbach has argued, addressed 'the problem of figuration' to exhort 'a literal-historical reading' of Biblical narrative: 'believe that what has been read to you actually happened as read, or else the foundation of an actual event will be removed [from the moral lesson], and you will be trying to build castles in the air'.[99] In a sense, the expression's later life in nineteenth-century English is unchanged from this original usage in their shared implication that ideals collapse without a foundation in actuality.[100] In another sense, however, Augustine's sermon also 'emphatically rejected those who would interpret Holy Scripture in a purely allegorical way', advocating a reading of religious narratives as accounts of material events.[101] This secondary meaning of the expression – an insistence to concretise language – introduces unintended ambiguities to its later and more narrow usage as a moralisation against imaginary objects, for instance, in Forbes Winslow's 1842 treatise *On the Preservation of the Health of Body and Mind*:

> The habit of what in common parlance is termed 'building castles in the air', has a most pernicious influence upon the health of the mind [...] when the fancy is allowed 'to body forth the form of things unknown', without being under proper discipline, much evil will result. Individuals endowed

with an unhealthy expansion of the imagination, create a world within themselves, in which the mind revels until all consciousness of the reality that surround them is lost.[102]

The passage is another formulaic diagnosis of psychological danger, complete with an allusion to Theseus and to the perniciousness of common habits, but Winslow's language also presages Stoehr and *Little Dorrit* in prompting us to suspect something literal about his reference to 'castles in the air', especially as it stands in relation to a spatial metaphor, 'an unhealthy expansion', and a description of hallucinatory space, 'a world within'. Much like in Dickens's novel, a proprioceptive sense of the castle attaches onto its figurative uses to denote acts of sensory unreality; as if, in memory of its philological origins, it inherently defies reduction into allegory.

While it is clear that most nineteenth-century usages of this phrase do not consciously refer to a fictional construction within imagined space, this slippage occurs remarkably often, especially when it is used (as it frequently was) to describe the real-but-not-actual experience of paracosmic play. 'All children who are forbidden by their rank, education, or clean pinafores, to make dirt-pies', writes a reviewer for *Fraser's Magazine*, 'indulge in the building of air-castles; but we never knew or heard of so persevering an architect as young Hartley'.[103] In speaking as if the difference were not only between mental and physical forms of play, but between the material substances involved – respectable children can avoid dirtying their clothes by using air instead of earth – does this review speak figuratively? Or do they take Hartley for literally imagining fictional structures (which he did), just as children literally make dirt-pies? The expression intrinsically blurs this distinction, compounded by the fact that (as we have seen on Vision Island) children do in fact delight to play at building: *The New Monthly Magazine*'s article on Jameson compares her to 'Hartley Coleridge with his dreamland Ejuxria, [and] Thomas de Quincey with his dreamland Gombroon', noting how she similarly 'imagined new worlds, and peopled them with life, and crowded them with air-castles, and constructed for the denizens [. . .] carefully evolved adventures'.[104] Embedded within a list of *fictional* activities literally performed (the creation of worlds, characters, and adventures), the *figurative* castle is functionally an abstraction for imaginative habit, but also difficult not to 'see' as something a character might inhabit in Ejuxria or Gombroon.

In its combination of the abstract and the sensuous, of transparency and tangibility, the aerial castle is a paradigmatic object of 'hypotyposis'; the antithesis to Davis's 'house in the novel' for which 'there is no "there" for a "there" to be'.[105] Its virtual presence in *Little Dorrit* – and not even in the world of *Little Dorrit* – exemplifies the power of language to conjure the reality of a 'there' as Dickens exercises it in an ambivalent reflection on fiction's less abstracting functions; ambivalent because Mr Dorrit is the novel's most prominent and deeply compromised analogy for such fantasmatic experiences. His sensuous over-investment in abstract plans, at the expense of his perception of the here-and-now, is mimetically doubled by the readerly temptation to build worlds out of an extended figure of speech; both we and Mr Dorrit become too distracted by particularities, too fixated on materialising details, to observe the 'text actual world' which surrounds him:

> *Not a fortified town* that they passed in all their journey was as strong, *not a Cathedral summit* was as high, as Mr Dorrit's castle. *Neither the Saone nor the Rhone* sped with the swiftness of that peerless building; *nor was the Mediterranean* deeper than its foundations; *nor were the distant landscapes* on the Cornice road, *nor the hills and bay* of Genoa the Superb, more beautiful. (*LD* 616, emphasis added)

The mechanics of descriptive attention in these two chapters, by capitalising on the attraction of imagining details both in the novel and in the mind of its character, model Platonic or psychological anxieties about misperceiving imaginary objects for real ones. Those habits which for Cavalletto provide the 'sauce' to life, adding an imagined dimension to material experience, becomes a mutually excluding relation wherein the real and unreal compete to be perceived: for every proliferating tower or ornament of the figurative castle, 'Not a fortified town [...] not a Cathedral summit [...] Neither the Saone nor the Rhone' (for the reader, of course, the passage oscillates between the imagined world of the idiom and the imagined world of the narrative). The tendency of abstract plans or language to assume a concrete presence no longer collides with a stone wall which reasserts the greater solidity of the diegetic world, but blots it out as hallucination.

The case of Mr Dorrit comes to represent the novel's paranoid position about projections (predictive and sensory), wherein the imagination's richness is revealed to be a mode of impoverishment, and its capacity for escapism as an imprisoning state of mind. The novel's titular heroine, Amy Dorrit, similarly experiences visions and misgivings which negate experiences of the world around her: while travelling through Italy, passing through deliberately unspecified environments of 'splendid rooms', 'heaps of wonders', 'great churches', and 'miles of palaces' (453), Amy finds that 'all she saw appeared unreal; the more surprising the scenes, the more they resembled the unreality of her own inner life' (451). Like her father's, her imagination is also dominated by visions which become inverse-proportionally real to her: 'the old room, and the old inmates, and the old visitors: all lasting realities that had never changed' (454). In another exemplification of hallucinatory logic, inner and outer worlds grow to resemble each other, and threaten to exchange places.[106]

Yet Mr Dorrit is not the novel's representative nor final case for the potential effects of investment in imaginary objects; he is not even the last to build mental pictures of the Marshalsea. His narrative moralises the dangers of realising the imagined with too much detail and force, of mistaking the inner world for the outer, but Dickens nonetheless maintains the value of experiencing fiction, for one, as explicitly fictional; and for another, in more than a 'vague schematic way'.[107] In Amy's own carriage-dreaming, and in Young John Chivery's plan to domesticate the debtors' prison, the novel returns from its case of hallucination back to more complementary relations between imagined and material life. Like Mr Dorrit, both Amy and John are in some way mistaken or disappointed in their fantasies of the present or future; but rather than diminishing their perceptions, the practice of imagining rooms and objects helps them to express constructive responses to circumstance. Through the castle in the air, the novel demonstrates the autonomous force of fictional realities with 'all the salient details obtruding themselves on [. . .] attention', embodied to its logical extreme by the tragedy of Mr Dorrit.[108] Through these other examples of characters sensuously imagining alternate worlds or lives, Dickens draws a more subtle distinction between artificial experience and delusional belief, pulling back (as Lewes would do) from an example of madness to an account of fiction's capacity to produce unrealistic, but useful images.

Playing Prison-House

Amy, appearing to suffer from an early stage of her father's condition, cannot help but look at Venice 'as if, in the general vision, it might run dry, and show her the prison again' (*LD* 454).[109] But in addition to the Marshalsea, which continually intrudes into her awareness as hiding underwater or behind mountains, she also envisions – and chooses to envision – other, more consoling fantasies of rooms where she and Arthur Clennam had shared warm encounters. She describes them to Clennam as idle and inexplicable visions, but her motives for seeing these specific places clearly derive from their affectionate association with him:

> I often felt [...] as if Mrs Clennam's room where I have worked so many days, and where I first saw you, must be just beyond that snow. Do you remember one night when I came with Maggy to your lodging in Covent Garden? That room I have often and often fancied I have seen before me, travelling along for miles by the side of our carriage, when I have looked out of the carriage-window after dark. (456)

The appearance of these rooms, suspended over the changing landscapes of the moving carriage, echo the aerial castle and forebode the hallucinatory prison. Investing her longings in these rooms, she not only reflects on their memories but fancies to 'see' them, rebuilding them in the dark and snow which recalls the dimness of the Clennam House and the cold night of her visit to Covent Garden. Unlike for her father, however, her sensuous engagement with such visions does not involve belief; they are neither plans for the future nor delusions about the present. Rather, in their explicit unreality, they are a way of confronting the reality of her desire for Clennam. His presence is brought impossibly out of time and space, affording an experience she knows to be wildly untrue, like the 'detachable set-piece' of Barthes's rhetoricians, for whose purposes of fantasmatic experiencing there need be 'no hesitation to put lions or olive trees in a northern country'.[110]

If the seeming omnipresence of the prison suggests the replication of its conditions everywhere in a 'world of "the mind-forg'd manacles"', by the same token, Amy's portable vision allows her to take consolation anywhere.[111] The thing that floats outside her window is not an accurate nor inaccurate projection, realistic nor unrealistic plan, nor (despite the distinctness of its vision) a hallucination that occludes her awareness of actual surroundings; it is a mental miniature or toy, a semblance which makes the original more accessible by remaking it as artifice. It is this kind of object, too, which novels can provide through the vicarious experience of their material details. If *Little Dorrit* is a novel constructed 'under the dominion of a great articulated idea', or composed within 'a subtle cellular structure', it is also one which offers relief, through the richness and vividness of the reading experience, from one's continual implication in the truths of material reality.[112] The clarity with which Amy sees and dwells on her floating rooms does not derive its value from a '*judgment* of the correspondence between a fiction and life', but from its combination of 'lifelikeness' and non-correspondence; a palpable vision which does not solicit belief.[113]

The difference between these models of sensuous projection, between the virtual or fictional and the hallucinatory or Platonic, is embodied finally in the case of Young John Chivery. John, whose unrequited love for Amy forms another recurring motif in the novel, contemplates his plans for marriage through his own castle in the air. Like Mr Dorrit, his obsession with idealising this future produces an image of 'the prison again' (*LD* 454); unlike Mr Dorrit, however, he is literally imagining the 'ornamental touches' (614) he wishes to put onto the prison as an architectural space, in a true conflation of narrative figure and character fantasy:

> Young John had considered the object of his attachment in all its lights and shades. Following it out to its blissful results [...] Say things prospered, and they were united. [...] Say he became a resident turnkey. She would officially succeed to the chamber she had rented for so long. There was a beautiful propriety in that. It looked over the wall, if you stood on tip-toe; and, with a trellis-work of scarlet beans and a canary or so, would become a very Arbour. There was a charming idea in that [...] with the Arbour above, and the Lodge below; they would glide down the stream of time, in pastoral domestic happiness. Young John drew tears from his eyes by finishing the picture with a tombstone in the adjoining churchyard, close against the prison wall, bearing the follow touching inscription: 'Sacred to the Memory Of JOHN CHIVERY, Sixty years Turnkey, and fifty years Head Turnkey [...] Also of his truly beloved and truly loving wife, AMY, whose maiden name was DORRIT, Who survived his loss not quite forty-eight hours['.] (206)

The passage requires quotation at length because it really does describe a multi-dimensional fantasy 'in all its lights and shades', combining time and space, text and vision, putting 'the Arbour above, and the Lodge below' while travelling 'down the stream of time' towards a 'finishing [...] picture' of their epitaphs. In the sense that John can already mentally occupy this space – drawing tears from his eyes, satisfaction from its 'charming idea' – his vision is both fantasy and forecast, valued as much for its predictive or preparatory nature as for the arrangement and construction already performed. It is both a plan or road-map for the future and a concrete, sensuous world which he has realised to himself in the present, and to the reader as a reality produced through description. Neither need wait for the actual 'blissful results' to 'see' them already assuming a detailed existence as a fictional object in the fictional world of the novel.

In another pointed example of the novel's many disappointed expectations – the personal and fluctuating prolepses which Hardy notes as a means of characterisation and narrative structure – John's hopes are quickly dashed by actuality. Yet, because of its vividness as a fiction, the *world* of his hopes survives this collapse of its misguided conjectural value. After Amy's rejection of his advances, John continues to imagine his future Marshalsea, not as a delusion in the face of harsh reality, but as an extended space for experiencing its harshness. Although it is unclear what happens (for instance) to the canary or the trellis of beans, immediately following his rebuff, the text on the tombstone is revised: John composes 'the following new inscription [. . .] "Here lie the mortal remains OF JOHN CHIVERY, Never anything worth mentioning, Who died about the end of the year [1826], Of a broken heart, Requesting with his last breath that the word AMY might be inscribed over his ashes, which was accordingly directed to be done, By his afflicted Parents"' (*LD* 213). As John does not in fact die within the year, this turns out to be no more accurate as a forecast than the first, touching picture – but to evaluate it by those terms is of course to misread the point of the new inscription as an immaterial monument to his disappointment. Much as his vision of domestic happiness was already satisfying in itself, his composition of a fictional tombstone suggests the vicarious emotional value of visualising his grief through a projection in imagined space, as one of Dickens's 'dreamlike amalgams of object and feeling'.[114] Like Amy herself, John holds on to visions which he knows to be unreal and untrue, but whose experience of detail nonetheless provides a real outlet for working through the painful exigencies of the real.

The fantasy world of Young John Chivery is the most explicit in the novel of what characters can *do* with fantasy objects. John is a decidedly minor character, relegated to his small corner of the novel's geographically and socially expansive narrative, whose choices (when he has any) rarely make real differences to the world in which he finds himself. Yet unlike more central characters like Mr Dorrit, who ultimately can do little with the real resources they have, John makes strategic use of his imaginary objects. His inner world, which begins as a plan of action to then become indulgently realised into fantasy, finally bears a different relation to life and action when it reappears, near the end of the novel, as he nobly aids Amy and Clennam to realise their love for each other. John falls asleep 'after composing and arranging the following monumental inscription on his pillow':

> Stranger! Respect the tomb of John Chivery, Junior, who died at an advanced age not necessary to mention. He encountered his rival, in a distressed state, and felt inclined to have a round with him; But, for the sake of the loved one, conquered those feelings of bitterness, and became magnanimous. (*LD* 714)

Playing Prison-House

What John demonstrates is not the ability to turn his plans into reality, or to forecast the direction of events – in one way or another, almost all of the characters fail to do so – but the ability to transform foiled expectations into a counterfactual (technically, counterfictional) reality, a miniature of the novel's world over which he asserts a kind of authorial autonomy alongside (and perhaps sometimes against) Dickens's narration.[115] The triumph of John Chivery, in the grand scheme of *Little Dorrit*'s globetrotting ambitions, consists of this reparative accommodation – between the intractable logic of the world around him and, within that, a little corner of life as he chooses to envision it to himself.

This, too, is the triumph of the novel's little world and its function as a medium for artificial experience. As I have argued, Brontë's fiction provides a version of the world in which it is possible to perform powerful, vicarious actions that acknowledge and defy material constraints; Trollope offers flexible realities whose facts and causations are open and responsive to human creativity, and which cultivate this as a generalisable moral perspective; Thackeray creates a holding-space, in the 'Fable-land' of the novel's world, into which readers can extend their social life as imaginary regions that ostensibly never end. In this final case study, I have attempted to show how nineteenth-century theorisations of fiction as analogous to hallucination presage this sense of its practical, but not necessarily 'realistic', experience. These palpable worlds are not solipsistic retreats nor psychological prisons, not symbolic nor historical representations, but fictions whose presence and experience afford an imaginative extension of life and its manifold resources for living.

Conclusion
Approaching Virtuality

>   Birds will once again appear when a bird feeder is placed.
>   Children no longer wake up in a panic every time they wake up.
>   The police chief can no longer be the suspect in a crime.[1]

Since its publication by the Electronic Arts corporation in 2014, the video game *The Sims 4* has accrued seventy-two 'patches': corrective updates to its programming code. In software development, the documentation of such electronic errata tends towards the technical; most users of Microsoft Word, for instance, would not be expected to know that in July 2018 it was repaired to prevent 'Memory leaks when you open and close a document that contains Embedded Object Linking and Embedding (OLE) objects'.[2] The developers of *The Sims 4*, however, have identified a unique opportunity in presenting their 'patch notes', rather than in terms of Boolean flags or subroutines, as a reflection on the fictionality of their own game.

Originally conceived by the developer Will Wright as a digital 'dollhouse for adults', the popular *Sims* franchise (currently on its fourth instalment) is a game of the everyday.[3] Players begin by designing one or more characters, determining their age, gender, ethnicity, hobbies, ambitions, and even psychological traits; then build a house for them to inhabit, putting in walls and windows, buying lamps and fridges and showerheads from an extensive inventory of options for each; then guide their characters through a virtual life, from prompting them to make dinner and clean the house, to fulfilling long-term objectives like starting a family or pursuing a career. As Diane Nutt and Diane Railton have argued, if this new medium can be analysed with traditional concepts of genre, the genre at hand is 'real life' ('albeit [...] a very Western suburban family life'), through whose language and conventions players parse the 'fiction' represented by the moving bits on screen, and perceive the narrative possibilities made available as well as delimited by the system.[4] Players know that *The Sims 4* will not allow them (as with other games) to kill a dragon or invade a country, because its priorities and limits are set around the material (and consumeristic) aesthetics of domestic life: there are six types of home coffee machine available in the game, each lovingly crafted by a graphic artist.

I give this idiosyncratic account not, as I attempt to do with the archives of worldplay, to suggest formal or historical affinities with literary works, but because the 'patch notes' of a digital everyday undergoing technical repair can help to place us into the logical or cognitive space which it has been my aim to recover as a reading practice of the novel and to cultivate as a critical perspective. That distinction of volitional imagining which I have called the double consciousness, explicit pretence, or virtuality of fiction is intuitively evoked by the observation, deadpan, that the children of *The Sims* have been collectively terrorised in the night by a misfiring line of code. The metaleptic humour of these notes arises from exposing the imagined world as one explicitly governed by systems (electronic and discursive) of representation, not in order to spoil the game, but to intensify the original, peculiar appeal of an artificial reality. The children are imaginary, and we must save them from distress; it is only because they are imaginary that we can. As Lewes pointed out in 1872, the wheels on a wooden horse make clear both its inadequacy as a portrayal and its utility as a toy, its appropriation of the image of a horse for encounters only an artificial animal can offer. It is one thing to go out and feed the pigeons; it is another, specific experience to participate in fictional or vicarious actions, to offer digital seeds to imaginary birds which 'will once again appear', as if a season has come in a way it never could in life.

Virtual Play has proposed this distinction as a significant intervention into the theory and criticism of mid-Victorian novel fiction, the preeminent literary form of 'believable stories that [do] not solicit belief'.[5] There is a 'patch notes' logic at work in Brontë's Glass Town, when her narrator complains that the author-gods of his universe are threatening to write its apocalypse, or in Trollope's explanations that his heroines behave as they do because they happen to live in a narrative world. Yet such reflections on the generic-metaphysical peculiarities of fictional worlds have long been sidelined in novel criticism, which frequently smooths over these admissions, or repudiates them as blandly ironic or artistically anomalous. Taking such reflections seriously, and recovering their anomalousness as features of a coherent imaginative practice, allows us to disrupt the complacent sense that novels are abstractly 'reflective', 'symbolic', or 'representative' of historical or universal conditions, or merely aesthetic arrangements of language.

The practice of virtual worlds, from Angria to *The Sims*, reveals other uses for verisimilitude than these. The case studies here of Brontë, Trollope, Thackeray, and Dickens have suggested the alternative social, ethical, and artistic functions novels in particular perform by virtue of their patchy, artificial realities: in a world which is known to be imaginary, even decades of alienated labour can be contemplated with desire and pleasure; the fulfilment of moral duties can become a matter of creative invention; feelings of dependency and attachment can be freed from material exigencies; lack and loss can be survived by extending the scope of living beyond one's immediate surroundings. The novel's simultaneous capacity for literality and unreality, concreteness and imaginariness, is an unacknowledged resource of the form which this book has only begun to explore but – more importantly – seeks to make available as a subject of criticism.

In making this case for the *useability* of novels, I have chosen in this book to offer a partial view: prioritising accounts of how the authors, readers, and characters of these texts employ the virtual for pleasure, sustenance, or agency (and how we can too). I choose to retrace these 'histories of use' over more suspicious interpretations of imaginative experience as ideological reproduction or interpolation, partly to respect the accounts of historical readers about how they make value out of such experiences, and partly to ally the participatory perspective of the virtual with recent projects of 'reparative' and 'postcritical' reading, a disciplinary shift from methods of suspicion and demystification to new phenomenologies of agency and possibility. A criticism of fictional experience (rather than of aesthetic experience more broadly) demands an especially involved version of this disciplinary call to replace 'looking behind the text – for its hidden causes, determining conditions, and noxious motives' with descriptions of 'what [the text] unfurls, calls forth, makes possible'.[6] Suppose we each had an island of our own, suggests eleven-year-old Charlotte Brontë, what could we do with it? What options become available? I have characterised my own approach as a 'vicarious' criticism because to hypothesise the possibilities of fictional experience, even if only to document its formal and historical affordances ('Well, I suppose one could . . . '), is already to start playing the game. If distance and detachment have become the default moods of literary analysis, the studies in this book conversely work hand in glove with the authors and readers it examines, understanding how they (and how to) put fiction to use, learning by doing.

Of course, not everything that a novel or game makes available for imaginative experience is good or desirable, or should be free from critical scrutiny. What remains importantly to be explored, and what I hope this work opens for exploration, are new approaches of scrutinisation which can account for the distinctiveness of virtual and vicarious experiences. The content of *The Sims* is indisputably shaped by a strong ideological picture of 'real' or 'normal' life, an argument which has also been made of nineteenth-century realism.[7] But as the patch notes show, encountering this picture as explicit artifice is an experience prone to accident and surprise. It is again one thing to believe that police chiefs do not commit crimes; it is another, much more ambiguous in motive and commitment, to reprogram an imaginary world so as to render police corruption metaphysically impossible; which is different also from a radical imagining of a world without police. Emma Butcher presents a strong test-case in the graphic descriptions of colonial violence featured in the Brontës' tales of Glass Town and Angria, deployed against a fictionalised version of the sub-Saharan Ashanti people, and borrowed (like so many of their non-physical 'toys') from their contemporary reading materials:

> It is through these horrifying descriptions that the siblings were able to convey the prejudices displayed in contemporary writings [...] their imaginations and writings were firmly grounded in the lurid language of published war reportage. Their mimicry of racism consolidates their positions as recorders of their society's prejudices[.][8]

The claims in *Virtual Play* about the distinction between virtuality and reference do not amount to an argument for dismissing the troubling nature of this violence. Rather, such claims suggest that this violence is troubling for more particular and ethically complicated reasons than the passive reproduction or mimicry of racist ideologies from reader to reader. There is a categorical difference between the racist reporting in *Blackwood's Magazine* and the racism of fictionalising native peoples as targets for explicitly imagined acts of violence, and this difference is morally significant (even if not morally mitigating) for how it complicates the relationship between cultural context and individual agency.

For critics of different generations, the further questions I begin to frame here may recall either the cultural, academic, and policy debates over pornography in the 1970s and 80s, or those over video game violence in the 1990s and the early millennium – or ones over the ethics of sex with robots, which are at this moment emerging even ahead of the technology itself.[9] Although the empirical and philosophical arguments underpinning those debates remain inconclusive and deeply divisive, the urgency of those around porn and gaming have in some ways already been overwhelmed by the ubiquity of these forms of vicarious experience.[10] In describing *The Professor* as a pornographic realism, I drew from the work of Nancy Bauer:

> [W]e are past the point, if we were ever there, at which a bipolar politics of pornography, for or against, could be of use to us [...] What we need now is not a new politics of porn but, rather, a candid phenomenology of it, an honest reckoning with its powers to produce intense pleasure and to color our ordinary sense of what the world is and ought to be like. Such a reckoning will have to involve a refocusing of our attention, from the male consumers who took center stage in the porn wars to the women for whom the pornutopia provides a new standard of beauty and of sexual fulfilment.[11]

What vicarious reading offers now is a similar project of understanding fiction's possibilities, for better or worse, and its history as part of a still-evolving tradition of simulated experience. Literary studies, with its attentiveness to individual texts and its long view of form and reception, has unique contributions to make alongside philosophy and the social sciences in the study of fictional actions literally performed.

To do this, we must advocate for the courage to approach our objects of study with intimate participation and a willingness to encounter, with the confidence that we will find something more surprising and useful than our reaffirmation as ideological subjects. Although the postcritical has sometimes been characterised as a replacement of cynicism with more positive critical affects, another way to consider this 'turn' may be as an increased tolerance for risk. Play, as the psychoanalyst Donald Winnicott proposed, is fundamentally a matter of trust.[12] Like many situations in life and some (well- or ill-intentioned) people we meet, novels call on us to do unreasonable things: to expand the geography of England, to place non-existent people into history, 'to perform the rather startling (upon examination) action of believing that inside the novel is not only a three-dimensional space but a person'.[13] Yet for Winnicott, an unwillingness to risk play can inhibit modes of action and knowledge that arise from the experience of being involved. Moreover, choosing to accept the imaginative premises of fiction does not amount to a conscription of 'belief' – only a conscious agreement in service of, and provisional on, a shared practice or activity for mutual use or value. In this book, I have tried to document the results of a literary criticism that steps forward to participate in the novel, which is no more than a child does by going along with a sibling's proposal for a make-believe. There is much that, as De Quincey bemoaned, one stands to suffer and lose by accepting. But there is also much that we stand to miss in the refusal.

Notes

Notes to the Introduction

1. See Nathan Hensley's summation in 'Figures of Reading', *Criticism* 54, no. 2 (2012): 329–42, especially 329–30. 'Should the reading we do be close or distant? Deep or superficial? Fast or slow? And is literature information or something, well, better?'
2. See the discussion on 'symptomatic' reading in Stephen Best and Sharon Marcus, 'Surface Reading: An Introduction', *Representations* 108, no. 1 (2009): 1–21; see also the discussions on 'critical' and 'suspicious' reading (and their alternatives) in Rita Felski, 'After Suspicion', *Profession* (2009): 28–35 and in Rita Felski, *The Limits of Critique* (Chicago: University of Chicago Press, 2015), especially 14–20 and 107–16.
3. Rita Felski, *Uses of Literature* (Oxford: Blackwell, 2009), 76.
4. Elaine Auyoung, *When Fiction Feels Real: Representation and the Reading Mind* (Oxford: Oxford University Press, 2018), 20.
5. Brigid Lowe, *Victorian Fiction and the Insights of Sympathy: An Alternative to the Hermeneutics of Suspicion* (London: Anthem Press, 2007), 12.
6. Charles Dickens, *David Copperfield*, ed. Nina Burgis (Oxford: Clarendon Press, 1981), 48.
7. William Makepeace Thackeray, *Vanity Fair*, ed. Helen Small (Oxford: Oxford University Press, 2015), 878.
8. Charlotte Brontë, *Jane Eyre*, ed. Jane Jack and Margaret Smith (Oxford: Clarendon Press, 1969), 132. Further references to this edition will be incorporated into the text.
9. Eve Kosofsky Sedgwick, *Touching Feeling: Affect, Pedagogy, Performativity* (Durham, NC: Duke University Press, 2003), 150.
10. George Henry Lewes, 'Dickens in Relation to Criticism', *Fortnightly Review* 11, no. 62 (1872): 146.
11. Sigmund Freud, 'Creative Writers and Day-Dreaming', in *Pelican Freud Library*, ed. James Strachey, vol. 14 (Harmondsworth: Penguin, 1985), 131.
12. Peter Brooks, *Realist Vision* (New Haven, CT: Yale University Press, 2005), 3.
13. Thomas Pavel, *Fictional Worlds* (Cambridge, MA: Harvard University Press, 1989), 55.

14 Gilles Deleuze, *Difference and Repetition*, trans. Paul Patton (London: Bloomsbury, 2014), 272. For Deleuze, however, the term refers more specifically to the reality of states of potential, rather than the sense of pretended, artificial, or mediated reality explored here and in the concept's broader usage in cultural studies (as I go on to explain). See Paul Patton, *Deleuze and the Political* (London: Routledge, 2000), 35–36.
15 John Plotz, *Semi-Detached: The Aesthetics of Virtual Experience since Dickens* (Princeton: Princeton University Press, 2018), 16.
16 Jean-Marie Schaeffer, *Why Fiction?*, trans. Dorrit Cohn (Lincoln: University of Nebraska Press, 2010), x: '[V]irtualisation is by no means an invention of the digital era [...] every mental representation is a virtual reality. There is thus definitely a link between the virtual and fiction; being a particular modality of representation, fiction is at the same time a specific form of the virtual'. See also Elizabeth A. Grosz's argument in *Architecture from the Outside: Essays on Virtual and Real Space* (Cambridge, MA: MIT Press, 2001), 77. '[T]he virtual reality of writing, reading, drawing or even thinking [...] loads the presence of the present with supplementarity, redoubling a world through parallel universes, universes that might have been', as quoted in Peter Otto, *Multiplying Worlds: Romanticism, Modernity, and the Emergence of Virtual Reality* (Oxford: Oxford University Press, 2011), 6.
17 Otto, *Multiplying Worlds*, 7–14.
18 Plotz, *Semi-Detached*, 16.
19 William Gibson, *Neuromancer* (New York: Berkley Publishing Group, 1989), 128.
20 William Makepeace Thackeray, *Roundabout Papers* (London: J. M. Dent & Sons, 1914), 273.
21 J. David Velleman, 'Bodies, Selves', *American Imago* 65, no. 3 (2008): 407, emphasis added; for other examples of fictional-literal actions in the context of ethics – e.g., virtual adultery with fictional persons – see Charles M. Ess, 'Ethics at the Boundaries of the Virtual', in *The Oxford Handbook of Virtuality*, ed. Mark Grimshaw (Oxford: Oxford University Press, 2014), 691.
22 Auyoung, *When Fiction Feels Real*, 2.
23 Terence Cave, *Thinking with Literature: Towards a Cognitive Criticism* (Oxford: Oxford University Press, 2016), 48, original emphasis; see also Caroline Levine, *Forms: Whole, Rhythm, Hierarchy, Network* (Princeton: Princeton University Press, 2015), 6.
24 Catherine Gallagher, 'The Rise of Fictionality', in *The Novel*, ed. Franco Moretti (Princeton: Princeton University Press, 2006), 340; Lennard J. Davis, *Factual Fictions: The Origins of the English Novel* (Philadelphia: University of Pennsylvania Press, 1983), 156.
25 Elaine Freedgood, 'Fictional Settlements: Footnotes, Metalepsis, the Colonial Effect', *New Literary History* 41, no. 2 (2010): 394.
26 Lennard J. Davis, *Resisting Novels* (New York: Routledge, 1987), 2.

27 Michael Saler, *As If: Modern Enchantment and the Literary Prehistory of Virtual Reality* (Oxford: Oxford University Press, 2011), 32; Lowe, *Insights of Sympathy*, 82.
28 Henry Fielding, *The Wesleyan Edition of the Works of Henry Fielding: Joseph Andrews*, ed. Martin C. Battestin (Oxford: Oxford University Press and Wesleyan University Press, 1966), 189; Gallagher, 'Rise of Fictionality', 342.
29 Lowe, *Insights of Sympathy*, 78; see Michael Warner's reflections on teaching critical reading, in 'Uncritical Reading', in *Polemic: Critical or Uncritical*, ed. Jane Gallop (New York: Routledge, 2004), 13–15.
30 As Richard Walsh similarly argues, 'What we understand, feel, and value [in fiction] may be ultimately grounded in the abstract and the general, but it is not in general terms that we experience understanding, feeling, or valuing it. Fiction enables us to go through that process, for the sake of its experience'. *The Rhetoric of Fictionality: Narrative Theory and the Idea of Fiction* (Columbus: Ohio State University Press, 2007), 51.
31 William Charles Macready, *The Journal of William Charles Macready, 1832–1851*, ed. J. C. Trewin (Carbondale: Southern Illinois University Press, 2009), 169; Charles Dickens, *The Letters of Charles Dickens, 1840–1841*, ed. Madeline House, Graham Storey, and Kathleen Tillotson, vol. 2 (Oxford: Clarendon Press, 1969), 181.
32 Macready, *Journal, 1832–1851*, 169.
33 Dickens, *Letters 1840–1841*, 2: x, original emphasis.
34 Lesley Anne Goodman, 'Indignant Reading' (PhD diss., Harvard University, 2013), 26, original emphasis.
35 Lowe, *Insights of Sympathy*, 12; Wayne Booth, *The Company We Keep: An Ethics of Fiction* (Berkeley: University of California Press, 1988), 256; see also Martha Nussbaum's reflections on experiencing love for *David Copperfield*'s Steerforth, from reciting the words of a besotted character (David himself) in the first person, in *Love's Knowledge* (Oxford: Oxford University Press, 1992), 335.
36 Velleman, 'Bodies, Selves', 407.
37 Charles Dickens, *The Mudfog Papers* (London: Richard Bentley and Son, 1880), 133–34.
38 Dickens, 135–36.
39 Charles Dickens, *The Letters of Charles Dickens, 1847–1849*, ed. Graham Storey, K. J. Fielding, and Anthony Laude, vol. 5 (Oxford: Clarendon Press, 1977), 640.
40 Rae Greiner, *Sympathetic Realism in Nineteenth-Century British Fiction* (Baltimore: Johns Hopkins University Press, 2012), 10.
41 Jonathan Farina, '"Dickens's As If": Analogy and Victorian Virtual Reality', *Victorian Studies* 53, no. 3 (2011): 429, original emphasis.
42 Freedgood, 'Fictional Settlements', 407–8.
43 Nicholas Dames, 'On Hegel, History, and Reading as If for Life: Response', *Victorian Studies* 53, no. 3 (2011): 437–44, https://doi.org/10.1353/vic.2011.0044.

Notes to Chapter One

1. William Makepeace Thackeray, *The History of Pendennis: His Fortunes and Misfortunes, His Friends and His Greatest Enemy*, ed. John A. Sutherland (Oxford: Oxford University Press, 1994), 531.
2. The most formalised version of this idea is known as the possible worlds theory of fiction, which uses the tools of modal logic to explain how we refer concretely to hypothetical, counterfactual, and fictional states of affairs. The narratological scholarship around this theory aims to solve other kinds of problems – of narrative semantics and typology – than this book's focus on the novel form and its criticism, but the two share an interest in the ontology of fictional language. See Marie-Laure's Ryan's bibliographical survey in 'Possible Worlds in Recent Literary Theory', *Style* 4, no. 26 (1992): 528–53; Ruth Ronen's study *Possible Worlds in Literary Theory* (Cambridge: Cambridge University Press, 1994). For a more recent discussion, see Marie-Laure Ryan, 'From Parallel Universes to Possible Worlds: Ontological Pluralism in Physics, Narratology, and Narrative', *Poetics Today* 27, no. 4 (2006): 633–74.
3. Michael McKeon, 'The Eighteenth-Century Challenge to Narrative Theory', in *Narrative Concepts in the Study of Eighteenth-Century Literature*, ed. Liisa Steinby and Aino Mäkikalli (Amsterdam: University of Amsterdam Press, 2017), 41.
4. Jonathan Rose, *The Intellectual Life of the British Working Classes* (New Haven, CT: Yale University Press, 2001), 94.
5. Rose quotes a range of examples, from a nineteenth-century joiner's son: 'characters in the book have always been historical characters with me, just as real as Caius Julius Caesar [. . .] I believed every word it contained. I never saw a novel before. I did not know the meaning of fiction.' The minister Joseph Barker: 'I doubted nothing that I found in books [. . .] I had no idea at the time I read Robinson Crusoe, that there were such things as novels, works of fiction, in existence.' See Rose, 92–102; for the philosophical confusion of Sherlock Holmes's fictional existence in factual London, see David Lewis, 'Truth in Fiction', *American Philosophical Quarterly* 15, no. 1 (1978): 37–46.
6. Gallagher, 'Rise of Fictionality', 341.
7. J. Jeffrey Franklin, *Serious Play: The Cultural Form of the Nineteenth-Century Realist Novel* (Philadelphia: University of Pennsylvania Press, 1999), 4; for an overview of play as a cultural concept more generally, see also Matthew Kaiser, *The World in Play: Portraits of a Victorian Concept* (Stanford, CA: Stanford University Press, 2011), 13–49.
8. Gallagher, 'Rise of Fictionality', 336–37.
9. Rose, *Intellectual Life*, 94.
10. Thomas De Quincey, 'Autobiographical Sketches' in *The Works of Thomas De Quincey*, ed. Daniel Sanjiv Roberts, vol. 19 (London: Pickering & Chatto, 2003), 45. Further references to this edition will be incorporated into the text.

11 Both of the brothers' islands lack a longitudinal coordinate because the universal Prime Meridian (the zero point of longitude) would not be established in Greenwich until 1884.
12 Sally Shuttleworth, *The Mind of the Child: Child Development in Literature, Science, and Medicine, 1840–1900* (Oxford: Oxford University Press, 2013), 82.
13 Daniel Defoe, *Robinson Crusoe*, ed. Thomas Keymer and James Kelly (Oxford: Oxford University Press, 2007), 4, 276n. The first and second editions have 'dispatch'd' instead of 'disputed'. See Keymer and Kelly's explanatory note.
14 Putting aside the ongoing contentiousness of his wider history of the form, Watt's account incisively identifies the novel's fictional informativeness as 'its most distinctive literary qualities': 'the premise, or primary convention, that the novel is a full and authentic report of human experience [...] with such details of the story as the individuality of the actors concerned, the particulars of the times and places of their actions [...] presented through a more largely referential use of language than is common in other literary forms'. *The Rise of the Novel: Studies in Defoe, Richardson and Fielding* (London: Pimlico, 2000), 32–33. As Michael Seidel has argued, despite the numerous revisions and criticisms on Watt's model of realism, 'no one, to my knowledge, has ever convincingly displaced Watt's notion of formal realism as a dominant characteristic of narrative during the early eighteenth century, particularly in England'. See 'The Man Who Came to Dinner: Ian Watt and the Theory of Formal Realism', *Eighteenth-Century Fiction* 12, no. 2–3 (2000): 194.
15 Walter Scott, *Introductions and Notes from the Magnum Opus: Waverley to A Legend of the Wars of Montrose*, ed. J. H. Alexander, P. D. Garside, and Claire Lamont (Edinburgh: Edinburgh University Press, 2012), 335, 343.
16 'Memoir of Hartley Coleridge' in Hartley Coleridge, *Poems*, ed. Derwent Coleridge, vol. 1 (London: Edward Moxon, 1851), xlii. Further references to this volume and edition will be incorporated into the text.
17 Benjamin Heath Malkin, *A Father's Memoirs of His Child* (London: Longman, Hurst, Rees, and Orme, 1806), 93–94.
18 Anna Jameson, *A Commonplace Book of Thoughts, Memories, and Fancies* (London: Longman, Brown, Green, and Longmans, 1855), 131.
19 Jameson, *Commonplace Book*, 135.
20 Jameson, *Commonplace Book*, 132. As Patricia Meyer Spacks has suggested of the eighteenth century, 'privacy is a peculiarly emphatic issue for [...] women, both within fiction (e.g., Clarissa) and as writers of fiction, poetry, and diaries'. Gendered implications of interiority, education, and sociality clearly intervene in Jameson's expression of this practice. See *Privacy: Concealing the Eighteenth-Century Self* (Chicago: University of Chicago Press, 2003), 25.
21 Charlotte Brontë, *Villette*, ed. Margaret Smith and Herbert Rosengarten (Oxford: Clarendon Press, 1984), 105.
22 Jameson, *Commonplace Book*, 135.

23 Shuttleworth, *Mind of the Child*, 79.
24 Shuttleworth, *Mind of the Child*, 79.
25 Their close succession led an anonymous reviewer of Jameson's *Commonplace Book* to recognise her account of play as the example of a known category, being 'like Hartley Coleridge with his dreamland Ejuxria, like Thomas De Quincey with his dreamland Gombroon'. 'Mrs Jameson's Common-Place Book', *The New Monthly Magazine* 103 (1855): 196.
26 See Michele Root-Bernstein's account of this study in *Inventing Imaginary Worlds: From Childhood Play to Adult Creativity Across the Arts and Sciences* (Lanham, MD: Rowman & Littlefield Education, 2014), 69–73.
27 'What, if any, effect [...] the elaboration of the imaginary land, may exert on character formation and habits of adjustment in adulthood is at present unknown'. The studies that follow might be seen as a taking-up of this challenge. Leta S. Hollingworth, *Children Above 180 IQ (Stanford-Binet): Origin and Development* (London: George G. Harrap & Company, 1942), 275.
28 David Cohen and Stephen A. MacKeith, *The Development of Imagination: The Private Worlds of Childhood* (London: Routledge, 1991), 11–14.
29 Cohen and MacKeith, *Development of Imagination*, 23.
30 See her hypotheses on 'Rates of Worldplay', 'Disciplinary Inclinations', and 'Perceptions of Connection' [between worldplay and creativity] in Root-Bernstein, *Inventing Imaginary Worlds*, 42–52.
31 Her study also produces a tabled list of historical cases, which organises the names and dates of children alongside columns on their 'Imaginary World' and 'Adult Endeavor'. See Root-Bernstein, *Inventing Imaginary Worlds*, 211–15.
32 Christine Alexander, 'Nineteenth-Century Juvenilia: A Survey', in *The Child Writer from Austen to Woolf*, ed. Christine Alexander and Juliet McMasters (Cambridge, UK: Cambridge University Press, 2005), 11.
33 Joetta Harty, 'The Islanders: Mapping Paracosms in the Early Writings of Hartley Coleridge, Thomas Malkin, Thomas De Quincey, and the Brontes' (PhD diss., The George Washington University, 2007), 3.
34 Although I describe this as a transmission of narrative convention and form from colonial adventure to play, Freedgood has argued that the fictionality of the realist novel involves 'an ontological imperialism' mimetic of (and involved in) other kinds of imperial relationality in this period. Freedgood, 'Fictional Settlements', 394.
35 Defoe, *Robinson Crusoe*, 4.
36 Kate E. Brown, 'Beloved Objects: Mourning, Materiality, and Charlotte Brontë's 'Never-Ending Story',' *ELH* 65, no. 2 (1998): 403; *The Letters of Mrs Gaskell*, ed. J. A. V. Chapple and Arthur Pollard (Manchester: Manchester University Press, 1966), 398.
37 Gaskell, *Letters*, 398. In the next chapter, I suggest Gaskell's ambivalences are grounded in a model of Brontë's realism, and of women's novel-writing more generally, which she seeks to defend.

38 Fannie Ratchford, *The Brontës' Web of Childhood* (New York: Columbia University Press, 1941), xiv.
39 'Introduction' in Charlotte Brontë et al., *Tales of Glass Town, Angria, and Gondal*, ed. Christine Alexander (Oxford: Oxford University Press, 2010), xliii.
40 See the account given in Ratchford, *The Brontës' Web of Childhood*, 65.
41 After receiving William's publication about the secret tails of his Gombroonians, De Quincey writes: 'Overwhelming to me and stunning was the ignominy of this horrible discovery' (*AS* 52).
42 'Then, around the turn of the nineteenth century, there was a last change – last in the sense that I think we are still in it, not last in the sense of perfect or final. This change is what I'm calling fiction – works that make no bones about their invention despite being set within contemporary reality. (This last trait clearly separates fiction from the 'fanciful' genres of the fairy tale or the oriental tale, as well as from allegory.)' Nicholas D. Paige, *Before Fiction: The Ancien Régime of the Novel* (Philadelphia: University of Pennsylvania Press, 2011), 26.
43 Catherine Gallagher, 'What Would Napoleon Do?: Historical, Fictional, and Counterfactual Characters', *New Literary History* 42, no. 2 (2011): 332.
44 Gallagher's study on the alternative history genre makes this distinction, against the narratological models of Ryan and Doležel, arguing that 'we don't read most novels as counterfactual conjectures; we intuitively make a distinction between the kind of hypothetical exercises involved in counterfactuals and mere fictionality.' Gallagher, 'What Would Napoleon Do?' 333. This chapter argues, however, that 'mere fictionality' is more distinct and complicated than Gallagher acknowledges.
45 Gallagher, 'Rise of Fictionality', 341.
46 Dickens, *David Copperfield*, 48.
47 Watt, *Rise of the Novel*, 19.
48 Gallagher, 'Rise of Fictionality', 337.
49 Jeremy Bentham, *The Works of Jeremy Bentham: Memoirs*, ed. John Bowring, vol. 10 (Edinburgh: William Tait, 1843), 21.
50 Jeremy Bentham, *The Works of Jeremy Bentham: Chrestomathia, Ontology, Logic*, ed. John Bowring, vol. 8 (Edinburgh: William Tait, 1841), 262fn.
51 Saler has also identified this moment of conceptualisation – the invention of explicitly imaginary facts – as an encounter between a Weberian model of modern disenchantment, exemplified here by Bentham's purge of non-actual or non-literal truths, and a re-enchantment of the world and everyday life through forms of make-believe. By using paracosmic play as the signal phenomenon, I locate this moment earlier in literary history than Saler's focus on the fictional worlds of Arthur Conan Doyle, H. P. Lovecraft, and J. R. R. Tolkien. See Saler, *As If*, 8–11.
52 Jason Pearl, *Utopian Geographies and the Early English Novel* (Charlottesville: University of Virginia Press, 2014), 11, 137.
53 Malkin, *Father's Memoir*, 69.

54 See Terence Cave's argument that 'The paratextual material [of Utopia] seems designed to foster the illusion of Utopia as a new or new-found island, but this is especially true of the map and the alphabet [...] [which] is of course essential to the way the work as a whole commutes between the 'ideal' world of Utopia and the lived reality of the early sixteenth century.' *Thomas More's Utopia in Early Modern Europe: Paratexts and Contexts* (Manchester: Manchester University Press, 2008), 21–22. For a discussion of belief and evidence in Utopia, see Emmanouil Aretoulakis, 'The Prefatory/Postscript Letters to St. Thomas More's *Utopia*: The Culture of 'Seeing' as a Reality-Conferring Strategy', *Journal of Early Modern Studies*, no. 3 (2014): 91–113.
55 Thomas More, *Utopia*, ed. George M. Logan, trans. Robert M. Adams (Cambridge: Cambridge University Press, 2016), 129.
56 Pearl, *Utopian Geographies*, 117.
57 Pearl, *Utopian Geographies*, 11.
58 "ideal, Adj. 4.", *OED Online* (Oxford University Press, 2010), www.oed.com/view/Entry/90958, accessed 19 June 2018.
59 Trollope writes that 'This had been the occupation of my life for six or seven years before I went to the Post Office', (*AA* 33) which he joined as a clerk in 1834 – placing the start of play around 1827 – and he later notes that 'Up to this time [1843] I had continued that practice of castle-building of which I have spoken' (49), making roughly sixteen years of castles in all.
60 Jameson, *Commonplace Book*, 131.
61 J. Hillis Miller, *On Literature* (London: Routledge, 2002), 53.
62 Cohen and MacKeith, *Development of Imagination*, 10–11.
63 Root-Bernstein, *Inventing Imaginary Worlds*, 41.
64 Eric Hayot, *On Literary Worlds* (Oxford: Oxford University Press, 2012), 66.
65 Hayot, *On Literary Worlds*, 65–66.
66 Hillis Miller similarly articulates the intuitive sense that the novel 'give[s] the reader access to a realm that seems to exist apart from the words, even though the reader cannot enter it except by way of the words'. *On Literature*, 54.
67 Paige, *Before Fiction*, 31–32.

Notes to Chapter 2

1 Gaskell, *Letters*, 398.
2 Elizabeth Gaskell, *The Life of Charlotte Bronte*, ed. Elisabeth Jay (London: Penguin, 1997), 69 Further references to this edition will be incorporated into the text.
3 That Eliot's essay, published during the writing of the *Life*, singles out Brontë and Gaskell (alongside Harriet Martineau) as women writers who do commit to these qualities of excellence may have given ballast to Gaskell's associations of Brontë's writing with manual and domestic labour, with the 'patient analysis of cause and effect', and with her own prose. George Eliot, 'Silly

Novels by Lady Novelists', in *Essays of George Eliot*, ed. Thomas Pinney (New York: Columbia University Press, 1963), 323.
4 Eliot, 'Silly Novels by Lady Novelists', 301–2; Eliot's focus on difficulty, both of novel-writing and of the feminine accomplishments indulgently represented in novels, reflects an antipathy to art's deprecation into facile recreation. Her critique is embodied by Gwendolen Harleth, who wishes 'I could write books to amuse myself [...] How delightful it must be to write books after one's own taste instead of reading other people's! Home-made books must be so nice'. Gwendolen discovers, in the same chapter, that her soprano is nothing extraordinary in the judgement of a trained musician. *Daniel Deronda*, ed. Graham Handley (Oxford: Clarendon Press, 1984), 39.
5 Q. D. Leavis, *Fiction and the Reading Public* (London: Chatto & Windus, 1978), 237.
6 Vladimir Nabokov, *Lectures on Russian Literature* (London: Weidenfeld and Nicolson, 1982), 106.
7 Lowe, *Insights of Sympathy*, 82.
8 Nabokov, *Russian Literature*, 106.
9 J. R. R. Tolkien, *Tolkien on Fairy-Stories*, ed. Verlyn Flieger and Douglas A. Anderson (London: HarperCollins, 2014), 52.
10 Tolkien, *Tolkien on Fairy-Stories*, 42.
11 M. H. Abrams, *The Mirror and the Lamp: Romantic Theory and the Critical Tradition* (London: Oxford University Press, 1953), 272.
12 Elder Olson, '"Sailing to Byzantium": Prolegomena to a Poetics of the Lyric', *The University of Kansas City Review* 8, no. 3 (1942): 216–17; quoted in Abrams, 284.
13 Abrams, *The Mirror and the Lamp*, 384fn.
14 Nabokov, *Russian Literature*, 106.
15 Gallagher, 'Rise of Fictionality', 337.
16 Charlotte Brontë, *The Letters of Charlotte Brontë, 1848–1851*, ed. Margaret Smith (Oxford: Clarendon Press, 2000), 98.
17 Brontë, *The Letters of Charlotte Brontë*, 98, emphasis added.
18 Charlotte Brontë, *The Early Writings of Charlotte Brontë, 1826–1832*, ed. Christine Alexander (Padstow: Shakespeare Head Press, 1987), 5–6. Further references to this edition will be incorporated into the text.
19 Firdous Azim, *The Colonial Rise of the Novel* (London: Routledge, 1993), 116.
20 Pavel, *Fictional Worlds*, 56.
21 Meg Harris Williams, 'Book Magic: Aesthetic Conflicts in Charlotte Brontë's Juvenilia', *Nineteenth-Century Literature* 42, no. 1 (1987): 32.
22 Olson, 'Sailing to Byzantium', 216–17; quoted in Abrams, 284.
23 See also Bock's and Heather Glen's respective discussions of 'Strange Events', a juvenilia tale where the protagonist begins to suspect their own nonexistence. Carol Bock, *Charlotte Brontë and the Storyteller's Audience* (Iowa City: University of Iowa Press, 1992), 33–36; Heather Glen, *Charlotte Brontë: The Imagination in History* (Oxford: Oxford University Press, 2004), 13–16.

24 Laura Forsberg, 'The Miniature World of Charlotte Brontë's Glass Town', in *Charlotte Brontë from the Beginnings: New Essays from the Juvenilia to the Major Works*, ed. Judith E. Pike and Lucy Morrison (Oxford: Routledge, 2016), 51.
25 Glen, *Imagination in History*, 11, 19.
26 Dickens, *Letters*, 620.
27 Forsberg, 'Miniature World', 57.
28 Eliot, 'Lady Novelists', 323; George Eliot, *Adam Bede*, ed. Carol A. Martin (Oxford: Clarendon Press, 2001), 7.
29 Frank Kermode, *Essays on Fiction 1971–82* (Oxford: Routledge Revivals, 2015), 114.
30 Jane Moore, 'Problematising Postmodernism', in *Critical Dialogues: Current Issues in English Studies in Germany and Britain*, ed. Isobel Armstrong and Hans-Werner Ludwig (Tubingen: Gunter Narr Verlag Tubingen, 1995), 139. The agent of this act, in Moore's analysis, is unclear; something which 'texts are compelled to perform' due to the inherent nature of fictional language. My own approach is to understand novelists as exploiting the authorial power afforded by fictional realities.
31 J. Hillis Miller, *Reading for Our Time: 'Adam Bede' and 'Middlemarch' Revisited* (Edinburgh: Edinburgh University Press, 2012), 13.
32 George Levine, *The Realistic Imagination: English Fiction from Frankenstein to Lady Chatterly* (Chicago: University of Chicago Press, 1981), 56.
33 Levine, *The Realistic Imagination*, 56.
34 Gérard Genette, *Narrative Discourse*, ed. Jane E. Lewin and Jonathan Culler (Oxford: Basil Blackwell, 1980), 234–35.
35 Genette, *Narrative Discourse*, 234–35.
36 Gustave Flaubert, *The Letters of Gustave Flaubert, 1830–1857*, ed. and trans. Francis Steegmuller (London: Faber & Faber, 1979), 173.
37 Dorothy L. Sayers, *The Mind of the Maker* (London: Methuen, 1941), 62–63.
38 Nabokov, *Russian Literature*, 106.
39 Jacques Rancière, *The Flesh of Words: The Politics of Writing*, trans. Charlotte Mandell (Stanford: Stanford University Press, 2004), 72.
40 Rancière, *The Flesh of Words*, 73.
41 Roland Barthes, *The Rustle of Language*, trans. Richard Howard (Berkeley: University of California Press, 1989), 54.
42 Barthes, *The Rustle of Language*, 52.
43 Rancière, *The Flesh of Words*, 72.
44 See Bock's similar reading of this moment: 'For young Charlotte, to make books was to stand in the epistemological space where the actual and the imaginary overlap, creating a third reality in the storytelling situation'. *Storyteller's Audience*, 31.
45 Levine, *Realistic Imagination*, 15, emphasis added.
46 Levine, *Realistic Imagination*, 8.
47 Levine, *Realistic Imagination*, 15.
48 Dames, 'On Hegel'.

49 'Introduction' in Charlotte Brontë, *Jane Eyre*, ed. Mary Augusta Arnold Ward (New York: Harper Bros., 1899), x.
50 Anne Thackeray Ritchie, *Chapters from Some Memoirs* (London: MacMillan and Co., 1894), 64.
51 Gaskell, *Letters*, 400–401.
52 'The Professor', *Examiner*, June 20, 1857, 388; R. H. Hutton, 'Novels by the Authoress of "John Halifax"', *North British Review*, no. 29 (1859): 474; 'The Professor', *Critic*, June 15, 1857, 271; quoted in Catherine Malone, '"We Have Learnt to Love Her More than Her Books": The Critical Reception of Brontë's Professor', *The Review of English Studies* 47, no. 186 (1996): 177, 181.
53 Henry Houston Bonnell, *Charlotte Brontë, George Eliot, and Jane Austen: Studies in Their Work* (New York: Longmans, Green, and Co., 1902), 35.
54 Barthes, *The Rustle of Language*, 54.
55 Charlotte Brontë, *The Professor*, ed. Margaret Smith and Herbert Rosengarten (Oxford: Clarendon Press, 1987), 221. Further references to this edition will be incorporated into the text.
56 Dames, 'On Hegel'.
57 Leavis, *The Reading Public*, 188.
58 Leavis, *The Reading Public*, 189–90.
59 'Introduction' in Charlotte Brontë, *The Professor*, ed. Heather Glen (London: Penguin, 2003), 31.
60 Glen, *Imagination in History*, 57–58.
61 Glen, *Imagination in History*, 58.
62 Leavis, *The Reading Public*, 188.
63 Barthes, *The Rustle of Language*, 54.
64 Levine, *Realistic Imagination*, 15; Brontë, *The Professor*, 2003, 31.
65 Charlotte Brontë, *The Letters of Charlotte Brontë, 1829–1847*, ed. Margaret Smith (Oxford: Clarendon Press, 1995), 574.
66 Levine, *Realistic Imagination*, 15.
67 Levine, *Realistic Imagination*, 15.
68 Glen, *Imagination in History*, 50.
69 Glen, *Imagination in History*, 46.
70 Glen, *Imagination in History*, 35.
71 Sally Shuttleworth, *Charlotte Brontë and Victorian Psychology* (Cambridge: Cambridge University Press, 1996), 24; for the textual history of *Self-Help*, and particularly its development throughout Smiles's editorship of *The Leeds Times* (a newspaper Brontë was known to have read), see Tim Travers, *Samuel Smiles and the Victorian Work Ethic* (New York: Garland Publishing, 1987), 76–80.
72 Samuel Smiles, *Self-Help; with Illustrations of Character and Conduct* (London: John Murray, 1859), 277–78.
73 Sedgwick, *Touching Feeling*, 131, original emphasis.
74 Shuttleworth, *Victorian Psychology*, 127.
75 Shuttleworth, *Victorian Psychology*, 146–47.

76 Glen, *Imagination in History*, 19, 43–44.
77 Terry Eagleton, *Myths of Power* (Basingstoke: MacMillan Press, 1988), 43.
78 Malone, '"We Have Learnt to Love Her More than Her Books": The Critical Reception of Brontë's Professor', 180.
79 Neville Newman, '"Workers, Gentlemen and Landowners": Identifying Social Class in The Professor and Wuthering Heights', *Brontë Society Transactions* 26, no. 1 (2001): 10–11.
80 Jennifer Ruth, 'Between Labor and Capital: Charlotte Bronte's Professional Professor', *Victorian Studies* 45, no. 2 (2003): 279–303, https://doi.org/10.1353/vic.2003.0098.
81 Glen, *Imagination in History*, 35.
82 Glen, *Imagination in History*, 43.
83 Asa Briggs, *Victorian People: A Reassessment of Persons and Themes, 1851–67* (Chicago: University of Chicago Press, 1973), 118.
84 Glen, *Imagination in History*, 35; Shuttleworth, *Victorian Psychology*, 146.
85 Nancy Bauer has recently argued that the ethical critique of pornography requires a more literal understanding of the logic of the fictional world depicted by pornographic representation, especially as it operates differently from the actual world which it superficially mimics: 'No one in the pornutopia has a reason to lose interest in or fear or get bored by sex; no one suffers in a way that can't be cured by it; no one is homeless or dispossessed or morally or spiritually abused or lost. When Daddy fucks Becky, she doesn't experience it as rape. She come'. *How to Do Things with Pornography* (Cambridge, MA: Harvard University Press, 2015), 5. Likewise, what it means for a novel character to experience years of abject labour conditions is not exactly the same as what it means for a historical person to do so; this book argues that a recognition of this flexible correspondence enriches, rather than deflates, the meaningful value and function of literature for life.
86 Brown, 'Beloved Objects', 400.
87 Barthes, *The Rustle of Language*, 129.
88 Ruth, 'Between Labor and Capital', 295.
89 Sedgwick, *Touching Feeling*, 150; see also Berlant's interpretation of reparative reading as 'a theory of being [...] Sedgwick's mode of reading is to deshame fantasmatic attachment so as to encounter its operations as knowledge'. Lauren Berlant, *Cruel Optimism* (Durham, NC: Duke University Press, 2011), 122.

Notes to Chapter Three

1 Henry James, *Literary Criticism: Essays on Literature, American Writers, English Writers*, ed. Leon Edel and Mark Wilson, vol. 1 (New York: The Library of America, 1984), 1331.
2 James, *Literary Criticism*, 1:1331–32.
3 James R. Kincaid, *The Novels of Anthony Trollope* (Oxford: Clarendon Press, 1977), 7.

Notes to pages 71–81

4 Anna Jameson, *The Diary of an Ennuyée* (London: Henry Colburn, 1826), 311; for the European history of the improvvisatore and their reception by the English Romantics, see Angela Esterhammer's work in 'The Cosmopolitan Improvvisatore: Spontaneity and Performance in Romantic Poetics', *European Romantic Review* 16, no. 2 (2005): 153–65; and in 'The Improvisation of Poetry, 1750–1850', in *The Oxford Handbook of Critical Improvisation Studies*, ed. George E. Lewis and Benjamin Piekut, vol. 1 (Oxford: Oxford University Press, 2016), 239–54.
5 'Improvvisatori', *The Penny Magazine of the Society for the Diffusion of Useful Knowledge*, April 20, 1839, 146–47.
6 Jameson, *Ennuyée*, 317.
7 Henry James, *The Tragic Muse* (London: MacMillan and Co., 1921), xi.
8 Anthony Trollope, *Barchester Towers*, ed. John Bowen (Oxford: Oxford University Press, 2014), 241. Further references to this edition will be incorporated into the text.
9 James, *Essays on Literature*, 1:1343.
10 Anthony Trollope, *Orley Farm*, ed. Francis O'Gorman (Oxford: Oxford University Press, 2018), 16.
11 Kincaid, *Anthony Trollope*, 3–4.
12 James, *Essays on Literature*, 1:1343.
13 'Anthony Trollope', *Macmillan's Magazine*, no. 44 (1883): 47–56; quoted in Robert D. Aguirre, 'Cold Print: Professing Authorship in Anthony Trollope's *An Autobiography*', *Biography* 25, no. 4 (2002): 569.
14 Carolyn Dever, 'Trollope, Seriality, and the "Dullness" of Form', *Literature Compass* 7, no. 9 (2010): 865.
15 William A. Cohen, 'The Palliser Novels', in *The Cambridge Companion to Anthony Trollope*, ed. Carolyn Dever and Lisa Niles (Cambridge: Cambridge University Press, 2010), 47; George Levine, *Darwin and the Novelists: Patterns of Science in Victorian Fiction* (Chicago: University of Chicago Press, 1991), 195; L. J. Swingle, *Romanticism and Anthony Trollope: A Study in the Continuities of Nineteenth-Century Literary Thought* (Ann Arbor: University of Michigan Press, 1990), 74–75.
16 James, *Essays on Literature*, 1:1338.
17 D. A. Miller, *Narrative and Its Discontents: Problems of Closure in the Traditional Novel* (Princeton: Princeton University Press, 1981), xiv, ix, emphasis added.
18 James, *Essays on Literature*, 1:1343.
19 Bertrand Russell, *The Problems of Philosophy*, ed. John Skorupski (Oxford: Oxford University Press, 1998), 47.
20 Russell, *The Problems of Philosophy*, 47.
21 In narratology, this is more usually framed as a problem of communication and pertinence (rather than, as I suggest here, a mechanism for narrative), or a way of typologising genres of fiction by degrees of implied incompleteness. See Marie-Laure Ryan, 'Fiction As a Logical, Ontological, and Illocutionary Issue', *Style* 18, no. 2 (1984): 129–31; see also Doležel's reviews of this

problem in 'Mimesis and Possible Worlds', *Poetics Today* 9, no. 3 (1988): 486–87; and in Lubomír Doležel, 'Fictional Worlds: Density, Gaps, and Inference', *Style* 29, no. 2 (1995): 201–14.
22 As I argued in the first chapter, to add an imaginary soldier to a historical military campaign, or posit an extra address (221B) to those which actually exist on London's Baker Street, is exemplary of the novel's distinctive, utopian fictionality.
23 Lewis, 'Truth in Fiction', 42; see a similar argument in Nicholas Wolterstorff's variation on a critical commonplace: 'We shall never know how many children had Lady Macbeth in the worlds of Macbeth [...] because there is nothing of the sort to know'. *Works and Worlds of Art* (Oxford: Clarendon Press, 1980), 133; cited by Doležel as an exemplary case of 'The property of incompleteness [which] implies that many conceivable statements about literary fictional worlds are undecidable'. 'Mimesis and Possible Worlds', 486.
24 Miller, *Discontents*, ix.
25 Jameson, *Commonplace Book*, 131, emphasis added.
26 Miller, *Discontents*, 365; for a similar model of narrative desire as moving from insufficiency towards totality, see Peter Brooks, *Reading for the Plot: Design and Intention in Narrative* (Cambridge, MA: Harvard University Press, 1996), 94. '[W]e are able to read present moments – in literature and, by extension, in life – as endowed with narrative meaning only because we read them in anticipation of the structuring power of those endings that will retrospectively give them the order and significance of plot'.
27 Anthony Trollope, *The Last Chronicle of Barset*, ed. Helen Small (Oxford: Oxford University Press, 2015), 729. Further references to this edition will be incorporated into the text.
28 Anthony Arthur, 'The Death of Mrs. Proudie: "Frivolous Slaughter" or Calculated Dispatch?', *Nineteenth-Century Fiction* 26, no. 4 (1972): 478; such criticism recurrently identifies as anomalous or idiosyncratic behaviours which novelists in this period clearly had in common. My broader argument is to reintegrate these anomalies into a coherent practice of fiction. 'Perhaps it is only Thackeray, among the great, who seems to find a positively wilful pleasure in damaging his own story [...] insisting in so many words on his freedom to say what he pleases about his men and women and to make them behave as he will'. Percy Lubbock, *The Craft of Fiction* (London: Jonathan Cape, 1954), 87–88.
29 Sophie Ratcliffe, 'The Episodic Trollope and *An Editor's Tales*', *Victorian Studies* 58, no. 1 (2015): 61.
30 Kincaid, *Anthony Trollope*, 3.
31 Arthur, 'Death of Mrs. Proudie', 482.
32 Arthur, 'Death of Mrs. Proudie', 484.
33 Arthur, 'Death of Mrs. Proudie', 480. While I emphasise this here as a practice of literary production, in the next chapter on Thackeray's novel series, I examine the reading experience engendered by such intertextual connections of a fictional world.

34 Sedgwick, *Touching Feeling*, 130.
35 Arthur, 'Death of Mrs. Proudie', 478.
36 John A. Sutherland, 'Trollope at Work on *The Way We Live Now*', *Nineteenth-Century Fiction* 37, no. 3 (1982): 439.
37 Sutherland, 'Trollope at Work', 439.
38 James, *Tragic Muse*, xi.
39 David Russell, *Tact: Aesthetic Liberalism and the Essay Form in Nineteenth-Century Britain* (Princeton: Princeton University Press, 2018), 29–30.
40 Russell, *Tact*, 29.
41 Russell, *Tact*, 29.
42 Ruth ApRoberts, *Trollope: Artist and Moralist* (London: Chatto, 1971), 52.
43 ApRoberts, *Trollope,* 52, 42, 39, original emphases.
44 On objections to apRoberts's 'relativist' view of Trollope, see Roger L Slakey, 'Trollope's Case for Moral Imperative', *Nineteenth-Century Fiction* 28, no. 3 (1973): 305–20; and Andrew Wright, *Anthony Trollope: Dream and Art* (London: MacMillan Press, 1983), 153.
45 ApRoberts, *Artist and Moralist*, 52.
46 ApRoberts, *Artist and Moralist*, 39.
47 Andrew H. Miller, *The Burdens of Perfection: On Ethics and Reading in Nineteenth-Century Literature* (Ithaca, NY: Cornell University Press, 2008), 95.
48 'casuistry, n.', *OED Online* (Oxford University Press, 2010), www.oed.com/view/Entry/28642, accessed 19 June 2018; see George Eliot's ambivalence on this point: 'The casuists have become a byword of reproach; but their perverted spirit of minute discrimination [...] discern[s] that the mysterious complexity of our life is not to be embraced by maxims[.]' *The Mill on the Floss*, ed. Gordon S. Haight (Oxford: Clarendon Press, 1980), 437–38.
49 Anthony Trollope, *Eustace Diamonds*, ed. Helen Small (Oxford: Oxford University Press, 2011), 33; quoted in Kincaid, *Anthony Trollope*, 15.
50 Anthony Trollope, *The Prime Minister*, ed. Nicholas Shrimpton (Oxford: Oxford University Press, 2011), 9; Miller, *Burdens of Perfection*, 95.
51 Miller, *Burdens of Perfection*, 95.
52 ApRoberts, *Artist and Moralist*, 52.
53 Matthew Sussman, 'Optative Form in Anthony Trollope's *The Small House at Allington*', *Nineteenth-Century Literature* 71, no. 4 (2017): 498.
54 Anthony Trollope, *The Small House at Allington*, ed. Dinah Birch (Oxford: Oxford University Press, 2015), xii, xiii. Further references to this edition will be incorporated into the text.
55 Amanda Anderson, 'Trollope's Modernity', *ELH* 74, no. 3 (2007): 509–34.
56 Stephen Wall, *Trollope and Character* (London: Faber & Faber, 1988), 34–35.
57 Sussman, 'Optative Form', 489.
58 J. Hillis Miller, *Communities in Fiction* (New York: Fordham University Press, 2015), 77.
59 As Betty Cannon puts it, one falls into Sartre's definition of bad faith 'if I take one or both of two positions about reality: If I pretend either to be free in a world without facts or to be a fact in a world without freedom'. *Sartre and*

Psychoanalysis: An Existential Challenge to Clinical Meta-Theory (Lawrence: University Press of Kansas, 1991), 46. The experience of an explicitly subjective world with consistent, objective facts represents the strategic redeployment of these operations of bad faith in an authentic act of play.
60 Wall, *Trollope and Character*, 34.
61 Anderson, 'Trollope's Modernity'; Wall, *Trollope and Character*, 59.
62 ApRoberts, *Artist and Moralist*, 43. It should be noted that apRoberts argues strongly against Trollope's arbitrariness or artificiality, which would constitute 'an unethical manipulation of data' in the moral situations he constructs. My argument, of course, is precisely that this manipulation constitutes an ethical process.
63 Miller, *Burdens of Perfection*, 94.
64 Quoted in Ratcliffe, 'Episodic Trollope', 61.
65 Helena Michie, 'Rethinking Marriage: Trollope's Internal Revision', in *The Routledge Research Companion to Anthony Trollope*, ed. Deborah Denenholz Morse, Margaret Markwick, and Mark W. Turner (Oxford: Routledge, 2017), 154.
66 Michie, 'Rethinking Marriage', 155.
67 Sussman, 'Optative Form', 493.
68 Anthony Trollope, *Can You Forgive Her?*, ed. Dinah Birch (Oxford: Oxford University Press, 2012), 95.
69 On the extent to which the difference between these two characters is a gendered one, see Michie's argument that 'Thinking for all Trollope characters, but especially for women, happens under a set of social and generic constraints' that are particularly palpable for middle- to upper-class women of Alice's position. 'Rethinking Marriage', 155; see also Margaret F. King's argument on Trollope's attitude towards contemporary 'learned ladies' bringing female decision-making into new scrutiny, in "Certain Learned Ladies': Trollope's Can You Forgive Her? And the Langham Place Circle', *Victorian Literature and Culture* 21 (1993): 307–26; for Sussman, 'Gender is among the variables that cause the surface details between the two novels to differ [...] but the underlying condition is the same [...] it is this universality of the optative[.]' 'Optative Form', 502.
70 Wall, *Trollope and Character*, 63.
71 Sussman, 'Optative Form', 496.
72 Miller, *Burdens of Perfection*, 95, 98.
73 Ratcliffe, 'Episodic Trollope', 59.
74 For a full account of Trollope's working process, see Mary Hamer, *Writing by Numbers: Trollope's Serial Fiction* (Cambridge: Cambridge University Press, 1987).

Notes to Chapter Four

1 G. K. Chesterton, *The Collected Works of G. K. Chesterton: Chesterton on Dickens*, ed. Alzina Stone Dale, vol. 15 (San Francisco: Ignatius Press, 1989), 403.

2. Chesterton, *On Dickens*, 15:404.
3. Chesterton, *On Dickens*, 15:403.
4. Chesterton, *On Dickens*, 15:403.
5. Chesterton, *On Dickens*, 15:403.
6. James, *Essays on Literature*, 1:1352.
7. Henry James, *Literary Criticism: French Writers, Other European Writers, the Prefaces to the New York Edition*, ed. Leon Edel and Mark Wilson, vol. 2 (New York: The Library of America, 1984), 41.
8. Geoffrey Tillotson, *Thackeray the Novelist* (London: Methuen & Co., 1954), 5.
9. 'stock, n. 3c.', *OED Online* (Oxford University Press, 2010), www.oed.com/view/Entry/190595, accessed 19 June 2018.
10. James, *Tragic Muse*, xi.
11. James, *Tragic Muse*, xi.
12. Chesterton, *On Dickens*, 15:404.
13. Tillotson, *Thackeray the Novelist*, 1–2.
14. James, *French Writers*, 2:41.
15. Chesterton, *On Dickens*, 15:403.
16. William Makepeace Thackeray, 'Proposals for a Continuation of Ivanhoe', *Fraser's Magazine for Town and Country* 34, no. 200 (August 1846): 237.
17. William Makepeace Thackeray, *A Collection of Letters of Thackeray, 1847–1855*, ed. Jane Octavia Brookfield (New York: Scribner, 1887), 87.
18. Thackeray, 'Proposals', 237.
19. Thackeray, 'Proposals', 237.
20. 'wallow, v.', *OED Online* (Oxford University Press, 2010), www.oed.com/view/Entry/225332, accessed 19 June 2018.
21. Gaskell, *Letters*, 602.
22. James, *Essays on Literature*, 1:977.
23. William Allingham, 'Visits to Aldsworth', in *Tennyson: Interviews and Recollections*, ed. Norman Page (London: MacMillan Press, 1983), 134.
24. Samuel Taylor Coleridge, *Biographia Literaria*, ed. J. Shawcross, vol. 1 (Oxford: Oxford University Press, 1907), 34, original emphasis.
25. Henrietta Eliza Vaughan Stannard, née Palmer, also wrote under the pseudonyms 'John Strange Winter' and 'Violet Whyte', and was also referred to by her husband's name, Mrs Arthur Stannard.
26. 'Novels and their Endings' in John Ruskin, *The Works of John Ruskin*, ed. E. T. Cook and Alexander Wedderburn, vol. 34 (London: George Allen, 1908), 605. Further references to this edition will be incorporated into the text.
27. James, *French Writers*, 2:41.
28. Allingham, 'Visits to Aldsworth', 134.
29. Auyoung, *When Fiction Feels Real*, 97.
30. F. R. Leavis, *The Great Tradition: George Eliot, Henry James, Joseph Conrad* (New York: George W. Stewart, 1950), 21.
31. John Strange Winter, *Bootles' Children* (London: F. V. White & Co., 1888), unpaginated.

32 John Plotz, 'Serial Pleasures: The Influence of Television on the Victorian Novel', *Romanticism on the Net*, no. 63 (2014): para. 26, http://id.erudit.org/iderudit/1025619ar.
33 Plotz, 'Serial Pleasures', para. 19.
34 James, *Essays on Literature*, 1:977.
35 Plotz, 'Serial Pleasures', para. 19.
36 Holly Furneaux, *Queer Dickens* (Oxford: Oxford University Press, 2009), 67.
37 Ben Winyard, '"May We Meet Again": Rereading the Dickensian Serial in the Digital Age', *19: Interdisciplinary Studies in the Long Nineteenth Century*, no. 21 (2015): para. 3, www.19.bbk.ac.uk/articles/10.16995/ntn.737/.
38 See John M. Picker, 'George Eliot and the Sequel Question', *New Literary History* 37, no. 2 (2006): 361–88.
39 Wolfgang Iser, *Prospecting: From Reader Response to Literary Anthropology* (Baltimore: Johns Hopkins University Press, 1989), 11.
40 Winyard, '"May We Meet Again"', para. 3.
41 Levine, *Realistic Imagination*, 143.
42 D. A. Miller, *The Novel and the Police* (Berkeley: University of California Press, 1988), 141.
43 Plotz, 'Serial Pleasures', para. 27.
44 Picker, 'George Eliot and the Sequel Question', 378.
45 Elisha Cohn, *Still Life* (Oxford: Oxford University Press, 2016), 62, 63.
46 Coleridge, *Biographia Literaria*, 1:34.
47 Brontë, *Villette*, 105.
48 Brown, 'Beloved Objects: Mourning, Materiality, and Charlotte Brontë's "Never-Ending Story"', 403.
49 Root-Bernstein, *Inventing Imaginary Worlds*, 41.
50 Jameson, *Commonplace Book*, 131.
51 Shuttleworth, *Mind of the Child*, 87.
52 Root-Bernstein, *Inventing Imaginary Worlds*, 23.
53 Berlant, *Cruel Optimism*, 24, original emphasis; Root-Bernstein, *Inventing Imaginary Worlds*, 23.
54 Allingham, 'Visits to Aldsworth', 134.
55 James, *Essays on Literature*, 1:977; Berlant, *Cruel Optimism*, 24, emphasis added.
56 Charles Dickens, *Master Humphrey's Clock*, vol. 1 (London: Chapman and Hall, 1840), iii.
57 Furneaux, *Queer Dickens*, 86–87.
58 Winter, *Bootles' Children*, unpaginated.
59 'Farewell to Angria' in Brontë et al., *Tales*, 314. Further references to this edition will be incorporated into the text.
60 Linda K. Hughes and Michael Lund, *The Victorian Serial* (Charlottesville: University Press of Virginia, 1991), 10.
61 Philip Collins, ed., *Thackeray: Interviews and Recollections*, vol. 2 (London: MacMillan Press, 1989), 250.

62 Amy Barter, *Stories of Pendennis and the Charterhouse, from Thackeray* (London: George G. Harrap & Company, 1912).
63 Leah Price, *The Anthology and the Rise of the Novel* (Cambridge: Cambridge University Press, 2000), 6–7.
64 Barter, *Stories of Pendennis*, 36–37.
65 Barter, 36.
66 William Makepeace Thackeray, *The Adventures of Philip On His Way through the World Shewing Who Robbed Him, Who Helped Him, and Who Passed Him By*, ed. Judith Law Fisher (Ann Arbor: University of Michigan Press, 2010), 533; see also Auyoung's flagging of this passage as self-reflexive of the reading experience of closure. 'The farewells expressed in this last scene double as a means by which the text figuratively takes leave of the reader'. *When Fiction Feels Real*, 99.
67 William Makepeace Thackeray, *The Newcomes: Memoirs of a Most Respectable Family*, ed. Andrew Sanders (Oxford: Oxford University Press, 1995), 17. Further references to this edition will be incorporated into the text.
68 Nicholas Dames, *The Physiology of the Novel: Reading, Neural Science, and the Form of Victorian Fiction* (Oxford: Oxford University Press, 2007), 109.
69 Juliet McMaster, 'Theme and Form in The Newcomes', *Nineteenth-Century Fiction* 23, no. 2 (1968): 180.
70 Dames, *Physiology*, 109.
71 Levine, *Forms*, 108.
72 Levine, *Forms*, 108.
73 Levine, *Forms*, 125; see also Levine's previous work in *The Serious Pleasures of Suspense* (Charlottesville: University of Virginia Press, 2003).
74 'The Newcomes', *Athenaeum*, August 4, 1855, 1499; quoted in Dames, *Physiology*, 106.
75 Levine, *Forms*, 108.
76 Levine, *Forms*, 128.
77 G. Levine, *Realistic Imagination*, 139–40.
78 Lawrence Charles Zygmunt, 'Thackeray and the Picaresque World' (PhD diss., University of Chicago, 2012), 46.
79 Thackeray, *Vanity Fair*, 2.
80 Gage McWeeny, *The Comfort of Strangers: Social Life and Literary Form* (Oxford: Oxford University Press, 2016), 65.
81 Chesterton, *On Dickens*; Zygmunt, 'Thackeray and the Picaresque World', 56.
82 Zygmunt, 'Thackeray and the Picaresque World', 56.
83 Collins, *Thackeray: Interviews and Recollections*, 2:216.
84 McWeeny, *Comfort of Strangers*, 66; G. Levine, *Realistic Imagination*, 153–54.
85 Thackeray, 'Proposals', 238.
86 Henry James, *Roderick Hudson* (London: MacMillan and Co., 1921), x.
87 Chesterton, *On Dickens*, 15:403.
88 Levine, *Forms*, 130.

89 Keren Eyal and Jonathan Cohen, 'When Good Friends Say Goodbye: A Parasocial Breakup Study', *Journal of Broadcasting & Electronic Media* 50, no. 3 (2006): 502–3.
90 Thackeray, *Roundabout Papers*, 272.
91 Thackeray, *Roundabout Papers*, 272–73.
92 Thackeray, *Roundabout Papers*, 273.
93 Thackeray, *Roundabout Papers*, 273.
94 Thackeray, *Roundabout Papers*, 272.
95 Edward W. Said, *Culture and Imperialism* (New York: Knopf, 1994), 74; or in Raymond Williams's very similar argument, as an 'available escape route [...] [where] characters whose destinies could not be worked out within the system as given were simply put on the boat', in *The Long Revolution* (Westport, CT: Greenwood Press, 1975), 115–16; both quoted in Maia McAleavey, *The Bigamy Plot: Sensation and Convention in the Victorian Novel* (Cambridge: Cambridge University Press, 2015), 116.
96 Said, *Culture and Imperialism*, 74; Chesterton, *On Dickens*, 15:403.
97 Barter, *Stories of Pendennis*, 36.
98 Tillotson has also called this the 'lack of an edged shape' in Thackeray's novels, produced by 'an aspiration towards rendering the vastness of the world and the never-endingness of time'. *Thackeray the Novelist*, 12.

Notes to Chapter Five

1 Lewes, 'Dickens in Relation', 144.
2 Lewes, 'Dickens in Relation', 144, original emphasis.
3 Lewes, 'Dickens in Relation', 145.
4 Lewes, 'Dickens in Relation', 144.
5 Tyson Michael Stolte, 'Mind Reflected on Paper: Dickens, Victorian Psychology, and the First-Person Novel' (PhD diss., University of British Columbia, 2009), 1.
6 Lewes, 'Dickens in Relation', 146; Henry James, 'Our Mutual Friend', *The Nation*, December 21, 1865.
7 Lewes, 'Dickens in Relation', 146.
8 Lewes, 'Dickens in Relation', 144.
9 Lewes, 'Dickens in Relation', 144.
10 Rosemarie Bodenheimer, *Knowing Dickens* (Ithaca, NY: Cornell University Press, 2007), 5.
11 As I have previously argued, such conflations of belief with experience misconceive the double consciousness involved in pretending and imagining (although Lewes distinguishes 'knowing' from 'being affected'). Lewes, 'Dickens in Relation', 145.
12 Lowe, *Insights of Sympathy*, 94.
13 It is hard to say for certain how much of this composition is the written record of a verbal game that occurred the year before, in 1828, and how much is

being invented with the composition in 1829. The Brontës in this period are in the process of transitioning from writing down records of previous play-narratives and writing new narratives as a form of play in itself.
14 Julia Mandell, 'Rules of the Games', *Architecture* 93, no. 7 (2004): 66.
15 Barthes, *The Rustle of Language*, 141, original emphasis.
16 Barthes, *The Rustle of Language*, 143, 145–46, original emphasis.
17 Barthes, *The Rustle of Language*, 144, 146.
18 Barthes, *The Rustle of Language*, 142.
19 Barthes, *The Rustle of Language*, 148.
20 James Wood, *How Fiction Works* (London: Vintage Books, 2010), 52, original emphasis.
21 As I argued in the second chapter, such repudiations are more ambivalent than they appear – Crimsworth and Frances in fact build an extravagantly successful boarding-school at the conclusion of *The Professor*.
22 James, *Tragic Muse*, xi.
23 Lowe, *Insights of Sympathy*, 91.
24 James, *Essays on Literature*, 1:958, 965.
25 Leavis, *The Great Tradition*, 21.
26 Davis, *Resisting Novels*, 24; quoted in Lowe, *Insights of Sympathy*, 76.
27 Davis, *Resisting Novels*, 24.
28 Sue Zemka, *Time and the Moment in Victorian Literature and Society* (Cambridge: Cambridge University Press, 2012), 19.
29 James Mill, *Analysis of the Phenomena of the Human Mind*, ed. Alexander Bain et al., vol. 1 (London: Longmans, Green, Reader, & Dyer, 1869), 52.
30 Mill, *Analysis*, 1:52.
31 Zemka, *Time and the Moment in Victorian Literature and Society*, 21.
32 Mill, *Analysis*, 1:65.
33 Jean-Marie Schaeffer has recently described these experiences – of memory, visualisation, and hallucination – as '"virtual realities" born with biological systems of representation'. *Why Fiction?*, xii.
34 James Cowles Prichard, *A Treatise on Diseases of the Nervous System, Part the First: Comprising Convulsive and Maniacal Affections* (London: Underwood, 1822), 126.
35 Robert MacNish, *The Philosophy of Sleep* (Glasgow: W. R. M'Phun, 1834), 243.
36 John Abercrombie, *Inquiries Concerning the Intellectual Powers, and the Investigation of Truth* (New York: Collins and Brother, 1849), 52.
37 Henry Holland, *Chapters on Mental Physiology* (London: Longman, Brown, Green, and Longmans, 1852), 113.
38 Prichard, *Diseases of the Nervous System*, 126.
39 [Francis Jacox,] 'Hartley Coleridge', *Bentley's Miscellany* 45 (1859): 584.
40 'Hartley Coleridge as Man, Poet, Essayist', *Fraser's Magazine for Town and Country* 43 (1851): 504.
41 'Hartley Coleridge', *The Gentleman's Magazine* (June 1851): 581.
42 'Review of "Poem, by Hartley Coleridge; with a Memoir of Life, by His Brother"', *The Christian Remembrancer* 22 (1851): 108–9.

43 Gallagher, 'Rise of Fictionality', 338.
44 Shuttleworth, *Mind of the Child*, 86–87; more or less the kind of moral failing Plato denounced as the effect of poetry in Book X of The Republic, as it appeals to our 'childish and pervasive' love for unreason. See Plato, *Republic*, trans. Robin Waterfield (Oxford: Oxford University Press, 2008), 606d–608b, 360–62.
45 J. Crichton-Browne, 'Psychical Diseases of Early Life', *British Journal of Psychology* 6 (1860): 303.
46 'Mrs Jameson's Common-Place Book', *The New Monthly Magazine*, 1855, 194; 'Mrs Jameson's Common-Place Book', *Chamber's Journal of Popular Literature, Science and Arts* 3, no. 53 (1855): 8.
47 'Hartley Coleridge', *The Gentleman's Magazine*, 581.
48 Davis, *Resisting Novels*, 24.
49 'Mrs Jameson's Common-Place Book', *Chamber's Journal*, 1855, 8.
50 Lewes, 'Dickens in Relation', 144, emphasis added; Lewes's own work had contributed to the consensus around mental perceptions by theorising the phenomena of 'subjective sensations; that is to say, we see objects very vividly, where no such objects exist; we hear sounds of many kinds, where none of their external causes exist [...] They are indistinguishable from the sensations caused by actual contact of the objects with our organs', which in intense forms 'produce Hallucinations'. *The Physiology of Common Life*, vol. 2 (London: William Blackwood and Sons, 1859), 308.
51 Lewes, 'Dickens in Relation', 145.
52 P. R. Marland, 'Seeing Things in Dickens: A Study of Representation and Hypotyposis' (PhD diss., University of Sydney, 2014), 6.
53 Charles Lamb, *Selected Prose*, ed. Adam Phillips (Harmondsworth: Penguin, 1985), 202.
54 See Adam Phillips, *Going Sane* (London: Penguin, 2006), 63.
55 Lamb, *Selected Prose*, 202.
56 Taylor Stoehr, *Dickens: The Dreamer's Stance* (Ithaca, NY: Cornell University Press, 1965), 38.
57 Lewes, 'Dickens In Relatio', 145.
58 'About Ejuxria and Gombroon', *Bentley's Miscellany*, no. 59 (1866): 75.
59 Jacox, 'Hartley Coleridge', 75–76.
60 Abercrombie, *The Intellectual Powers*, 52.
61 Marland, 'Seeing Things', 69.
62 Marland, 'Seeing Things', 67.
63 Lowe, *Insights of Sympathy*, 94.
64 Barthes, *The Rustle of Language*, 148.
65 Barthes, *The Rustle of Language*, 143.
66 Marie-Laure Ryan, 'The Modes of Narrativity and Their Visual Metaphors', *Style* 26, no. 3 (1992): 375; see also Erik Van Ooijen's discussion of Ryan in relation to Barthes's changing concepts of textual economy, in 'The Affluence of Literature', in *Narrativity, Fictionality and Literariness: The Narrative Turn*

and the Study of Literary Fiction, ed. Lars-Åke Skalin (Örebro: Örebro University Press, 2008), 125–27.
67 Lowe, Insights of Sympathy, 94.
68 Ryan, 'Modes of Narrativity', 375.
69 Lewes, 'Dickens in Relation', 146; Lewes seems therefore to be reversing associationism's terms for objects of direct sensory presence (sensations) and recalled or mental presence (ideas). As Mill despairingly admits, both 'sensation' and 'idea' are words of 'inconvenience [...] used with great latitude of meaning, both in ordinary, and in philosophical discourse'. Mill, Analysis, 1:152.
70 Lewes, 'Dickens in Relation', 146.
71 'wooden, Adj. 2a.', OED Online (Oxford University Press, 2010), www.oed.com/view/Entry/230028, accessed 19 June 2018.
72 Crichton-Browne, 'Psychical Diseases', 303.
73 Charles Dickens, Little Dorrit, ed. Harvey Peter Sucksmith (Oxford: Clarendon Press, 1979), 5–6. Further references to this edition will be incorporated into the text.
74 Philip Collins, 'Little Dorrit: The Prison and the Critics', Times Literary Supplement, April 18, 1980, 446; Lionel Trilling, 'Little Dorrit', The Kenyon Review 15, no. 4 (1953): 589.
75 Trilling, 'Little Dorrit', 578–79.
76 Edmund Wilson, The Wound and the Bow: Seven Studies in Literature (Cambridge: Houghton Mifflin Company, 1941), 56; J. Hillis Miller, Charles Dickens: The World of the His Novels (Cambridge, MA: Harvard University Press, 1958), 228–29.
77 For which, see John Carey's strong contention: 'We're told that the repetition [of the prison symbol] unifies the novel, and that it reveals a deeper meaning. This deep meaning is represented by maxims like "Society is a prison" or "All the world's a prison", [...] using the word "prison", we realize, only in some enfeebled figurative sense – a sense which no one who had ever really been in prison would condone'. The Violent Effigy: A Study of Dickens' Imagination (London: Faber & Faber, 1979), 114.
78 Barthes, The Rustle of Language, 146.
79 'Introduction' in Charles Dickens, Little Dorrit, ed. John Holloway (Harmondsworth: Penguin, 1973), 15; Charles Dickens, The Letters of Charles Dickens, 1856–1858, ed. Graham Storey and Kathleen Tillotson, vol. 8 (Oxford: Clarendon Press, 1995), 79, 280; quoted in Collins, 'Little Dorrit: The Prison and the Critics', 446.
80 See Paul D. Herring, 'Dickens' Monthly Number Plans', Modern Philology 64, no. 1 (1966): 26.
81 Trilling, 'Little Dorrit', 578.
82 George Orwell, Critical Essays (London: Secker & Warburg, 1946), 52.
83 Michel Foucault, Discipline and Punish, trans. Alan Sheridan (London: Harmondsworth, 1979), 205.

84 F. R. Leavis and Q. D. Leavis, *Dickens the Novelist* (London: Chatto & Windus, 1972), 222.
85 George Gissing, *Charles Dickens: A Critical Study* (New York: Dodd, Mead and Company, 1898), 134.
86 As with Jane Eyre, going hungry at the Lowood School, who makes a habit of 'prepar[ing] in imagination the Barmecide supper of hot roast potatoes, or white bread and new milk, with which I was wont to amuse my inward cravings' (*JE* 87). Or with Lamb's depiction of 'Captain Jackson', maintaining a spirit of hospitality in poverty: 'You saw with your bodily eyes indeed what seemed a bare scrag – cold savings from the foregone meal – remnant hardly sufficient [...] But in the copious will – the revelling imagination of your host [...] no end appeared to the profusion'. To drink, 'Wine we had none [...] but the sensation of wine was there [...] Shut your eyes, and you would swear a capacious bowl of punch was foaming in the centre'. *Essays of Elia, Letters, and Rosamund, A Tale* (Paris: Baudry's European Library, 1835), 209. Such studies in illusory food are clearly interested in the potential resources of a sensuous imagination in historical conditions of need.
87 Ryan, 'Modes of Narrativity', 375.
88 Barbara Hardy, *Dickens and Creativity* (London: Continuum, 2008), 124.
89 'castle, n. 11.', *OED Online* (Oxford University Press, 2010), www.oed.com/view/Entry/28581, accessed 19 June 2018.
90 Ryan, 'Parallel Universes to Possible Worlds', 156.
91 Hardy, *Dickens and Creativity*, 109.
92 Trilling, 'Little Dorrit', 579.
93 Crichton-Browne, 'Psychical Diseases', 303.
94 Prichard, *Diseases of the Nervous System*, 128; or as Abercrombie noted, 'Visions of the imagination which have formerly been indulged in, of that kind which we call waking dreams, or castle-building [...] [are] now believed to have a real existence'. *The Intellectual Powers*, 234.
95 Exemplifying, as Robert Douglas-Fairhurst puts it, 'how adept Dickens was becoming at creating complications for himself and then tidying them away'. *Charles Dickens*, ed. Adrian Poole, *The Cambridge Companion to English Novelists* (Cambridge: Cambridge University Press, 2009), 136.
96 Stoehr, *The Dreamer's Stance*, 64.
97 See Stoehr, *The Dreamer's Stance*, 63–64.
98 Trilling, 'Little Dorrit', 578.
99 Quoted and translated in Erich Auerbach, *Time, History, and Literature: Selected Essays of Erich Auerbach*, ed. James I. Porter, trans. Jane O. Newman (Princeton: Princeton University Press, 2014), 86.
100 See also Wolfgang Mieder, *Behold the Proverbs of a People* (Jackson: University Press of Mississippi, 2014), 422–25.
101 Auerbach, *Time, History, and Literature*, 86.
102 Forbes Winslow, *On the Preservation of the Health of Body and Mind* (London: Henry Renshaw, 1842), 172, emphasis added.
103 'Hartley Coleridge as Man, Poet, Essayist', 605.

104 'Mrs Jameson's Common-Place Book', *The New Monthly Magazine*, 1855, 196.
105 Davis, *Resisting Novels*, 24.
106 See also Elaine Scarry's discussion about the projections from Proust's magic lantern, as a metonym for how *Swann's Way* materialises the solid walls of Marcel's childhood bedroom. *Dreaming by the Book* (Princeton: Princeton University Press, 2001), 12.
107 Lewes, 'Dickens in Relation', 145.
108 Lewes, 'Dickens in Relation', 145.
109 Venice seems to represent, for Dickens, a particularly apt setting for this kind of mental state. His accounts of visiting the city emphasise the hallucinogenic quality of 'this strange Dream upon the water', wondering at the architecture that rises unstably – like the aerial castle – from its 'unsubstantial ground'. Charles Dickens, *Pictures from Italy*, ed. Kate Flint (London: Penguin, 1998), 249, 256.
110 Barthes, *The Rustle of Language*, 144.
111 Leavis and Leavis, *Dickens the Novelist*, 222.
112 Trilling, 'Little Dorrit', 589; Hardy, *Dickens and Creativity*, 109.
113 Stoehr, *The Dreamer's Stance*, 38.
114 Stoehr, *The Dreamer's Stance*, 64.
115 As Jolene Zigarovich has pointed out, 'in the manuscripts, proofs, and first editions of the novel, the names in all the epitaphs are small-capped, which resembles epitaph typography [...] Chivery's depresentification, his spatial self-distance, is not confined to a mode of verbal narration'. 'Proleptic Death in Dickens's A Christmas Carol and Little Dorrit', *ANQ: A Quarterly Journal of Short Articles, Notes and Reviews* 29, no. 2 (2016): 80. Alongside the 'hypotyposis' of John's verbal description of his future, these epitaphs form a graphic representation of what he imagines, such that – bizarrely – the character's imagined objects achieve a more visual, spatial, and material existence in the novel's print than in the novel's world. Like the extended metaphor of the castle in the air, the imagined world of John's prison-churchyard assumes its own reality for the reader as its objects materialise on the page.

Notes to the Conclusion

1 Grant Rodiek, 'The Sims 4 Patch Notes', The Sims 4, 2018, https://help.ea.com/en-gb/help/the-sims/the-sims-4/the-sims-4-updates/, accessed 19 June 2018.
2 'Description of the Security Update for Word 2016: July 10, 2018', Microsoft Support, 2018, https://support.microsoft.com/en-us/help/4022218/description-of-the-security-update-for-word-2016-july-10–2018.
3 Chris Baker, 'Will Wright Wants to Make a Game out of Life Itself', *Wired Magazine*, July 2012, https://www.wired.com/2012/07/mf_iconswright/.
4 Diane Nutt and Diane Railton, 'The Sims: Real Life as Genre', *Information, Communication & Society* 6, no. 4 (2003): 584.

5 Gallagher, 'Rise of Fictionality', 340.
6 Felski, *Limits of Critique*, 12.
7 'The work of ideology is to present the position of the subject as fixed and unchangeable [...] [in] human nature and the world of human experience, and to show possible action as an endless repetition of "normal", familiar action. To the extent that the classic realist text performs this work, classical realism is an ideological practice'. Catherine Belsey, *Critical Practice* (London: Routledge, 2001), 74.
8 Emma Butcher, *The Brontës and War: Fantasy and Conflict in Charlotte and Bronwell Brontë's Youthful Writings* (London: Palgrave Macmillan, 2019), 135.
9 See Robert Sparrow, 'Robots, Rape, and Representation', *International Journal of Social Robotics* 9, no. 4 (2017): 465–77.
10 These subjects have also explicitly converged in recent scholarship. See S. L. Patridge, 'Pornography, Ethics, and Video games', *Ethics and Information Technology* 15 (2013): 25–34; A. W. Eaton, 'A Sensible Antiporn Feminism', *Ethics* 117, no. 4 (2007): 674–715.
11 Bauer, *How to Do Things with Pornography*, 6.
12 'The thing about playing is always the precariousness of the interplay of personal psychic reality and the experience of control of actual objects. This is the precariousness of magic itself, magic that arises from intimacy, in a relationship that is found to be reliable'. D. W. Winnicott, *Playing and Reality* (London: Routledge Classics, 2005), 64.
13 Davis, *Resisting Novels*, 103.

Bibliography

Abercrombie, John. *Inquiries Concerning the Intellectual Powers, and the Investigation of Truth*. New York: Collins and Brother, 1849.
Abrams, Meyer H. *The Mirror and the Lamp: Romantic Theory and the Critical Tradition*. London: Oxford University Press, 1953.
Aguirre, Robert D. 'Cold Print: Professing Authorship in Anthony Trollope's *An Autobiography*'. *Biography* 25, no. 4 (2002): 569–92.
Alexander, Christine. 'Nineteenth-Century Juvenilia: A Survey'. In *The Child Writer from Austen to Woolf*. Edited by Christine Alexander and Juliet McMasters, 11–30. Cambridge: Cambridge University Press, 2005.
Allingham, William. 'Visits to Aldsworth'. In *Tennyson: Interviews and Recollections*. Edited by Norman Page, 130–54. London: MacMillan Press, 1983.
Anderson, Amanda. 'Trollope's Modernity'. *ELH* 74, no. 3 (2007): 509–34.
'Anthony Trollope'. *Macmillan's Magazine*, no. 44 (1883): 47–56.
apRoberts, Ruth. *Trollope: Artist and Moralist*. London: Chatto, 1971.
Aretoulakis, Emmanouil. 'The Prefatory/Postscript Letters to St. Thomas More's Utopia: The Culture of "Seeing" as a Reality-Conferring Strategy'. *Journal of Early Modern Studies* 3 (2014): 91–113.
Arthur, Anthony. 'The Death of Mrs. Proudie: "Frivolous Slaughter" or Calculated Dispatch?' *Nineteenth-Century Fiction* 26, no. 4 (1972): 477–84.
Auerbach, Erich. *Time, History, and Literature: Selected Essays of Erich Auerbach*. Edited by James I. Porter. Translated by Jane O. Newman. Princeton, NJ: Princeton University Press, 2014.
Auyoung, Elaine. *When Fiction Feels Real: Representation and the Reading Mind*. Oxford: Oxford University Press, 2018.
Azim, Firdous. *The Colonial Rise of the Novel*. London: Routledge, 1993.
Baker, Chris. 'Will Wright Wants to Make a Game out of Life Itself'. *Wired Magazine*. New York, July 2012. www.wired.com/2012/07/mf_iconswright/.
Barter, Amy. *Stories of Pendennis and the Charterhouse, from Thackeray*. London: George G. Harrap & Company, 1912.
Barthes, Roland. *The Rustle of Language*. Translated by Richard Howard. Berkeley: University of California Press, 1989.
Bauer, Nancy. *How to Do Things with Pornography*. Cambridge, MA: Harvard University Press, 2015.

Belsey, Catherine. *Critical Practice*. London: Routledge, 2001.
Bentham, Jeremy. *The Works of Jeremy Bentham: Chrestomathia, Ontology, Logic*. Edited by John Bowring. Vol. 8. Edinburgh: William Tait, 1841.
  The Works of Jeremy Bentham: Memoirs. Edited by John Bowring. Vol. 10. Edinburgh: William Tait, 1843.
Berlant, Lauren. *Cruel Optimism*. Durham, NC: Duke University Press, 2011.
Best, Stephen, and Sharon Marcus. 'Surface Reading: An Introduction'. *Representations* 108, no. 1 (2009): 1–21.
Bock, Carol. *Charlotte Brontë and the Storyteller's Audience*. Iowa City: University of Iowa Press, 1992.
Bodenheimer, Rosemarie. *Knowing Dickens*. Ithaca, NY: Cornell University Press, 2007.
Bonnell, Henry Houston. *Charlotte Brontë, George Eliot, and Jane Austen: Studies in Their Work*. New York: Longmans, Green, and Co., 1902.
Booth, Wayne. *The Company We Keep: An Ethics of Fiction*. Berkeley: University of California Press, 1988.
Briggs, Asa. *Victorian People: A Reassessment of Persons and Themes, 1851–67*. Chicago: University of Chicago Press, 1973.
Brontë, Charlotte. *The Early Writings of Charlotte Brontë, 1826–1832*. Edited by Christine Alexander. Padstow: Shakespeare Head Press, 1987.
  Jane Eyre. Edited by Mary Augusta Arnold Ward. New York: Harper Bros., 1899.
  Jane Eyre. Edited by Jane Jack and Margaret Smith. Oxford: Clarendon Press, 1969.
  The Letters of Charlotte Brontë, 1829–1847. Edited by Margaret Smith. Oxford: Clarendon Press, 1995.
  The Letters of Charlotte Brontë, 1848–1851. Edited by Margaret Smith. Oxford: Clarendon Press, 2000.
  The Professor. Edited by Margaret Smith and Herbert Rosengarten. Oxford: Clarendon Press, 1987.
  The Professor. Edited by Heather Glen. London: Penguin, 2003.
  Villette. Edited by Margaret Smith and Herbert Rosengarten. Oxford: Clarendon Press, 1984.
Brontë, Charlotte, Branwell Brontë, Emily Brontë, and Anne Brontë. *Tales of Glass Town, Angria, and Gondal*. Edited by Christine Alexander. Oxford: Oxford University Press, 2010.
Brooks, Peter. *Reading for the Plot: Design and Intention in Narrative*. Cambridge, MA: Harvard University Press, 1996.
  Realist Vision. New Haven, CT: Yale University Press, 2005.
Brown, Kate E. 'Beloved Objects: Mourning, Materiality, and Charlotte Brontë's "Never-Ending Story"'. *ELH* 65, no. 2 (1998): 395–421.
Butcher, Emma. *The Brontës and War: Fantasy and Conflict in Charlotte and Branwell Brontë's Youthful Writings*, London: Palgrave MacMillan, 2019.
Cannon, Betty. *Sartre and Psychoanalysis: An Existential Challenge to Clinical Meta-Theory*. Lawrence: University Press of Kansas, 1991.

Carey, John. *The Violent Effigy: A Study of Dickens' Imagination*. London: Faber & Faber, 1979.
'castle, n. 11'. *OED Online*. Oxford University Press, 2010. www.oed.com/view/Entry/28581. Accessed 19 July 2018.
'casuistry, n.' *OED Online*. Oxford University Press, 2010. www.oed.com/view/Entry/28642. Accessed 19 July 2018.
Cave, Terence. *Thinking with Literature: Towards a Cognitive Criticism*. Oxford: Oxford University Press, 2016.
Thomas More's Utopia in Early Modern Europe: Paratexts and Contexts. Manchester: Manchester University Press, 2008.
Chesterton, G. K. *The Collected Works of G. K. Chesterton: Chesterton on Dickens*. Edited by Alzina Stone Dale. Vol. 15. San Francisco: Ignatius Press, 1989.
Cohen, David, and Stephen A. MacKeith. *The Development of Imagination: The Private Worlds of Childhood*. London: Routledge, 1991.
Cohen, William A. 'The Palliser Novels'. In *The Cambridge Companion to Anthony Trollope*. Edited by Carolyn Dever and Lisa Niles, 44–57. Cambridge: Cambridge University Press, 2010.
Cohn, Elisha. *Still Life*. Oxford: Oxford University Press, 2016.
Coleridge, Hartley. *Poems*. Edited by Derwent Coleridge. Vol. 1. London: Edward Moxon, 1851.
Coleridge, Samuel Taylor. *Biographia Literaria*. Edited by J. Shawcross. Vol. 1. Oxford: Oxford University Press, 1907.
Collins, Philip. 'Little Dorrit: The Prison and the Critics'. *Times Literary Supplement*. April 18, 1980.
Collins, Philip, ed. *Thackeray: Interviews and Recollections*. Vol. 2. London: MacMillan Press, 1989.
Crichton-Browne, James. 'Psychical Diseases of Early Life'. *British Journal of Psychology* 6 (1860): 284–320.
Dames, Nicholas. 'On Hegel, History, and Reading As If for Life: Response'. *Victorian Studies* 53, no. 3 (2011): 437–44. https://doi.org/10.1353/vic.2011.0044.
The Physiology of the Novel: Reading, Neural Science, and the Form of Victorian Fiction. Oxford: Oxford University Press, 2007.
Davis, Lennard J. *Factual Fictions: The Origins of the English Novel*. Philadelphia: University of Pennsylvania Press, 1983.
Resisting Novels. New York: Routledge, 1987.
Defoe, Daniel. *Robinson Crusoe*. Edited by Thomas Keymer and James Kelly. Oxford: Oxford University Press, 2007.
Deleuze, Gilles. 'Description of the Security Update for Word 2016: July 10, 2018'. Microsoft Support, 2018. https://support.microsoft.com/en-us/help/4022218/description-of-the-security-update-for-word-2016-july-10-2018.
Difference and Repetition. Translated by Paul Patton. London: Bloomsbury, 2014.
Dever, Carolyn. 'Trollope, Seriality, and the "Dullness" of Form'. *Literature Compass* 7, no. 9 (2010): 861–66.

Dickens, Charles. *David Copperfield*. Edited by Nina Burgis. Oxford: Clarendon Press, 1981.
  The Letters of Charles Dickens, 1840–1841. Edited by Madeline House, Graham Storey, and Kathleen Tillotson. Vol. 2. Oxford: Clarendon Press, 1969.
  The Letters of Charles Dickens, 1847–1849. Edited by Graham Storey, K. J. Fielding, and Anthony Laude. Vol. 5. Oxford: Clarendon Press, 1977.
  The Letters of Charles Dickens, 1856–1858. Edited by Graham Storey and Kathleen Tillotson. Vol. 8. Oxford: Clarendon Press, 1995.
  Little Dorrit. Edited by John Holloway. Harmondsworth: Penguin, 1973.
  Little Dorrit. Edited by Harvey Peter Sucksmith. Oxford: Clarendon Press, 1979.
  Master Humphrey's Clock. Vol. 1. London: Chapman and Hall, 1840.
  The Mudfog Papers. London: Richard Bentley and Son, 1880.
  Pictures from Italy. Edited by Kate Flint. London: Penguin, 1998.
Doležel, Lubomír. 'Fictional Worlds: Density, Gaps, and Inference'. *Style* 29, no. 2 (1995): 201–14.
  'Mimesis and Possible Worlds'. *Poetics Today* 9, no. 3 (1988): 475–96.
Douglas-Fairhurst, Robert. *Charles Dickens*. Edited by Adrian Poole. *The Cambridge Companion to English Novelists*. Cambridge: Cambridge University Press, 2009.
Eagleton, Terry. *Myths of Power*. Basingstoke: MacMillan Press, 1988.
Eaton, Anne W. 'A Sensible Antiporn Feminism'. *Ethics* 117.4 (2007): 674–715.
Eliot, George. *Adam Bede*. Edited by Carol A. Martin. Oxford: Clarendon Press, 2001.
  Daniel Deronda. Edited by Graham Handley. Oxford: Clarendon Press, 1984.
  The Mill on the Floss. Edited by Gordon S. Haight. Oxford: Clarendon Press, 1980.
  'Silly Novels by Lady Novelists'. In *Essays of George Eliot*. Edited by Thomas Pinney, 300–324. New York: Columbia University Press, 1963.
Ess, Charles M. 'Ethics at the Boundaries of the Virtual'. In *The Oxford Handbook of Virtuality*. Edited by Mark Grimshaw, 683–97. Oxford: Oxford University Press, 2014.
Esterhammer, Angela. 'The Cosmopolitan Improvvisatore: Spontaneity and Performance in Romantic Poetics'. *European Romantic Review* 16, no. 2 (2005): 153–65.
  'The Improvisation of Poetry, 1750–1850'. In *The Oxford Handbook of Critical Improvisation Studies*. Edited by George E. Lewis and Benjamin Piekut, 1:239–54. Oxford: Oxford University Press, 2016.
Eyal, Keren, and Jonathan Cohen. 'When Good Friends Say Goodbye: A Parasocial Breakup Study'. *Journal of Broadcasting & Electronic Media* 50, no. 3 (2006): 502–23.
Farina, Jonathan. '"Dickens's As If": Analogy and Victorian Virtual Reality'. *Victorian Studies* 53, no. 3 (2011): 427–36.
Felski, Rita. 'After Suspicion'. *Profession*, 2009, 28–35.
  The Limits of Critique. Chicago: University of Chicago Press, 2015.

Uses of Literature. Oxford: Blackwell Publishing, 2009.
Fielding, Henry. *The Wesleyan Edition of the Works of Henry Fielding: Joseph Andrews*. Edited by Martin C. Battestin. Oxford: Oxford University Press and Wesleyan University Press, 1966.
Flaubert, Gustave. *The Letters of Gustave Flaubert, 1830–1857*. Edited and translated by Francis Steegmuller. London: Faber & Faber, 1979.
Forsberg, Laura. 'The Miniature World of Charlotte Brontë's Glass Town'. In *Charlotte Brontë from the Beginnings: New Essays from the Juvenilia to the Major Works*. Edited by Judith E. Pike and Lucy Morrison, 44–58. Oxford: Routledge, 2016.
Foucault, Michel. *Discipline and Punish*. Translated by Alan Sheridan. London: Harmondsworth, 1979.
Franklin, J. Jeffrey. *Serious Play: The Cultural Form of the Nineteenth-Century Realist Novel*. Philadelphia: University of Pennsylvania Press, 1999.
Freedgood, Elaine. 'Fictional Settlements: Footnotes, Metalepsis, the Colonial Effect'. *New Literary History* 41, no. 2 (2010): 393–411.
Freud, Sigmund. 'Creative Writers and Day-Dreaming'. In *Pelican Freud Library*. Edited by James Strachey, 14:129–41. Harmondsworth: Penguin, 1985.
Furneaux, Holly. *Queer Dickens*. Oxford: Oxford University Press, 2009.
Gallagher, Catherine. 'The Rise of Fictionality'. In *The Novel*. Edited by Franco Moretti, 336–63. Princeton, NJ: Princeton University Press, 2006.
"What Would Napoleon Do?: Historical, Fictional, and Counterfactual Characters'. *New Literary History* 42, no. 2 (2011): 315–36.
Gaskell, Elizabeth. *The Letters of Mrs Gaskell*. Edited by J. A. V. Chapple and Arthur Pollard. Manchester: Manchester University Press, 1966.
The Life of Charlotte Bronte. Edited by Elisabeth Jay. London: Penguin, 1997.
Genette, Gérard. *Narrative Discourse*. Edited by Jane E. Lewin and Jonathan Culler. Oxford: Basil Blackwell, 1980.
Gibson, William. *Neuromancer*. New York: Berkley Publishing Group, 1989.
Gissing, George. *Charles Dickens: A Critical Study*. New York: Dodd, Mead and Company, 1898.
Glen, Heather. *Charlotte Brontë: The Imagination in History*. Oxford: Oxford University Press, 2004.
Goodman, Lesley Anne. 'Indignant Reading'. PhD diss., Harvard University, 2013.
Greiner, Rae. *Sympathetic Realism in Nineteenth-Century British Fiction*. Baltimore: Johns Hopkins University Press, 2012.
Grosz, Elizabeth A. *Architecture from the Outside: Essays on Virtual and Real Space*. Cambridge, MA: MIT Press, 2001.
Hamer, Mary. *Writing by Numbers: Trollope's Serial Fiction*. Cambridge: Cambridge University Press, 1987.
Hardy, Barbara. *Dickens and Creativity*. London: Continuum, 2008.
'Hartley Coleridge'. *The Gentleman's Magazine*, June (1851): 579–88.
'Hartley Coleridge as Man, Poet, Essayist'. *Fraser's Magazine for Town and Country* 43 (1851): 604–15.

Harty, Joetta. 'The Islanders: Mapping Paracosms in the Early Writings of Hartley Coleridge, Thomas Malkin, Thomas De Quincey, and the Brontës'. PhD diss., George Washington University, 2007.
Hayot, Eric. *On Literary Worlds*. Oxford: Oxford University Press, 2012.
Hensley, Nathan K. 'Figures of Reading'. *Criticism* 54, no. 2 (2012): 329–42.
Herring, Paul D. 'Dickens' Monthly Number Plans'. *Modern Philology* 64, no. 1 (1966): 22–63.
Hillis Miller, J. *Charles Dickens: The World of the His Novels*. Cambridge, MA: Harvard University Press, 1958.
Communities in Fiction. New York: Fordham University Press, 2015.
On Literature. London: Routledge, 2002.
Reading for Our Time: 'Adam Bede' and 'Middlemarch' Revisited. Edinburgh: Edinburgh University Press, 2012.
Holland, Henry. *Chapters on Mental Physiology*. London: Longman, Brown, Green, and Longmans, 1852.
Hollingworth, Leta S. *Children Above 180 IQ (Stanford-Binet): Origin and Development*. London: George G. Harrap & Company, 1942.
Hughes, Linda K., and Michael Lund. *The Victorian Serial*. Charlottesville: University Press of Virginia, 1991.
Hutton, Richard H. 'ideal, adj. 4'. *OED Online*. Oxford University Press, 2010. www.oed.com/view/Entry/90958, 19 June 2018.
'Improvvisatori'. *The Penny Magazine of the Society for the Diffusion of Useful Knowledge*, April 20, 1839.
'Novels by the Authoress of "John Halifax"'. *North British Review*, no. 29 (1859): 466–81.
Iser, Wolfgang. *Prospecting: From Reader Response to Literary Anthropology*. Baltimore: Johns Hopkins University Press, 1989.
Jacox, Francis. 'About Ejuxria and Gombroon'. *Bentley's Miscellany*, no. 59 (1866): 68–78.
'Hartley Coleridge'. *Bentley's Miscellany* 45 (1859): 581–92.
James, Henry. *Literary Criticism: Essays on Literature, American Writers, English Writers*. Edited by Leon Edel and Mark Wilson. Vol. 1. New York: The Library of America, 1984.
Literary Criticism: French Writers, Other European Writers, the Prefaces to the New York Edition. Edited by Leon Edel and Mark Wilson. Vol. 2. New York: The Library of America, 1984.
'Our Mutual Friend'. *The Nation*. December 21, 1865.
Roderick Hudson. London: MacMillan and Co., 1921.
The Tragic Muse. London: MacMillan and Co., 1921.
Jameson, Anna. *A Commonplace Book of Thoughts, Memories, and Fancies*. London: Longman, Brown, Green, and Longmans, 1855.
The Diary of an Ennuyée. London: Henry Colburn, 1826.
Kaiser, Matthew. *The World in Play: Portraits of a Victorian Concept*. Stanford, CA: Stanford University Press, 2011.
Kermode, Frank. *Essays on Fiction 1971–82*. Oxford: Routledge Revivals, 2015.

Kincaid, James R. *The Novels of Anthony Trollope*. Oxford: Clarendon Press, 1977.
King, Margaret F. '"Certain Learned Ladies": Trollope's Can You Forgive Her? And the Langham Place Circle'. *Victorian Literature and Culture* 21 (1993): 307–26.
Lamb, Charles. *Essays of Elia, Letters, and Rosamund, A Tale*. Paris: Baudry's European Library, 1835.
  Selected Prose. Edited by Adam Phillips. Harmondsworth: Penguin, 1985.
Leavis, Frank R. *The Great Tradition: George Eliot, Henry James, Joseph Conrad*. New York: George W. Stewart, 1950.
Leavis, Frank R., and Queenie D. Leavis. *Dickens the Novelist*. London: Chatto & Windus, 1972.
Leavis, Queenie. D. *Fiction and the Reading Public*. London: Chatto & Windus, 1978.
Levine, Caroline. *Forms: Whole, Rhythm, Hierarchy, Network*. Princeton, NJ: Princeton University Press, 2015.
  The Serious Pleasures of Suspense. Charlottesville: University of Virginia Press, 2003.
Levine, George. *Darwin and the Novelists: Patterns of Science in Victorian Fiction*. Chicago: University of Chicago Press, 1991.
  The Realistic Imagination: English Fiction from Frankenstein to Lady Chatterly. Chicago: University of Chicago Press, 1981.
Lewes, George Henry. 'Dickens in Relation to Criticism'. *Fortnightly Review* 11, no. 62 (1872): 141–54.
  The Physiology of Common Life. Vol. 2. London: William Blackwood and Sons, 1859.
Lewis, David. 'Truth in Fiction'. *American Philosophical Quarterly* 15, no. 1 (1978): 37–46.
Lowe, Brigid. *Victorian Fiction and the Insights of Sympathy: An Alternative to the Hermeneutics of Suspicion*. London: Anthem Press, 2007.
Lubbock, Percy. *The Craft of Fiction*. London: Jonathan Cape, 1954.
MacNish, Robert. *The Philosophy of Sleep*. Glasgow: W. R. M'Phun, 1834.
Macready, William Charles. *The Journal of William Charles Macready, 1832–1851*. Edited by J. C. Trewin. Carbondale: Southern Illinois University Press, 2009.
Malkin, Benjamin Heath. *A Father's Memoirs of His Child*. London: Longman, Hurst, Rees, and Orme, 1806.
Malone, Catherine. '"We Have Learnt to Love Her More than Her Books": The Critical Reception of Brontë's Professor'. *The Review of English Studies* 47, no. 186 (1996): 175–87.
Mandell, Julia. 'Rules of the Games'. *Architecture* 93, no. 7 (2004): 66.
Marland, Patrick R. 'Seeing Things in Dickens: A Study of Representation and Hypotyposis'. PhD diss., University of Sydney, 2014.
McAleavey, Maia. *The Bigamy Plot: Sensation and Convention in the Victorian Novel*. Cambridge: Cambridge University Press, 2015.
McKeon, Michael. 'The Eighteenth-Century Challenge to Narrative Theory'. In *Narrative Concepts in the Study of Eighteenth-Century Literature*. Edited

by Liisa Steinby and Aino Mäkikalli, 39–78. Amsterdam: University of Amsterdam Press, 2017.

McMaster, Juliet. 'Theme and Form in The Newcomes'. *Nineteenth-Century Fiction* 23, no. 2 (1968): 177–88.

McWeeny, Gage. *The Comfort of Strangers: Social Life and Literary Form*. Oxford: Oxford University Press, 2016.

Michie, Helena. 'Rethinking Marriage: Trollope's Internal Revision'. In *The Routledge Research Companion to Anthony Trollope*. Edited by Deborah Denenholz Morse, Margaret Markwick, and Mark W. Turner, 154–65. Oxford: Routledge, 2017.

Mieder, Wolfgang. *Behold the Proverbs of a People*. Jackson: University Press of Mississippi, 2014.

Mill, James. *Analysis of the Phenomena of the Human Mind*. Edited by Alexander Bain, Andrew Findlater, George Grote, and John Stuart Mill. Vol. 1. London: Longmans, Green, Reader, & Dyer, 1869.

Miller, Andrew H. *The Burdens of Perfection: On Ethics and Reading in Nineteenth-Century Literature*. Ithaca, NY: Cornell University Press, 2008.

Miller, David A. *Narrative and Its Discontents: Problems of Closure in the Traditional Novel*. Princeton, NJ: Princeton University Press, 1981.

The Novel and the Police. Berkeley: University of California Press, 1988.

Moore, Jane. 'Problematising Postmodernism'. In *Critical Dialogues: Current Issues in English Studies in Germany and Britain*. Edited by Isobel Armstrong and Hans-Werner Ludwig, 131–41. Tubingen: Gunter Narr Verlag Tubingen, 1995.

More, Thomas. *Utopia*. Edited by George M. Logan. Translated by Robert M. Adams. Cambridge: Cambridge University Press, 2016.

'Mrs Jameson's Common-Place Book'. *The New Monthly Magazine* 103 (1855): 193–201.

'Mrs Jameson's Common-Place Book'. *Chamber's Journal of Popular Literature, Science and Arts* 3, no. 53 (1855): 7–10.

Nabokov, Vladimir. *Lectures on Russian Literature*. London: Weidenfeld and Nicolson, 1982.

'The Newcomes'. *Athenaeum*. August 4, 1855.

Newman, Neville. '"Workers, Gentlemen and Landowners": Identifying Social Class in The Professor and Wuthering Heights'. *Brontë Society Transactions* 26, no. 1 (2001): 10–18.

Nussbaum, Martha. *Love's Knowledge*. Oxford: Oxford University Press, 1992.

Nutt, Diane, and Diane Railton. 'The Sims: Real Life as Genre'. *Information, Communication & Society* 6, no. 4 (2003): 577–92.

Olson, Elder. '"Sailing to Byzantium": Prolegomena to a Poetics of the Lyric'. *The University of Kansas City Review* VIII, no. 3 (1942): 210–11, 216–17.

Ooijen, Erik Van. 'The Affluence of Literature'. In *Narrativity, Fictionality and Literariness: The Narrative Turn and the Study of Literary Fiction*. Edited by Lars-Åke Skalin, 113–29. Örebro: Örebro University Press, 2008.

Orwell, George. *Critical Essays*. London: Secker & Warburg, 1946.

Otto, Peter. *Multiplying Worlds: Romanticism, Modernity, and the Emergence of Virtual Reality*. Oxford: Oxford University Press, 2011.
Paige, Nicholas D. *Before Fiction: The Ancien Régime of the Novel*. Philadelphia: University of Pennsylvania Press, 2011.
Patridge, Stephanie L. 'Pornography, Ethics, and Video Games'. *Ethics and Information Technology* 15 (2013): 25–34.
Patton, Paul. *Deleuze and the Political*. London: Routledge, 2000.
Pavel, Thomas. *Fictional Worlds*. Cambridge, MA: Harvard University Press, 1989.
Pearl, Jason. *Utopian Geographies and the Early English Novel*. Charlottesville: University of Virginia Press, 2014.
Phillips, Adam. *Going Sane*. London: Penguin, 2006.
Picker, John M. 'George Eliot and the Sequel Question'. *New Literary History* 37, no. 2 (2006): 361–88.
Plato. *Republic*. Translated by Robin Waterfield. Oxford: Oxford University Press, 2008.
Plotz, John. *Semi-Detached: The Aesthetics of Virtual Experience since Dickens*. Princeton, NJ: Princeton University Press, 2018.
  'The Semi-Detached Provincial Novel'. *Victorian Studies* 53, no. 3 (2011): 405–16.
  'Serial Pleasures: The Influence of Television on the Victorian Novel'. *Romanticism on the Net*, no. 63 (2014). http://id.erudit.org/iderudit/1025619ar.
Price, Leah. *The Anthology and the Rise of the Novel*. Cambridge: Cambridge University Press, 2000.
Prichard, James Cowles. *A Treatise on Diseases of the Nervous System, Part the First: Comprising Convulsive and Maniacal Affections*. London: Underwood, 1822.
'The Professor'. *Critic*, June 15, 1857.
'The Professor'. *Examiner*, June 20, 1857.
Quincey, Thomas De. *The Works of Thomas De Quincey*. Edited by Daniel Sanjiv Roberts. Vol. 19. London: Pickering & Chatto, 2003.
Rancière, Jacques. *The Flesh of Words: The Politics of Writing*. Translated by Charlotte Mandell. Stanford, CA: Stanford University Press, 2004.
Ratchford, Fannie. *The Brontës' Web of Childhood*. New York: Columbia University Press, 1941.
Ratcliffe, Sophie. 'The Episodic Trollope and An Editor's Tales'. *Victorian Studies* 58, no. 1 (2015): 57.
'Review of "Poem, by Hartley Coleridge; with a Memoir of Life, by His Brother"'. *The Christian Remembrancer* 22 (1851): 102–42.
Ritchie, Anne Thackeray. *Chapters from Some Memoirs*. London: MacMillan and Co., 1894.
Rodiek, Grant. 'The Sims 4 Patch Notes'. The Sims 4, 2018. https://help.ea.com/en-gb/help/the-sims/the-sims-4/the-sims-4-updates/.
Ronen, Ruth. *Possible Worlds in Literary Theory*. Cambridge: Cambridge University Press, 1994.

Root-Bernstein, Michele. *Inventing Imaginary Worlds: From Childhood Play to Adult Creativity Across the Arts and Sciences*. Lanham: Rowman & Littlefield Education, 2014.

Rose, Jonathan. *The Intellectual Life of the British Working Classes*. New Haven, CT: Yale University Press, 2001.

Ruskin, John. *The Works of John Ruskin*. Edited by E. T. Cook and Alexander Wedderburn. Vol. 34. London: George Allen, 1908.

Russell, Bertrand. *The Problems of Philosophy*. Edited by John Skorupski. Oxford: Oxford University Press, 1998.

Russell, David. *Tact: Aesthetic Liberalism and the Essay Form in Nineteenth-Century Britain*. Princeton, NJ: Princeton University Press, 2018.

Ruth, Jennifer. 'Between Labor and Capital: Charlotte Bronte's Professional Professor'. *Victorian Studies* 45, no. 2 (2003): 279–303. https://doi.org/10.1353/vic.2003.0098.

Ryan, Marie-Laure. 'Fiction As a Logical, Ontological, and Illocutionary Issue'. *Style* 18, no. 2 (1984): 121–39.

 'From Parallel Universes to Possible Worlds: Ontological Pluralism in Physics, Narratology, and Narrative'. *Poetics Today* 27, no. 4 (2006): 633–74.

 'The Modes of Narrativity and Their Visual Metaphors'. *Style* 26, no. 3 (1992): 368–87.

 'Possible Worlds in Recent Literary Theory'. *Style* 4, no. 26 (1992): 528–53.

Said, Edward W. *Culture and Imperialism*. New York: Knopf, 1994.

Saler, Michael. *As If: Modern Enchantment and the Literary Prehistory of Virtual Reality*. Oxford: Oxford University Press, 2011.

Sayers, Dorothy L. *The Mind of the Maker*. London: Methuen, 1941.

Scarry, Elaine. *Dreaming by the Book*. Princeton, NJ: Princeton University Press, 2001.

Schaeffer, Jean-Marie. *Why Fiction?* Translated by Dorrit Cohn. Lincoln: University of Nebraska Press, 2010.

Scott, Walter. *Introductions and Notes from the Magnum Opus: Waverley to A Legend of the Wars of Montrose*. Edited by J. H. Alexander, P. D. Garside, and Claire Lamont. Edinburgh: Edinburgh University Press, 2012.

Sedgwick, Eve Kosofsky. *Touching Feeling: Affect, Pedagogy, Performativity*. Durham, NC: Duke University Press, 2003.

Seidel, Michael. 'The Man Who Came to Dinner: Ian Watt and the Theory of Formal Realism'. *Eighteenth-Century Fiction* 12, no. 2–3 (2000): 193–212.

Shuttleworth, Sally. *Charlotte Brontë and Victorian Psychology*. Cambridge: Cambridge University Press, 1996.

 The Mind of the Child: Child Development in Literature, Science, and Medicine 1840–1900. Oxford: Oxford University Press, 2013.

Slakey, Roger L. 'Trollope's Case for Moral Imperative'. *Nineteenth-Century Fiction* 28, no. 3 (1973): 305–20.

Smiles, Samuel. *Self-Help; with Illustrations of Character and Conduct*. London: John Murray, 1859.

Spacks, Patricia Meyer. *Privacy: Concealing the Eighteenth-Century Self*. Chicago: University of Chicago Press, 2003.

Sparrow, Robert. 'Robots, Rape, and Representation'. *International Journal of Social Robotics* 9, no. 4 (2017): 465–77.

Stewart, Garrett. *Dear Reader: The Conscripted Audience in Nineteenth-Century British Fiction*. Baltimore: Johns Hopkins University Press, 1996.

'stock, n. 3c'. *OED Online*. Oxford University Press, 2010. www.oed.com/view/Entry/190595, 19 June 2018.

Stoehr, Taylor. *Dickens: The Dreamer's Stance*. Ithaca, NY: Cornell University Press, 1965.

Stolte, Tyson Michael. 'Mind Reflected on Paper: Dickens, Victorian Psychology, and the First-Person Novel'. PhD diss., University of British Columbia, 2009.

Sussman, Matthew. 'Optative Form in Anthony Trollope's The Small House at Allington'. *Nineteenth-Century Literature* 71, no. 4 (2017): 485–515.

Sutherland, John A. 'Trollope at Work on The Way We Live Now'. *Nineteenth-Century Fiction* 37, no. 3 (1982): 472–93.

Swingle, Larry J. *Romanticism and Anthony Trollope: A Study in the Continuities of Nineteenth-Century Literary Thought*. Ann Arbor: University of Michigan Press, 1990.

Thackeray, William Makepeace. *The Adventures of Philip on His Way through the World Shewing Who Robbed Him, Who Helped Him, and Who Passed Him By*. Edited by Judith Law Fisher. Ann Arbor: University of Michigan Press, 2010.

A Collection of Letters of Thackeray, 1847–1855. Edited by Jane Octavia Brookfield. New York: Scribner, 1887.

The History of Pendennis: His Fortunes and Misfortunes, His Friends and His Greatest Enemy. Edited by John A. Sutherland. Oxford: Oxford University Press, 1994.

The Newcomes: Memoirs of a Most Respectable Family. Edited by Andrew Sanders. Oxford: Oxford University Press, 1995.

'Proposals for a Continuation of Ivanhoe'. *Fraser's Magazine for Town and Country* 34, no. 200 (August 1846): 237–45.

Roundabout Papers. London: J. M. Dent & Sons, 1914.

Vanity Fair. Edited by Helen Small. Oxford: Oxford University Press, 2015.

Tillotson, Geoffrey. *Thackeray the Novelist*. London: Methuen & Co., 1954.

Tolkien, J. R. R. *Tolkien On Fairy-Stories*. Edited by Verlyn Flieger and Douglas A. Anderson. London: HarperCollins, 2014.

Travers, Tim. *Samuel Smiles and the Victorian Work Ethic*. New York: Garland Publishing, 1987.

Trilling, Lionel. 'Little Dorrit'. *The Kenyon Review* 15, no. 4 (1953): 577–90.

Trollope, Anthony. *Barchester Towers*. Edited by John Bowen. Oxford: Oxford University Press, 2014.

Can You Forgive Her? Edited by Dinah Birch. Oxford: Oxford University Press, 2012.

Eustace Diamonds. Edited by Helen Small. Oxford: Oxford University Press, 2011.

The Last Chronicle of Barset. Edited by Helen Small. Oxford: Oxford University Press, 2015.

Orley Farm. Edited by Francis O'Gorman. Oxford: Oxford University Press, 2018.

The Prime Minister. Edited by Nicholas Shrimpton. Oxford: Oxford University Press, 2011.

The Small House at Allington. Edited by Dinah Birch. Oxford: Oxford University Press, 2015.

Velleman, J. David. 'Bodies, Selves'. *American Imago* 65, no. 3 (2008): 405–26.

Wall, Stephen. *Trollope and Character*. London: Faber & Faber, 1988.

'wallow, v.' *OED Online*. Oxford University Press, 2010. www.oed.com/view/Entry/225332, 19 June 2018.

Walsh, Richard. *The Rhetoric of Fictionality: Narrative Theory and the Idea of Fiction*. Columbus: Ohio State University Press, 2007.

Warner, Michael. 'Uncritical Reading'. In *Polemic: Critical or Uncritical*. Edited by Jane Gallop, 13–38. New York: Routledge, 2004.

Watt, Ian. *The Rise of the Novel: Studies in Defoe, Richardson and Fielding*. London: Pimlico, 2000.

Williams, Meg Harris. 'Book Magic: Aesthetic Conflicts in Charlotte Brontë's Juvenilia'. *Nineteenth-Century Literature* 42, no. 1 (1987): 29–45.

Williams, Raymond. *The Long Revolution*. Westport, CT: Greenwood Press, 1975.

Wilson, Edmund. *The Wound and the Bow: Seven Studies in Literature*. Cambridge, MA: Houghton Mifflin Company, 1941.

Winnicott, Donald W. *Playing and Reality*. London: Routledge Classics, 2005.

Winslow, Forbes. *On the Preservation of the Health of Body and Mind*. London: Henry Renshaw, 1842.

Winter, John Strange. *Bootles' Children*. London: F. V. White & Co., 1888.

Winyard, Ben. '"May We Meet Again": Rereading the Dickensian Serial in the Digital Age'. *19: Interdisciplinary Studies in the Long Nineteenth Century*, no. 21 (2015): 1–21. http://www.19.bbk.ac.uk/articles/10.16995/ntn.737/.

Wolterstorff, Nicholas. *Works and Worlds of Art*. Oxford: Clarendon Press, 1980.

Wood, James. *How Fiction Works*. London: Vintage Books, 2010.

'wooden, adj. 2a'. *OED Online*. Oxford University Press, 2018. www.oed.com/view/Entry/230028, 19 June 2018.

Wright, Andrew. *Anthony Trollope: Dream and Art*. London: MacMillan Press, 1983.

Zemka, Sue. *Time and the Moment in Victorian Literature and Society*. Cambridge: Cambridge University Press, 2012.

Zigarovich, Jolene. 'Proleptic Death in Dickens's A Christmas Carol and Little Dorrit'. *ANQ: A Quarterly Journal of Short Articles, Notes and Reviews* 29, no. 2 (2016): 79–83.

Zygmunt, Lawrence Charles. 'Thackeray and the Picaresque World'. PhD diss., University of Chicago, 2012.

Index

Abercrombie, John, 148
actuality, 4, 6–7
affordance, 5, 137, 176
   and disjunction, 109, 112
anthologies, 123–25
apRoberts, Ruth
   on situation ethics, 88–89, 91
   on the aesthetics of casuistry, 89–90
   on Trollope's characterisation, 96
architecture, imaginary, 31, 142–43, 164
Arthur, Anthony, 84–87
   as imaginative-logical structure, 28
associationism (philosophy), 147
attachment (affect), 117–18, *See also* parasociality
Auerbach, Erich, 50, 166
authorial power, 37–40, 44–46, 48–49, 68
Auyoung, Elaine, 2, 5, 110
Azim, Firdous, 42

Balzac, Honoré de, 105, 144
Barter, Amy, 123–25, 138
Barthes, Roland
   'The Death of the Author', 51
   'The Reality Effect', 143–45, 170
belief, as literary response, 37, 74, 142, 148–50, 153–54, 178, *See also* double consciousness
Bentham, Jeremy, 28–29, 160
Berlant, Lauren, 117
Bodenheimer, Rosemary, 141
book history, 112–14
Brontë siblings, 25–27, 40–41, 47, 51, *See also* Brontë Charlotte
Brontë, Charlotte
   critical reception of, 54, 56–57
   'Farewell to Angria', 119–21, 135
   identification with characters, 43–45, 54
   Jane Eyre, 2, 14, 22, 27–28, 114
   juvenilia, 25–26, 40–41, 43–44, 46–47, 51, 115, 142–43
   recounts of play, 40–43, 51
   reputation for disinterestedness and indulgence, 37, 56–58, 68
   Shirley, 63
   The Professor, *See Professor* The (main entry)
   transition from juvenilia to novels, 25–26, 119–21
   Villette, 22, 54, 114
Brooks, Peter, 3
Brown, Kate, 25, 66, 115

castle-building (idiom), 150, 163, 166–67
casuistry, 88, 96, 102
causation, narrative, 87, 91, 95, 102
Cave, Terence, 5
Cervantes, Miguel de, 6
Chesterton, Gilbert Keith, 104, 106
children
   anxieties about imaginativeness, 148–50
   capacity for imitation, 148–50
   consistency in play, 33
   inclination for participation, 49
   possessiveness, 41, 117, *See also* developmental psychology
closure, in paracosmic play, 120
Cohen, David, 23–24, 33, *See also* Root-Bernstein, Michele
Cohn, Elisha, 114
Coleridge, Derwent, *See* Coleridge, Hartley
Coleridge, Hartley, 20, 82, 142
   critical reception of, 148–49, 167
Coleridge, Samuel Taylor, 108
colonialism, 10, 136, 177
Crichton-Browne, James, 149–51

Dames, Nicholas
   on contextualist literary studies and Hegel, 53–54
   on *The Newcomes*, 127–29
   on virtuality and literary studies, 10
Davis, Lennard, 5–7, 145–46, 168, 178

daydream, 2, 16, 32, 114, 120, 141, See also castle-building (idiom)
De Quincey, Thomas, 17–18, 21, 79–81, 117, 148
  obligations to characters, 117
De Quincey, William, See De Quincey, Thomas
Defoe, Daniel
  Robinson Crusoe, 19, 24, 30
Deleuze, Gilles, 3
delusion,
  history of medicine, 150–51
  in *Little Dorrit*, 164 See also double consciousness; hallucination, as analogy
description
  pleasures of, 144–46, 161–62
  theory and purpose, 143–46
developmental psychology, 23–24
  in the nineteenth century, 148–51, See also Crichton-Browne, James
Dickens, Charles
  Bleak House, 15, 154
  critical reception of, 7–8, 139–41
  David Copperfield, 2, 26–27
  Letters, 9
  Little Dorrit, See *Little Dorrit* (main entry)
  Master Humphrey's Clock, 104–5, 118
  Mudfog Papers, 9
  The Old Curiosity Shop, 7–8, 140
diluted narrative, 114, 155
disenchantment, 28–29, 49
domestic fiction
  as basis of realism, 36
  as phantasmatic pleasure, 155, 161, 171
  and utopian fiction, 30–31
  as virtual game genre, 175
double consciousness, 7, 21, 37–38, 149, 170, 175–76
Doyle, Arthur Conan, 15, 81–82
Duma, Alexandre, 107–8

Eagleton, Terry, 62
ecphrasis, See hypotyposis
Eliot, George
  Adam Bede, 48
  Daniel Deronda, 108, 113–14
  Middlemarch, 130, 132
  Scenes of Clerical Life, 155
  "Silly Novels by Lady Novelists", 36, 39
  and sequels, 113–14
  ethics of fiction, 44–46, 89–90, 176–78, See also casuistry

Fables (Aesop), 41
Felski, Rita, 1–2, 176
fictional facts
  history and ubiquity, 18–19
  ontological incompleteness, 79–81, 85–86
fictionality,
  development of, 28–30
  as distinguished from literariness, 8, 39, 107, 117, 119, 154, See also novel, history of
Fielding, Henry, 7, 9, 19
Flaubert, Gustave, 6, 50
Foucault, Michel, 161
Freud, Sigmund, 3
Furneaux, Holly, 113, 119

Gallagher, Catherine
  'fictionality in its infancy', 16–17
  on novel referentiality and non-referentiality, 5–7, 27
  on the ambivalence of novel fictionality, 39
Gaskell, Elizabeth
  Letters, 26, 108
  The Life of Charlotte Brontë, 25–26, 35–36
Genette, Gérard, 49–50
genius, literary, 35
  as contrasted with Genii, 37
  as empirical ability, 35
  as experiential ability, 153–54
  Brontë on Thackeray, 40
  historical relationship with madness, 140, 151–53
  in children participating in paracosmic play, 21, 149
geography
  history of, 24
  imaginary, 14–15, 21, 26, 29–30, 142–43, 158
Gibson, William, 4
giftedness, See genius, literary; development psychology
Gissing, George, 161
Glen, Heather
  on *Jane Eyre*, 56–57
  on the Brontë juvenilia, 44–45
  on *The Professor*, 58–59, 61–62
god-like author,
  incarnation, 52
  use of narrative miracles, 46–50 See also authorial power
Goodman, Lesley, 8
Greiner, Rae, 10

hallucination,
  as analogy, 139–41, 153 See also perception, theories of
Hardy, Barbara, 162–63, 171
Hayot, Eric, 33

Index

hermeneutics of suspicion, 2, 176, *See also* post-critical reading
Hillis Miller, Joseph
  on Anthony Trollope's play, 32
  on Dickens and the prison, 158
  on George Eliot and performative writing, 48
  on Trollope's characters, 93
history of science, 147–48
  problems of pathologisation, 150–53
Holland, Henry, 148
homosociality, 123
hypotyposis, 144–45, 167, 170

improvisation
  narrative, 71–73, 75, 87
  poetic, 70–71
  relationship to restriction, 76–79
improvvisatore, *See* improvisation, poetic
incompleteness, narrative, 81–82
intertextuality, 130, 133–34
ironic imagination, *See* double consciousness

Jacox, Francis
  anxieties about play, 149
  rethinking of play and genius, 154
James, Henry
  'Anthony Trollope', 70
  'Daniel Deronda A Conversation', 108
  'Honoré de Balzac', 105
  Roderick Hudson, 134
  The Tragic Muse, 105, 126, 144
Jameson, Anna
  'A Revelation of Childhood', 22
  critical reception of, 167
  on the improvvisatore, 82

labour
  fictional, 64
  intellectual and physical, 63–64
  representations of, 62–64, 66–67
  writing as, 36, 79
Lamb, Charles, 88
  family history, 152
  'The Sanity of True Genius', 152–53
law of non-contradiction, Aristotelian, 81
law of the excluded middle, Aristotelian, 81
Leavis, F. R.
  on *Little Dorrit*, 161
  on Thackeray, 110–11, 146
Leavis, Q. D.
  on *Jane Eyre* and wish-fulfilment, 37, 56
  on *Little Dorrit*, 161
Levine, Caroline, 134
  on affordances, 5
  on *Bleak House* and networks, 128–29, 134

Levine, George
  on 'another realism, 52
  on anti-literary manifestos, 58, 113
  on realist disenchantment, 49
  on Thackeray and belatedness, 129
  on Thackeray's intertextuality, 132
  on Trollope's variations, 76
Lewes, George Henry
  on Dickens and hallucination, 139–41, 151–52
  on play and fiction, 3, 155–56
literality, 4–5, 15, 63–64, 164–67, 171, *See also* metaphor
literary form
  as imaginative-logical structure, 9, 34, 175
  as logical-imaginative structure, 9, 34, 175
  imagined and impossible, 107–9
  limits of, 112–14, 121
  networks as, 128–30
literary value, 2, 178
  of imaginative experience, 154
  of ingenuity, 71–73, 87, 89–90
  of juvenilia, 25–26
  of vicariousness, 37, 44–46
  of wallowing in fiction, 106, 108–9, *See also* fictionality, as distinguished from literariness
Little Dorrit (Dickens)
  Amy's fantasies, 169–71
  Clennam's room, 170
  conflict between reality and fantasy, 164
  imagined objects, 159–62, 168–69, 171–73
  Mr Dorrit's castle, 163
  Mr Dorrit's death, 164
  narrative forecasting, 163, 171, 173
  prisons and imprisonment, 160, 164, 171
  Rigaud and Cavalletto, 158–62
  thematic structure, 158–59, 163
  Young John Chivery, 171–73
Lowe, Brigid, 10
  on belief and imagining, 7, 37–38
  on fiction's sensuous imaginative function, 154–55
  on fiction's sensuous imaginative function, 142, 145
  on subjective participation in literature, 2, 8

MacKeith, Stephen, *See* Cohen, David
MacNish, Robert, 148
Malkin, Benjamin Heath, 20.*See also* paracosms, Allestone
Malkin, Thomas, *See* paracosms, Allestone
Malone, Catherine, 62
Marland, P. R., 152–53
marriage plot, 97–98, 129–32

metalepsis, 49–52, 74, 165
metaphor, 63, 164–67
Michie, Helena, 97
Miller, Andrew H., 89–90
Miller, D. A.
  on the limits of the narratable, 113–14
  on the novel's logic of insufficiency, 82
  on the novel's need for restrictions, 78–79
miniaturisation, 8–9, 45–46, 156, 159–60, 170, 173, *See also* toys
More, Thomas, 29

Nabokov, Vladimir, 38, 50
narrative closure, 83, 107, 112
  and the serial, 112–14
  in paracosmic play, 114–16, *See also* paracosmic play, ending or ceasing
  reader discontent with, 134
narrative detail, 144–45
narratology, 15, 81–82
New Formalism, 128
Newman, Neville, 63
non-fictional forms, 6, 19, 21, 27
novel, history of, 5–7, 15–20, 26–28

omnipotence, *See* authorial power
Otto, Peter, 4

paracosmic play
  ending or ceasing, 117, 119–22
  history and psychology of, 22–24, 116–18, 148–49
  nineteenth-century responses to, 148–49
  rules of, 18, 33, 77, 79–81
paracosms
  Allestone, 20–21, 24, 29
  Anna Jameson's, *See* Jameson, Anna, 'A Revelation of Childhood'
  Ejuxria, *See* Coleridge, Hartley
  Glasstown, Angria, Gondal, and Gaaldine, *See* Brontë, Charlotte, juvenilia
  Gombroon and Tigrosylvania, *See* De Quincey, Thomas
  the castle in the air, 31–33
parasociality, 7–8, 106, 118–19
patch notes (software), 174
Pavel, Thomas, 51
  on dolls and *Anna Karenina*, 3
  on the double consciousness of play, 42
Pearl, Jason, 29–30
perception, theories of, 147–48
persistence, virtual, 33, 106, 125
  in paracosmic play, 116–17
Picker, John, 114
Plato, 6, 18

play
  as analogy, 3, 42, 146–49, 153–54, 156, 178
  definitions, 16
Plotz, John
  on defining the virtual, 3–5
  on iterativeness and seriality, 112
  on the non-serial novel, 114
pornography, 66, 177–78
post-critical reading, 1–2, 176–78
proprioception, 159, 165–66, *See also* perception
pseudofactual posture, 27, 29, *See also* double consciousness

Rancière, Jacques, 50
Ratcliffe, Sophie, 84, 96, 103
reading, modes of, 1, 108–9
realism
  and theology, 50–52
  as social representation, 61
  empiricism and imaginativeness, 36–37, 47–48, 102, 140
  history of term, 140
  self-consciousness, 58, 114
referentiality (and non-referentiality), 5–8, 21, 27–28, 39, 41–42, 64
robotics, 177, *See also* toys, Dickens's automatons
Root-Bernstein, Michele
  on paracosmic play and creativity, 24
  on paracosmic play's emotional significance, 117
  on paracosmic play's consistency, 32–33, 116
Rose, Jonathan, 15, 17, 27
Ruskin, John, 110, 134
Russell, David, 88
Ruth, Jennifer, 63–64, 67–68
Ryan, Marie-Laure, 163

Said, Edward, 136
Saler, Michael, 7
Sayers, Dorothy, 50
Schaeffer, Jean-Marie, 4
Scott, Walter, 19, 107
Second Life (game), 4
Sedgwick, Eve Kosofsky
  paranoid reading, 62, 86
  reparative reading, 68
self-help, 60–61
Self-Help (Smiles), *See* Smiles, Samuel
self-narrativisation, 103
sequels and series, 104–6, 112–14
seriality, 103, 112–13
Shakespeare, William, 150, 167

Shuttleworth, Sally
  on medical anxieties around paracosmic play, 116, 149
  on the history of paracosmic play, 22–23
  on *The Professor*, 61–62
  on the rules of paracosmic play, 18
simulation, 8–10
situation ethics, *See* casuistry
Smiles, Samuel, 60–61, 65
sophistry, 89, 91, 99, 102, *See also* casuistry
Stannard, Henrietta (John Strange Winter), 109, 111–12
Stoehr, Taylor, 153, 165–67
suspension of disbelief, *See* double consciousness
Sussman, Matthew, 91–92, 97–98, 100
sustenance, 161–62, 173, *See also* Sedgwick, Eve Kosofky (reparative reading)
Sutherland, John, 87
Swift, Jonathan, 27–28
sympathy, 8–9

Tennyson, Alfred Lord, 108, 110, 118
Thackeray, William
  'De Finibus', 135–36
  'Proposals for a Continuation of *Ivanhoe*', 107–8, 133
  and Charterhouse School, 123, 138
  and Fable-land, 138
  attachment to characters, 105–6
  critical reception of, 40
  Pendennis, 15, 130, 132
  relationship with characters, 108–9, 135–36
  revisiting of characters, 105–6, 130, 133
  The Newcomes, *See The Newcomes* (main entry)
  Vanity Fair, 2, 130
The Newcomes (Thackeray)
  Colonel Newcome's history, 127, 131–32
  Coventry Island, 136–37
  Dobbin's cameo, 130
  ending, 135, 138
  family tree, 126–27
  Grey Friars, 123–25, 137
  Mrs Mackenzie, 131
  replaceability and irreplaceability of relationships, 129–30, 133
  thematic structure, 127–28
The Professor (Brontë)
  contrast to *Jane Eyre*, 58–59, 68
  Crimsworth and Frances's school, 66
  Crimsworth and gifts, 60
  ending, 66–67
  individualism, 59–61
  mise-en-abyme, 55–56
  narrative erotics, 64–66

  narrative frame, 59
  narrative style, 58–60
  preface, 58–59, 144
  publication history, 58
  realism, 68
  relationship between the Crimsworth brothers, 59–60
  representations of work, 62–63, 66–67
  the 'Hill of Difficulty', 58–59, 65–66
  Zoraide Reuter, 64–65
The Sims (game), 174–76
The Small House at Allington (Trollope)
  Adolphus Crosbie, 99–102
  dilemma of moving, 93
  Joseph Cradell, 95
  Lily's dilemma, 95–96
  Mrs Dale, 95
  retracting of decisions, 93–94, 99–102
  stubbornness of characters, 91–96
Tillotson, Geoffrey, 105–6
Tolkien, J. R. R., 38
Tolstoy, Leo, 3
toys
  as analogy for realism, 3
  Branwell Brontë's soldiers, 40–42, 51
  Dickens's automatons, 8–9
  George Henry Lewes's wooden horse, 2–3, 175
  Thackeray's puppets, 2
  The Sims as adult dollhouse, 174
Trilling, Lionel, 158–59
Trollope, Anthony
  'On English Novelists of the Present Day', 31
  An Autobiography, 2, 8, 31–33, 79, 85, 87, 96, 103
  and Mrs Proudie, 8, 84–86
  and narrative formulas, 73, 75–77
  and prolifixity, 70
  and psychological characterisation, 91–93
  Barchester Towers, 73, 84
  Can You Forgive Her?, 98–99
  Chronicles of Barsetshire (series), 83, 121
  compositional process, 75, 78–79, 86–87
  critical reception of, 70, 75–76, 84, 87
  Framley Parsonage, 75, 108
  Orley Farm, 73, 87
  revision process, 96–97, 103
  revisiting of characters, 105
  The Eustace Diamonds, 87, 90
  The Last Chronicle of Barset, 84–85, 121, 135
  The Prime Minister, 90
  The Small House at Allington, *See The Small House at Allington* (main entry)

utopias, *See* geography, imaginary

Velleman, J. David, 5
vicarious reading, 2, 8, 146–47, 155, 178, *See also* post-critical reading
vicariousness, 8, *See also* wish-fulfilment
video gaming, *See* virtuality, digital
virtuality
  definition, 3–5
  digital, 6, 33, 142, 177, *See also* The Sims
  social and political, 4

Wall, Stephen, 92, 95, 100
Walton, Kendall, 3
Watt, Ian, 19, 27
Wellesley, Arthur (Duke of Wellington), 40–42, 46, 51–52
Williams, William Smith, 40
Winnicott, Donald, 178
wish-fulfilment, 53, 56
Wood, James, 144

Zygmunt, Lawrence, 130–31

CAMBRIDGE STUDIES IN NINETEENTH-CENTURY LITERATURE AND CULTURE

GENERAL EDITORS
Kate Flint, *University of Southern California*
Clare Pettitt, *King's College London*

Titles published

1. *The Sickroom in Victorian Fiction: The Art of Being Ill*
   MIRIAM BAILIN, *Washington University*
2. *Muscular Christianity: Embodying the Victorian Age* edited by
   DONALD E. HALL, *California State University, Northridge*
3. *Victorian Masculinities: Manhood and Masculine Poetics in Early Victorian Literature and Art*
   HERBERT SUSSMAN, *Northeastern University, Boston*
4. *Byron and the Victorians*
   ANDREW ELFENBEIN, *University of Minnesota*
5. *Literature in the Marketplace: Nineteenth-Century British Publishing and the Circulation of Books* edited by
   JOHN O. JORDAN, *University of California, Santa Cruz*
   and ROBERT L. PATTEN, *Rice University, Houston*
6. *Victorian Photography, Painting and Poetry*
   LINDSAY SMITH, *University of Sussex*
7. *Charlotte Brontë and Victorian Psychology*
   SALLY SHUTTLEWORTH, *University of Sheffield*
8. *The Gothic Body: Sexuality, Materialism and Degeneration at the* Fin de Siècle
   KELLY HURLEY, *University of Colorado at Boulder*
9. *Rereading Walter Pater*
   WILLIAM F. SHUTER, *Eastern Michigan University*
10. *Remaking Queen Victoria* edited by
    MARGARET HOMANS, *Yale University*
    and ADRIENNE MUNICH, *State University of New York, Stony Brook*
11. *Disease, Desire, and the Body in Victorian Women's Popular Novels*
    PAMELA K. GILBERT, *University of Florida*
12. *Realism, Representation, and the Arts in Nineteenth-Century Literature*
    ALISON BYERLY, *Middlebury College, Vermont*
13. *Literary Culture and the Pacific*
    VANESSA SMITH, *University of Sydney*
14. *Professional Domesticity in the Victorian Novel*
    MONICA F. COHEN

15. *Victorian Renovations of the Novel: Narrative Annexes and the Boundaries of Representation*
    SUZANNE KEEN, *Washington and Lee University, Virginia*
16. *Actresses on the Victorian Stage: Feminine Performance and the Galatea Myth*
    GAIL MARSHALL, *University of Leeds*
17. *Death and the Mother from Dickens to Freud: Victorian Fiction and the Anxiety of Origin*
    CAROLYN DEVER, *Vanderbilt University, Tennessee*
18. *Ancestry and Narrative in Nineteenth-Century British Literature: Blood Relations from Edgeworth to Hardy*
    SOPHIE GILMARTIN, *Royal Holloway, University of London*
19. *Dickens, Novel Reading, and the Victorian Popular Theatre*
    DEBORAH VLOCK
20. *After Dickens: Reading, Adaptation and Performance*
    JOHN GLAVIN, *Georgetown University, Washington DC*
21. *Victorian Women Writers and the Woman Question* edited by
    NICOLA DIANE THOMPSON, *Kingston University, London*
22. *Rhythm and Will in Victorian Poetry*
    MATTHEW CAMPBELL, *University of Sheffield*
23. *Gender, Race, and the Writing of Empire: Public Discourse and the Boer War*
    PAULA M. KREBS, *Wheaton College, Massachusetts*
24. *Ruskin's God*
    MICHAEL WHEELER, *University of Southampton*
25. *Dickens and the Daughter of the House*
    HILARY M. SCHOR, *University of Southern California*
26. *Detective Fiction and the Rise of Forensic Science*
    RONALD R. THOMAS, *Trinity College, Hartford, Connecticut*
27. *Testimony and Advocacy in Victorian Law, Literature, and Theology*
    JAN-MELISSA SCHRAMM, *Trinity Hall, Cambridge*
28. *Victorian Writing about Risk: Imagining a Safe England in a Dangerous World*
    ELAINE FREEDGOOD, *University of Pennsylvania*
29. *Physiognomy and the Meaning of Expression in Nineteenth-Century Culture*
    LUCY HARTLEY, *University of Southampton*
30. *The Victorian Parlour: A Cultural Study*
    THAD LOGAN, *Rice University, Houston*
31. *Aestheticism and Sexual Parody 1840-1940*
    DENNIS DENISOFF, *Ryerson University, Toronto*
32. *Literature, Technology and Magical Thinking, 1880-1920*
    PAMELA THURSCHWELL, *University College London*

33. *Fairies in Nineteenth-Century Art and Literature*
    NICOLA BOWN, *Birkbeck, University of London*
34. *George Eliot and the British Empire*
    NANCY HENRY *The State University of New York, Binghamton*
35. *Women's Poetry and Religion in Victorian England: Jewish Identity and Christian Culture*
    CYNTHIA SCHEINBERG, *Mills College, California*
36. *Victorian Literature and the Anorexic Body*
    ANNA KRUGOVOY SILVER, *Mercer University, Georgia*
37. *Eavesdropping in the Novel from Austen to Proust*
    ANN GAYLIN, *Yale University*
38. *Missionary Writing and Empire, 1800–1860*
    ANNA JOHNSTON, *University of Tasmania*
39. *London and the Culture of Homosexuality, 1885–1914*
    MATT COOK, *Keele University*
40. *Fiction, Famine, and the Rise of Economics in Victorian Britain and Ireland*
    GORDON BIGELOW, *Rhodes College, Tennessee*
41. *Gender and the Victorian Periodical*
    HILARY FRASER, *Birkbeck, University of London*
    JUDITH JOHNSTON and STEPHANIE GREEN, *University of Western Australia*
42. *The Victorian Supernatural* edited by
    NICOLA BOWN, *Birkbeck College, London*
    CAROLYN BURDETT, *London Metropolitan University*
    and PAMELA THURSCHWELL, *University College London*
43. *The Indian Mutiny and the British Imagination*
    GAUTAM CHAKRAVARTY, *University of Delhi*
44. *The Revolution in Popular Literature: Print, Politics and the People*
    IAN HAYWOOD, *Roehampton University of Surrey*
45. *Science in the Nineteenth-Century Periodical: Reading the Magazine of Nature*
    GEOFFREY CANTOR, *University of Leeds* GOWAN DAWSON, *University of Leicester* GRAEME GOODAY, *University of Leeds* RICHARD NOAKES, *University of Cambridge* SALLY SHUTTLEWORTH, *University of Sheffield* and JONATHAN R. TOPHAM, *University of Leeds*
46. *Literature and Medicine in Nineteenth-Century Britain from Mary Shelley to George Eliot*
    JANIS MCLARREN CALDWELL, *Wake Forest University*
47. *The Child Writer from Austen to Woolf* edited by
    CHRISTINE ALEXANDER, *University of New South Wales*
    and JULIET MCMASTER, *University of Alberta*

48. *From Dickens to Dracula: Gothic, Economics, and Victorian Fiction*
    GAIL TURLEY HOUSTON, University of New Mexico
49. *Voice and the Victorian Storyteller*
    IVAN KREILKAMP, University of Indiana
50. *Charles Darwin and Victorian Visual Culture*
    JONATHAN SMITH, University of Michigan-Dearborn
51. *Catholicism, Sexual Deviance, and Victorian Gothic Culture*
    PATRICK R. O'MALLEY, Georgetown University
52. *Epic and Empire in Nineteenth-Century Britain*
    SIMON DENTITH, University of Gloucestershire
53. *Victorian Honeymoons: Journeys to the Conjugal*
    HELENA MICHIE, Rice University
54. *The Jewess in Nineteenth-Century British Literary Culture*
    NADIA VALMAN, University of Southampton
55. *Ireland, India and Nationalism in Nineteenth-Century Literature*
    JULIA WRIGHT, Dalhousie University
56. *Dickens and the Popular Radical Imagination*
    SALLY LEDGER, Birkbeck, University of London
57. *Darwin, Literature and Victorian Respectability*
    GOWAN DAWSON, University of Leicester
58. *'Michael Field': Poetry, Aestheticism and the* Fin de Siècle
    MARION THAIN, University of Birmingham
59. *Colonies, Cults and Evolution: Literature, Science and Culture in Nineteenth-Century Writing*
    DAVID AMIGONI, Keele University
60. *Realism, Photography and Nineteenth-Century Fiction*
    DANIEL A. NOVAK, Lousiana State University
61. *Caribbean Culture and British Fiction in the Atlantic World, 1780–1870*
    TIM WATSON, University of Miami
62. *The Poetry of Chartism: Aesthetics, Politics, History*
    MICHAEL SANDERS, University of Manchester
63. *Literature and Dance in Nineteenth-Century Britain: Jane Austen to the New Woman*
    CHERYL WILSON, Indiana University
64. *Shakespeare and Victorian Women*
    GAIL MARSHALL, Oxford Brookes University
65. *The Tragi-Comedy of Victorian Fatherhood*
    VALERIE SANDERS, University of Hull
66. *Darwin and the Memory of the Human: Evolution, Savages, and South America*
    CANNON SCHMITT, University of Toronto

67. *From Sketch to Novel: The Development of Victorian Fiction*
    AMANPAL GARCHA, *Ohio State University*
68. *The Crimean War and the British Imagination*
    STEFANIE MARKOVITS, *Yale University*
69. *Shock, Memory and the Unconscious in Victorian Fiction*
    JILL L. MATUS, *University of Toronto*
70. *Sensation and Modernity in the 1860s*
    NICHOLAS DALY, *University College Dublin*
71. *Ghost-Seers, Detectives, and Spiritualists: Theories of Vision in Victorian Literature and Science*
    SRDJAN SMAJIĆ, *Furman University*
72. *Satire in an Age of Realism*
    AARON MATZ, *Scripps College, California*
73. *Thinking About Other People in Nineteenth-Century British Writing*
    ADELA PINCH, *University of Michigan*
74. *Tuberculosis and the Victorian Literary Imagination*
    KATHERINE BYRNE, *University of Ulster, Coleraine*
75. *Urban Realism and the Cosmopolitan Imagination in the Nineteenth Century: Visible City, Invisible World*
    TANYA AGATHOCLEOUS, *Hunter College, City University of New York*
76. *Women, Literature, and the Domesticated Landscape: England's Disciples of Flora, 1780-1870*
    JUDITH W. PAGE, *University of Florida*
    ELISE L. SMITH, *Millsaps College, Mississippi*
77. *Time and the Moment in Victorian Literature and Society*
    SUE ZEMKA, *University of Colorado*
78. *Popular Fiction and Brain Science in the Late Nineteenth Century*
    ANNE STILES, *Washington State University*
79. *Picturing Reform in Victorian Britain*
    JANICE CARLISLE, *Yale University*
80. *Atonement and Self-Sacrifice in Nineteenth-Century Narrative*
    JAN-MELISSA SCHRAMM, *University of Cambridge*
81. *The Silver Fork Novel: Fashionable Fiction in the Age of Reform*
    EDWARD COPELAND, *Pomona College, California*
82. *Oscar Wilde and Ancient Greece*
    IAIN ROSS, *Colchester Royal Grammar School*
83. *The Poetry of Victorian Scientists: Style, Science and Nonsense*
    DANIEL BROWN, *University of Southampton*
84. *Moral Authority, Men of Science, and the Victorian Novel*
    ANNE DEWITT, *Princeton Writing Program*

85. *China and the Victorian Imagination: Empires Entwined*
    ROSS G. FORMAN, *University of Warwick*
86. *Dickens's Style* edited by
    DANIEL TYLER, *University of Oxford*
87. *The Formation of the Victorian Literary Profession*
    RICHARD SALMON, *University of Leeds*
88. *Before George Eliot: Marian Evans and the Periodical Press*
    FIONNUALA DILLANE, *University College Dublin*
89. *The Victorian Novel and the Space of Art: Fictional Form on Display*
    DEHN GILMORE, *California Institute of Technology*
90. *George Eliot and Money: Economics, Ethics and Literature*
    DERMOT COLEMAN, *Independent Scholar*
91. *Masculinity and the New Imperialism: Rewriting Manhood in British Popular Literature, 1870–1914*
    BRADLEY DEANE, *University of Minnesota*
92. *Evolution and Victorian Culture* edited by
    BERNARD LIGHTMAN, *York University, Toronto*
    and BENNETT ZON, *University of Durham*
93. *Victorian Literature, Energy, and the Ecological Imagination*
    ALLEN MACDUFFIE, *University of Texas, Austin*
94. *Popular Literature, Authorship and the Occult in Late Victorian Britain*
    ANDREW MCCANN, *Dartmouth College, New Hampshire*
95. *Women Writing Art History in the Nineteenth Century: Looking Like a Woman*
    HILARY FRASER *Birkbeck, University of London*
96. *Relics of Death in Victorian Literature and Culture*
    DEBORAH LUTZ, *Long Island University, C. W. Post Campus*
97. *The Demographic Imagination and the Nineteenth-Century City: Paris, London, New York*
    NICHOLAS DALY, *University College Dublin*
98. *Dickens and the Business of Death*
    CLAIRE WOOD, *University of York*
99. *Translation as Transformation in Victorian Poetry*
    ANNMARIE DRURY, *Queens College, City University of New York*
100. *The Bigamy Plot: Sensation and Convention in the Victorian Novel*
    MAIA MCALEAVEY, *Boston College, Massachusetts*
101. *English Fiction and the Evolution of Language, 1850–1914*
    WILL ABBERLEY, *University of Oxford*
102. *The Racial Hand in the Victorian Imagination*
    AVIVA BRIEFEL, *Bowdoin College, Maine*

103. *Evolution and Imagination in Victorian Children's Literature*
    JESSICA STRALEY, *University of Utah*
104. *Writing Arctic Disaster: Authorship and Exploration*
    ADRIANA CRACIUN, *University of California, Riverside*
105. *Science, Fiction, and the* Fin-de-Siècle *Periodical Press*
    WILL TATTERSDILL, *University of Birmingham*
106. *Democratising Beauty in Nineteenth-Century Britain: Art and the Politics of Public Life*
    LUCY HARTLEY, *University of Michigan*
107. *Everyday Words and the Character of Prose in Nineteenth-Century Britain*
    JONATHAN FARINA, *Seton Hall University, New Jersey*
108. *Gerard Manley Hopkins and the Poetry of Religious Experience*
    MARTIN DUBOIS, *Newcastle University*
109. *Blindness and Writing: From Wordsworth to Gissing*
    HEATHER TILLEY, *Birkbeck College, University of London*
110. *An Underground History of Early Victorian Fiction: Chartism, Radical Print Culture, and the Social Problem Novel*
    GREGORY VARGO, *New York University*
111. *Automatism and Creative Acts in the Age of New Psychology*
    LINDA M. AUSTIN, *Oklahoma State University*
112. *Idleness and Aesthetic Consciousness, 1815-1900*
    RICHARD ADELMAN, *University of Sussex*
113. *Poetry, Media, and the Material Body: Autopoetics in Nineteenth-Century Britain*
    ASHLEY MILLER, *Albion College, Michigan*
114. *Malaria and Victorian Fictions of Empire*
    JESSICA HOWELL, *Texas A&M University*
115. *The Brontës and the Idea of the Human: Science, Ethics, and the Victorian Imagination* edited by
    ALEXANDRA LEWIS, *University of Aberdeen*
116. *The Political Lives of Victorian Animals: Liberal Creatures in Literature and Culture*
    ANNA FEUERSTEIN, *University of Hawai'i-Manoa*
117. *The Divine in the Commonplace: Recent Natural Histories and the Novel in Britain*
    AMY KING, *St John's University, New York*
118. *Plagiarizing the Victorian Novel: Imitation, Parody, Aftertext*
    ADAM ABRAHAM, *Virginia Commonwealth University*
119. *Literature, Print Culture, and Media Technologies, 1880-1900: Many Inventions*
    RICHARD MENKE, *University of Georgia*

120. *Aging, Duration, and the English Novel: Growing Old from Dickens to Woolf*
    JACOB JEWUSIAK, *Newcastle University*
121. *Autobiography, Sensation, and the Commodification of Identity in Victorian Narrative: Life upon the Exchange*
    SEAN GRASS, *Rochester Institute of Technology*
122. *Settler Colonialism in Victorian Literature: Economics and Political Identity in the Networks of Empire*
    PHILLIP STEER, *Massey University, Auckland*
123. *Mimicry and Display in Victorian Literary Culture: Nature, Science and the Nineteenth-Century Imagination*
    WILL ABBERLEY, *University of Sussex*
124. *Victorian Women and Wayward Reading: Crises of Identification*
    MARISA PALACIOS KNOX, *University of Texas Rio Grande Valley*
125. *The Victorian Cult of Shakespeare: Bardology in the Nineteenth Century*
    CHARLES LAPORTE, *University of Washington*
126. *Children's Literature and the Rise of 'Mind Cure': Positive Thinking and Pseudo-Science at the Fin de Siècle*
    ANNE STILES, *Saint Louis University, Missouri*
127. *Virtual Play and the Victorian Novel: The Ethics and Aesthetics of Fictional Experience*
    TIMOTHY GAO, *Nanyang Technological University*

CPSIA information can be obtained
at www.ICGtesting.com
Printed in the USA
LVHW080919030821
694401LV00004B/283